MAILING ADDRESS

Maritime Studies Research Unit
Memorial University of Newfoundland
St. John's, Newfoundland A1C 5S7, Canada

RESEARCH IN MARITIME HISTORY
NO. 5

THE DIARY OF JOHN HOLT

Edited by
Peter N. Davies

International Maritime Economic History Association

St. John's, Newfoundland
1993

ISSN -1188-3928
ISBN -0-9695885-5-0

Research in Maritime History is available free of charge to members of the International Maritime Economic History Association. The price to others is US$15 per copy.

Back issues of *Research in Maritime History* are available:

No. 1 (1991)	David M. Williams and Andrew P. White (comps.), *A Select Bibliography of British and Irish University Theses about Maritime History, 1792-1990*
No. 2 (1992)	Lewis R. Fischer (ed.), *From Wheel House to Counting House: Essays in Maritime Business History in Honour of Professor Peter Neville Davies*
No. 3 (1992)	Lewis R. Fischer and Walter Minchinton (eds.), *People of the Northern Seas*
No. 4 (1993)	Simon Ville (ed.), *Shipbuilding in the United Kingdom in the Nineteenth Century: A Regional Approach*

Research in Maritime History would like to thank the Friends of the Merseyside Maritime Museum and Memorial University of Newfoundland for their generous financial assistance in support of this volume.

CONTENTS

Foreword

Today the partnership between the Coast and Liverpool is not dissimilar to the organisation established by John Holt when he returned to Britain from Africa in 1874. In Nigeria John Holt's creation, which now trades as John Holt Plc and is quoted on the Lagos Stock Exchange, has over fifty thousand Nigerian shareholders and approximately 2800 employees. The name John Holt is known and respected throughout the federation. Indeed, a local folk song includes the line, "It happened a long long time ago before John Holt." From that nearly every Nigerian would know the period reference.

I am sure this new edition of *The Diary of John Holt* will interest many people in Nigeria and England, as well as readers around the world. I would like to thank Professor Davies and the International Maritime Economic History Association for arranging this new publication of what in my view is a fascinating historical document.

John Garnett
Managing Director
John Holt Group

Introduction to the 1993 Edition

Peter N. Davies

Any list of the pioneers of West Africa's modern deep-sea trade would include John Holt. His was the career to which many nineteenth-century Britons aspired but few achieved. From modest beginnings in Lincolnshire to an apprenticeship in Liverpool was a useful first step, but since this required his family's financial support it was not the beginning of a traditional "rags to riches" story. Indeed, the terms of his indenture specified that his father, Thomas, had to "bind himself to find and provide for the said John Holt good and sufficient meat, drink, washing, lodging and all necessary and proper wearing apparel of all sorts suitable for such an apprentice during the aforesaid term of five years."[1] While William Laird was bound by these articles to pay a total of £160 in wages over the period, it is unclear if these represented the return of a premium paid by Thomas Holt or a genuine contribution to John's living expenses.[2]

The firm of William and Hamilton Laird, which Holt joined in 1857, was founded originally to deal in coal. Links with the family shipbuilding firm helped to develop the bunkering side of the business; after their brother, Macgregor Laird, formed the African Steam Ship Company they were appointed its Liverpool agents.[3] At first the line used London as its terminus, but when sailings were transferred to the Mersey in 1856 their responsibility grew rapidly. This was not only because of the additional effort required to ensure an efficient turnaround, which involved the agency in all aspects of staffing, victualling and repairs, but also because control of the company gradually fell into their hands.[4] From John Holt's perspective this expansion came at an opportune moment, for it created the vacancy which he subsequently filled. Moreover, it also shifted the focus of the firm's activities toward West Africa and thus played a significant role in influencing his later career.

John Holt's decision to accept a position with James Lynslager on the island of Fernando Po has been discussed elsewhere.[5] The diaries he kept provide a fascinating account of his life from 23 June 1862 to 19 December 1864, and from 30 January 1869 to 2 January 1872. The earlier part of this period has been summarised as follows:

---

[1]The indenture between John Holt and William Laird is reproduced in *Merchant Adventure* (Liverpool, 1948), 12.

[2]See Cecil Holt, "Introduction," 3. Most such apprenticeships required payment of a premium during the indenture.

[3]*Builders of Great Ships* (Birkenhead, 1959).

[4]P.N. Davies, *The Trade Makers. Elder Dempster in West Africa, 1852-1972* (London, 1973), 52.

[5]See Holt, "Introduction," 5-8; and *Merchant Adventure*, 13-14.

> John Holt began his career as a shop assistant. Since he was, by nature, a meticulous, careful young man, the disorder of his employer's affairs offended him, and in the latter's absence, he set himself to put them to rights. He tidied up the books, sternly put an end to Mrs. Lynslager's casual dippings into both the cash box and the store, and re-organised the shop so that customers might be more attracted by its goods. When Lynslager returned from England in the middle of 1863 he found his affairs in a much happier state. When he died in 1864 Holt remained as manager for his widow. Three years later, with savings accumulated from his earnings, Holt bought out Mrs. Lynslager and began trading on his own account.[6]

Holt's early experience was therefore not that of the typical Coaster; he did not begin buying produce, for example, until 1868. Yet his knowledge of retailing taught him to appreciate the importance of catering to customers' needs and tastes.[7] This empathy enabled him to expand on Fernando Po and gave him a competitive advantage when he extended his activities to the mainland. This expansion was greatly assisted by the possession of his own ship, *Maria*, for by controlling his transport he was able to avoid many problems which plagued his rivals.[8]

A final factor in his success was the somewhat fortuitous choice of a trading centre that was one of the healthiest on the entire coast. Fernando Po lies in the Bight of Biafra, approximately twenty miles off the mainland.[9] The capital, Port Clarence (known to the Spanish as Santa Isabel), has a mean temperature of 78° F. and experiences much fever despite the sea breezes. While its climate was not ideal for Europeans, it was by West African standards reasonable. In addition, its fine natural harbour made it attractive for a trader and shipowner and explains why it was selected in 1853 as the southern terminus for the African Steam Ship Company. But it was not a perfect site. The island is small and the interest of the limited populace in commerce was quickly sated. Still, some African traders did cross from nearby coastal areas to obtain better prices for their produce and Holt did what he could to encourage this. He also exchanged trade goods for produce to accommodate European merchants on occasion, but such transactions did little more than convince him of the need to expand onto the continent.

The diaries contain many references to the way in which the purchase of the *Maria* and the regular sailings of the African Steam Ship Company permitted Holt to diversify into mainland trades:

---

[6] C. Gertzel, *The Early Years of an African Trader* (Ibadan, 1960), 13.

[7] *Ibid.*, 14.

[8] The *Maria* is discussed below, 137-189.

[9] *Encyclopedia Britannica* (11th ed.), X, 280-281.

> The *Maria* arrived from the South Coast with a cargo of rubber &c., on the 15th, which was discharged into the *Terrier* and she left at once for Bimbia, arriving back again on the 20th with thirty-three casks of palm oil on board. On the 22nd the [SS] *Mandingo* arrived and her outward cargo for the *Maria* had to be discharged and the produce shipped for her.[10]

The convenience of the liner service to Liverpool, reinforced in 1869 by ships of the newly-established British and African Steam Navigation Company, was thus a major factor in Holt's expansion.[11] From the start these scheduled services did much to open West African trade to merchants with insufficient capital to justify the purchase or charter of a suitable vessel.[12] Holt's activities were not exceptional in this respect--it was the existence of his own "feeder" line which provided the basis for the substantial growth which his business enjoyed.

During the period that Holt directed his enterprise from Fernando Po, the purchase of trade goods and disposal of produce was handled by Irvine and Woodward in Liverpool.[13] Correspondence with these agents was comparatively easy, for the ships treated mail as the first priority; queries could thus be answered and goods received within little more than a month of any request. Although the arrangements proved quite satisfactory, they were terminated in 1874 as a result of Holt's decision to return to England. By then he had reached the age of thirty-three and:

> could reflect on many positive achievements as a credit to his twelve years in Africa. He was the owner of a large newly-built store (insured with its contents in 1875 for £2,000) doing a lucrative business on Fernando Po, together with his coaling agencies and other interests there. His factories on the Coast were firmly entrenched, notwithstanding the sort of setbacks previously described, and he now had a miniature fleet of his own, including his first steamer *Pioneer*, plying the Coast. He had acted as British Consul and was already a man of considerable weight in local affairs.[14]

---

[10]See *Diary*, 117, entry for 22 August 1870.

[11]Davies, *The Trade Makers*, 56-59.

[12]P.N. Davies, "The Impact of the Expatriate Shipping Lines on the Economic Development of British West Africa," *Business History*, XIX, No. 1 (January 1977), 3-17.

[13]See Holt, "Introduction," 9-10; *Diary*, 105, fn. 64.

[14]*Merchant Adventure*, 25.

Having dispensed with the services of Irvine and Woodward, Holt established his own office to control his expanding business on the coast and in Fernando Po. Again the services of the two British lines were invaluable, especially after they had been integrated by Alfred Jones.[15] This made direction and communication even simpler; with the aid of his two brothers, who still spent much time in Africa, Holt was able to manage without difficulty. When at a later stage both Jonathan and Thomas Holt returned to Britain, John Holt appointed James Deeming as his Agent-General on the coast.[16]

Although these arrangements helped the company to prosper, Jonathan's death in 1896 at the young age of fifty-two led to a re-organisation.[17] John Holt and Company (Liverpool) Limited was established the next year with John Holt as Chairman and Managing Director and Thomas Holt and Thomas Welsh as Board members. All the shares were held by the Holts and their close friends, a pattern of ownership that was maintained until the Company joined the Lonrho Group in 1969.[18]

The new organisation did not, of course, affect John Holt's position. From his return to Liverpool in 1874 through the first decade of the twentieth century he was in personal control, leading the firm to grow and diversify into a wide range of new areas. Such expansion would likely have been even greater but for the stand he took against the concessionaire system established by the French in their part of the Congo. This disagreement expanded into a more general struggle in which Holt supported attempts by the Congo Reform Association to modify the exploitation of the Congo Free State. On both accounts he ultimately reaped rewards. The French compensated him for his losses by the grant of a forest concession in Gabon which could supply valuable hardwoods for export. The Congo Reform Association also succeeded in achieving its main aims and was dissolved in 1913. But these successes entailed cost, in Holt's case a stroke which in 1910 effectively ended his leadership of the firm.[19]

John Holt's illness left him virtually paralysed and he took little further part in the running of his company. His remaining years were spent on his farm at Broughton Grange in Lincolnshire, where he died on 22 June 1915, at the age of seventy-three.[20] The many tributes which followed his death indicated the esteem in which he was held:

---

[15] Davies, *The Trade Makers*, 88.

[16] "Autobiography of James Deeming," in P.N. Davies (ed.), *Trading in West Africa* (London, 1976), 93-136.

[17] *Merchant Adventure*, 36.

[18] It should be noted that the firm was by then valued at about £8 million and was held in such esteem that the agreement provided that it would continue to operate under its own separate identity. S. Cronje, *et al.*, *Lonrho: Portrait of a Multinational* (Harmondsworth, 1976), 43.

[19] *Merchant Adventure*, 41-44.

[20] *Ibid.*

> The pioneer trader building his fortune was succeeded by the merchant-statesman, not merely enlarging and consolidating the business he had hewn out of jungle and swamp but imbued with a deep and understanding interest in the country where his enterprise had struck root and in the relations of that country and its peoples with his own.

An African observed noted that:

> He experienced a sense of sincere gratitude towards the West African for the latter's share in building up his own fortunes and those of his family. 'They made me what I am', he used to say. 'Their labour, their muscles, their enterprise, have given me everything I possess. I am bound to try to protect them against outrage and injustice.'[21]

His confidence in the ability of Africans and of the need to deal with them equitably was repeated in the obituary by Mrs. J.R. Green:

> Mr. Holt was not a man for Associations and Companies. His intense individuality, his resentment at control, his scorn of assistance, made him repudiate any interference, whether by Companies or the State. He wanted no backing either of politician or of soldier. He had absolute confidence in his own method of dealing with the African, apart from all Government complications. Such a merchant as John Holt, far-sighted, self-reliant, guided by an unfailing instinct for good business, was never lured, by the plea of quick profits, to the exploitation of the native. He was pledged, if only by his sense of successful commerce, to a system of free labour for the inhabitants of the country. He saw no prospect of any enduring trade except through the development of equitable exchange to the profit alike of European and African. His appreciation of the African capacity for commerce guided him in creating a traffic in which the native was of necessity called to play his honourable and independent part, and the natural ability of the people had opportunity to develop on its own lines.[22]

These views by Europeans were also echoed by an African trader:

> His genuine interest in West Africa and its people forcibly arrested my attention. It was the genuine regard of a recipient for a donor. It

---

[21] *African Mail*, 2 July 1915.

[22] J.R. Green, "A Founder of the Society," *Journal of the African Society*, XV (October 1915), 12-13.

> was as it should be. Africa gave him wealth, he was mindful of her. His iron will stood in bold relief. I found the man as I thought he was. There was no half measures about him. It was neck or nothing. Once he had made up his mind about a thing, he was going to see it through at any cost...His knowledge of things Lagos, and the doings at Onitsha fairly took my breath away. We rambled through the principal streets of Lagos as if he had only just returned from there. He knew to an inch the length of the Marina and am sorry to say, more about Wilmot Point than I did. He discussed the advantages and disadvantages of his beach at Onitsha, as if he had superintended the loading and unloading of ships there. As was to be expected the details of his business were at his fingers end.[23]

Despite his major contributions, little has been written about either Holt or the Company he founded. This is surprising, if only because of the attention lavished on many contemporaries in recent years. Joseph Chamberlain, George Goldie, Alfred Jones, Mary Kingsley, Frederick Lugard, E.D. Morel and Henry Tyrer have all been the recipients of substantial studies, while the Bank of British West Africa, Elder Dempster, the Palm Line and the United Africa Company have received scholarly treatment.[24] John Holt and his company, on the other hand, have had only *Merchant Adventure*, an admirable but limited outline giving only a brief account of the firm's development, and the first edition of these *Diaries*. This neglect was not due to a paucity of source materials, since John Holt's considerable personal and company records have been well catalogued and are readily accessible at Rhodes House Library in Oxford.[25] This extensive archive has, however, been used to produce two informative theses: by C.J. Gertzel on "John Holt: A British Merchant in West Africa in the Era of Imperialism" and by R. Glover on "James Deemin and the Organisation of West African Trade, 1880-1913."[26] Unfortunately, neither has been published. The failure to produce more than

---

[23]*Nigerian Pioneer*, 16 July 1915.

[24]See the bibliography in P.N. Davies, *Sir Alfred Jones, Shipping Entrepreneur Par Excellence* (London, 1978) 151-154. Many of these works are also cited in the footnotes in this volume.

[25]The John Holt manuscripts were catalogued by Professor J.E. Flint, now of Dalhousie University; the associated papers of a prominent John Holt employee, James Deemin, were catalogued by Professor P.N. Davies of the University of Liverpool and are also held at Rhodes House Library.

[26]C.J. Gertzel, "John Holt: A British Merchant in West Africa in the Era of Imperialism" (Unpublished DPhil thesis, University of Oxford, 1959); R. Glover, "James Deemin and the Organisation of West African Trade, 1880-1913" (Unpublished MA thesis, University of Liverpool, 1978).

a few articles from this material means that we know more about lesser characters, such as Harry Cotterell, than about a principal figure like John Holt.[27]

What makes this lacunae even more surprising is the great upsurge since the 1960s in interest in all aspects of West African history. The achievement of independence by the four British possessions on the coast, together with parallel movements within other empires, transformed the perception of West Africa and promoted an increased concern for the past, one aspect of which was the development of a fresh academic interest into many previously neglected topics. This, in turn, resulted in a large number of important publications which have attempted to describe and analyze these themes.

Sadly, this scholarly outpouring has contained many incidental references to John Holt but little of real substance. At the same time the two publications produced privately by the Company have been long out of print. In these circumstances the decision to reprint the 1948 version of the John Holt Diaries, together with the valuable introduction by Cecil Holt and the account of the voyages of the *Maria*, will be widely welcomed. While this could have been reproduced in its original format without modification, the gap of over forty years since it was issued suggested that a fundamental revision would be both advisable and beneficial.

As a first step the handwritten *Diaries* so carefully compiled by John Holt were compared with the printed version.[28] Changes and omissions, in fact, proved to be so negligible that it was considered in general unnecessary to make significant alterations. In the few instances where it was felt that understanding could be improved new footnotes have been superimposed on the text. The opportunity has also been taken to include a fresh section on the sailings of the *Peep o'Day*. This, it is hoped, will give further perspective to the work as a whole, while the additional annotations may well aid a generation now far removed from the world described so aptly by the young John Holt to understand his role in an important and exciting time.

---

[27] See Harry Cotterell, "Reminiscences of One Connected with the West African Trade from 1863 to 1910," in Davies (ed.), *Trading in West Africa*.

[28] The original diaries are in the possession of D.J. Holt, who kindly made them available for this project.

Foreword

Eighty-five years have passed since this diary commenced, and with it began an enterprise that has grown to proportions which even its creator could hardly have envisaged when he embarked upon a career in West Africa.

John Holt was the product of that great age we now term the Victorian era, and apart from the gift of a first-class brain, he possessed, as the reader will perceive, the sturdy qualities of the time, coupled with a simple religious faith, which lasted him to the end.

In these days it is opportune that occasion be afforded to look back at the beginnings of this family business, particularly for all those concerned with its fortunes. May it be that they, and all who read, shall derive inspiration from the pages that follow.

John Holt, Jr.
Chairman
John Holt & Co. (Liverpool) Ltd.
March 1948

Introduction

Cecil R. Holt

John Holt, the eldest son of Thomas Godfrey Holt, was born in the village of Garthorpe, in Lincolnshire, on the 31st October, 1841. He was educated at the local village school which he left at the age of fourteen to enter the employ of his grandfather, Thomas Holt, and he went to sea on a schooner owned by his grandfather, which plied between Goole and London and the Northern French ports, carrying coals, cement, and tiles. The name of the schooner was the *Thomas Holt*. He apparently did not find this employment to his liking, and on the 1st July, 1857, his father signed an agreement with William Laird, of Messrs. W.H. Laird, Coal Dealers, Castle Street, Liverpool, to employ him as an apprentice for a period of five years.[1]

> In the words of the indenture, "John Holt, by his own freewill and with the consent of his father Thomas Holt, of Garthorpe, doth put, place, and bind himself a covenant servant or apprentice...and doth covenant promise and agree...that he shall and will faithfully serve his said master, his secrets keep, his lawful commands gladly obey and do; hurt to his said master he shall not do, or suffer to be done by others...His Master's goods he shall not waste or embezzle, the same give or lend without leave; day or night absent himself from his said master's service; nor do any other Act, Matter, or Thing whatsoever to the prejudice of his said master.... In consideration hereof the said William Laird shall and will pay the wages following, viz:--£20 for the first year, £25 for the second year, £30 for the third year, £35 for the fourth year, £50 for fifth and last year of the said term."[2]

William Laird was one of the well-known family of Lairds, who had shipping and shipbuilding interests in Liverpool, and was a brother of Macgregor Laird, the explorer.[3] In Laird's office together with John Holt was Alfred Jones who later became Sir Alfred Jones, of West African fame.[4]

---

[1]P.N. Davies, *The Trade Makers. Elder Dempster in West Africa, 1852-1972* (London, 1973), 52-55.

[2]The original indenture is in the possession of Mr. D.J. Holt. A reproduction can be found in the John Holt and Company (Liverpool) Limited publication, *Merchant Venture* (Liverpool, 1948), 12.

[3]*Builders of Great Ships*, published by Cammell Laird and Company (Birkenhead, 1959), provides a useful guide to the family and its shipbuilding business.

[4]P.N. Davies, *Sir Alfred Jones, Shipping Entrepreneur Par Excellence* (London, 1978).

At the beginning of his apprenticeship John Holt lodged in Price Street, Birkenhead, and spent his spare time improving his education by attending night schools, and visiting the public library. Later he moved to Tranmere.

As his apprenticeship drew towards a close he must have decided that the future prospects offered by a commercial career with Lairds were not sufficiently attractive for his ambitious nature, and that he must seek his fortune elsewhere. It is clear from his correspondence that he had been reading a great deal about West African exploration as there are references in his letters quoting the travels of Mungo Park, and the explorations of Macgregor Laird.[5] His first inclination, however, was to go to sea as a purser, and his thoughts and feelings are clearly set out in a letter he wrote to his father in the early months of 1862:

23, Castle Street
Liverpool

My Dear Father,

I enclose you Jonathan's letter for perusal, after which please return. The *Beechworth* I saw by our *Telegraph* a few days ago arrived at Bombay on the 31st January, after a very protracted voyage.

Mr. Laird wishes me to stay until I am out of my apprenticeship before I go to sea. Of course, it is my duty to do so, and I cannot but submit. However, I am writing to him in a day or two and shall not let the matter rest. I spoke to an old purser on the subject this morning and he advised me not to got--he considers it a bad place for a young man--a place I suppose in which virtues are scarce and vices abundant. This may be the case, but so far I have been able to avoid many of the rocks on which young men are wrecked, and I think by the exercise of a little common sense and fortitude I should be able to make myself proof against such things.

Mankind is like a lot of hungry pigs fighting over a trough of milk--everybody seems to be trying to pull the piece of food out of his neighbour's mouth. The common pursuits of life are full of earnest aspirants for the use of their peculiar craft--so full indeed that in England we have a great many people starving on account of being unable to get bread, and consequently work. What am I to do? If I stay where I am I have the prospect of a £60 salary which to my ambitious nature is beggary. No! it is money I want and money I must have if I go through fire and water for it. When I say I want money it is not for the pleasure of simply having a certain sum of gold. It is not the gold, but the independence it brings and the cares it drives away. I am not miserly, and do not want to hoard money, but I should like to have as much as would enable me to satisfy my own peculiar fancies, and exonerate me from thoughts of future

---

[5]Mungo Park, *Travels in the Interior of Africa* (London, 1799; reprint, Edinburgh, 1858). See also Sir Harry Johnson, *Pioneers in West Africa* (London, n.d.), 111-167.

beggary. This is hard to get. It seems to me as if I were just entering the world and commencing a struggle with everybody for a bit of bread. Every way I look I find thousands busy eating and it appears as if I must go and struggle with them or pine. This is my idea of life so far as I can at present see it.

I am much obliged for the bag and its contents, which were very nice, and, I assure you, properly appreciated. I should have been all the more pleased had I received a note from you, but as fate denied me that happiness it strikes me I am having my revenge by giving you plenty of it in return. I am very busy now with a concert to be given by our society on the 20th inst, so you will please be satisfied with this for a week or two, for what with one thing and another I am kept at work until all hours.

I am affectionately yours,

John Holt

In June, 1862, he mentions in a letter to Mr. Laird that he had applied to the P. and O. Co. asking for a position on one of their steamers as a purser, mentioning that he would be prepared to do one voyage on trial, without remuneration.

Before anything could come of this, however, he received an offer from a Mr. J.B. Lynslager, who was at that time in England, and who was the British Consul in the Spanish Island of Fernando Po.[6] Fernando Po is off the West Coast of Africa, about twenty miles from the mainland of the Cameroons. It is about 44 miles long, and 20 miles broad. It was first discovered by the Portuguese Fernao de Pao, in about 1471. It was ceded to Spain in 1778, but there was no colony founded there until the British founded a settlement in 1827.

J.B. Lynslager, or "Daddy" as he is called in the Diary, was born in London in 1810 and was one of the early colonisers of Fernando Po. The entry in the Diary for 14th September, 1864, contains many biographical details and an appreciation of his character and it is sufficient to say here that he was obviously a man of great and forceful personality. Mrs. Lynslager, who is referred to practically throughout the Diary as "Mammy," was a black woman but unfortunately little is known of her history subsequent to the ending of the Diary. As a result of this offer the following letters passed between John Holt and Mr. Laird:

23, Castle Street
Liverpool
12th June 1862

W. Laird Esq.,
Dear Sir,

Since writing you yesterday I have had an offer to go out to Fernando Po as Secretary to the British Consul there--J.W.B. Lynslager Esq., who is now in London, which having duly con-

---

[6]A brief account of Lynslager's background is provided in *Diary*, 84-86. See also p. 129.

sidered I have agreed conditionally to accept. These conditions are that I shall first write you on the subject begging your permission to leave on the 24th of this month, before giving a final answer to London.

The climate, I am told, is more healthy on this island than on any other part of the coast, and M. Laird Esq., in his narrative of the Niger Expedition, also gives the same testimony.[7] The salary (£100 per an) will also be much more than I could hope to obtain by going out as under-purser, and as I have made full enquiries respecting my duties & c. there, with which I am perfectly satisfied, and as I have also long desired to go to Africa, I think I have now an opportunity offered me which should not be missed.

I have, therefore, once more to trespass on your kindness, and to beg your permission to end the term of my apprenticeship on the 24th instead of the 30th instant.

I have explained the circumstances in which I am situated to Mr. Laughland, who has the appointing of this situation, and he has consented to wait until Saturday for my reply before taking any further steps in the affair.

May I be allowed to beg an answer by return, which I shall anxiously wait, and which, judging from your past indulgences will I have every hope, be favourable?

I remain, Dear Sir,
Your Faith Servt.
John Holt

At the same time he wrote the following letter to his parents telling them the offer he had received, and of his acceptance providing Laird released him:

Liver Villa,
Tranmere,
12th June, 1862

My Dear Parents,

It is very uncertain whether I shall be able to go home on Saturday. I have this day had an offer from a gentleman in Liverpool to go out to Fernando Po on the 24th of this month. I have written to Mr. Laird for permission to do so. As you are aware, he is my Master until the 30th instant and I am waiting his reply, which will arrive I expect on Saturday. If his reply is favourable I can come on Saturday. If not, I shall have to write to Glasgow explaining how I am situated and begging them to wait until the sailing of the July steamer when I shall be on my own master, and shall have to wait their answer, but you can tell the carrier to wait in any case as I

---

[7]M. Laird and R.A.K. Oldfield, *Narrative of an Expedition into the Interior of Africa by the River Niger...* (London, 1837).

suppose it will only be a matter of 1/6d.[8] I have agreed to accept this offer on condition that I can get off, of course. The principal feature are--I shall go for 3 years for which I receive at the rate of £100 per annum; I shall have board and lodging found me, my only expenses will be for clothes. My duties will be those of a clerk combined with those of overseer and storekeeper; my employer is the British Consul there and I shall be his only white assistant. The climate is more healthy than that of any other part of the coast. The purser through whom I received the offer says the situation is worth £300 a year. But whether it be so or not I think as I have long had a great desire to go to Africa, as this is the most healthy part of it, and as I may not early have the like opportunity, I hope you will agree with me that I have been prudent in accepting it, or rather in doing so conditionally as it is not settled yet. I have written only yesterday (for a situation as under-purser) to the P. and O. Co. where I should perhaps have been sent to the China Seas at £40 or £50 per annum for five years before being promoted to the office of purser, or I have no doubt I could have gone in the African Service for a voyage or two in that capacity which I had offered to do for nothing if they would only give me a trial, and might then have been made a purser when a vacancy was open. But at all times under such circumstances as I find myself placed in, I think it better to accept a certainty in preference to an uncertainty. If I do not like the situation I can return. If I am too ill to stay I can return also by paying half the passage money, supposing it is within the first twelve months. If any illness occurs after that time I shall be sent home at his expense and as 1st cabin passenger. If I go out it will also be at his expense, the passage money alone amounts to £40.

I am, my dear parents,
Your affectionate son,
John Holt

Laird replied to his letter on the 13th June in the following terms:

Conservative Club, London, S.W.
13th June, 1862

Mr. John Holt,
Liverpool
Dear Sir,

I am in receipt of your note of the 12th inst., and have written to Mr. Higginson on the subject of your leaving on the 24th inst.

---

[8]Holt is referring to the regular sailings from Liverpool to West Africa of the African Steam Ship Company. See P.N. Davies, "The African Steam Ship Company," in J. R. Harris (ed.), *Liverpool and Merseyside* (London, 1969).

Fernando Po is one of the best places to go to on the Coast, and I sincerely trust that you will keep your health.

I forward by this post some remarks on the Niger drawn up by my late brother, and call your attention to appendix No. 1 in which you will find some observations as to the best means of keeping your health, which may be of use.

Before finally accepting the offer from Mr. Lynslager, I think you had better enquire whether Messrs. Horsfall[9] or Harrison have any opening in their establishments on the Coast, as with them you would be likely to succeed better than with Mr. L.

I write Mr. Fletcher to ask him to be good enough to introduce you to some of these parties--going to them you would learn the mode of trading on the Coast which might lead to your obtaining a good position eventually.

I shall be glad to hear from you from time to time how you get on, and wishing you health and success,

I am

Very truly yours,

Wm. Laird.[10]

In spite of Laird's advice, John Holt did not hesitate any further and accepted Lynslager's offer.

From that time his diary takes up the story until just after his employer dies in September, 1864.

From the 30th September, 1864, to the 1st March, 1867, his employer's business was carried on by Mrs. Lynslager, under John Holt's management. During this time he allowed his salary to accumulate and invested it as capital in the business thus enabling him finally to purchase the business from Mrs. Lynslager. And so at the sage of twenty-five he set up in business on his own account.

In April, 1867, he returned to England for the first time, having previously persuaded his brother Jonathan to look after his business during his absence.

Jonathan Holt, the second son, was born on the 27th July, 1844, also at Garthorpe. Leaving school at 14, he became apprenticed to this uncle John Holt Snr., on board his uncle's sailing vessel *Wave*, which coasted between Hull and London. One of the conditions of his apprenticeship was that he bound himself "not to frequent Taverns or Ale Houses unless upon his master's business, nor play at unlawful games." His pay for this work was £7 for the first year, and £10, £13, and £20 for the second, third, and fourth years respectively.

---

[9]These were the Horsfall Brothers (Charles and Thomas) and Thomas Harrison and Company, both prominent Liverpool firms in the West African trade. See F.R. Wharton, unpublished Mss., in the possession of Dr. P.N. Davies, University of Liverpool, 59, 169-172 and 176-177.

[10]William and Hamilton Laird acted as Liverpool agents for the African Steam Ship Company, but after Hamilton's death in 1860 J.T. Fletcher was taken into partnership. See Davies, *The Trade Makers*, 52.

In September, 1861, he made a voyage to Bombay on the *Beechworth* and left her at Bombay in June, 1862, signing on the barque *Victoria*, and on his discharge from this vessel was referred to as "a particularly smart, steady, sober and moral young man and well deserving of advancement." He made a further voyage to New Zealand on the *Wild Duck*, as A.B., and thereafter, until 1866, was in the employ of his grandfather in command of the *Thomas Holt* sailing in coastal waters.

He obtained his Master's Certificate in October, 1868, but in January of the previous year he had sailed out the Cutter *Edmund* as Master, to Fernando Po, the *Edmund* being owned by Mr. Charles Townsend, of Fernando Po. It was during his stay on the Coast with this vessel that he was able to relieve his brother who returned home.

When John Holt returned to England his first action was to appoint Agents to act for him in Liverpool, and he chose Messrs. Irvine and Woodward, of The Temple, Dale Street,[11] with whom he had a few transactions during the time he had been managing Mrs. Lynslager's business, and the letter setting out his terms is worth quoting here:--

Liverpool
2nd September, 1867

Messrs. Irvine and Woodward,
The Temple, Liverpool.
Dear Sirs,

Having deciding upon commencing business on my own account in Fernando Po and having had the pleasure of a few transactions with you when acting as the manager of the Estate of the late Mr. Lynslager, all of which gave me the greatest satisfaction both in price selection and terms, I feel disposed to constitute you my sole agents on this side if you are agreeable, and beg to offer the following proposals for your kind consideration:--

1. I propose to begin by placing in your hands half the estimated amount of invoice of goods proposed to be shipped to my consignment--to an extent not exceeding two thousand pounds nor less than one thousand--an equal sum being advanced by you to enable you to make the required consignments.

2. The advance on your part is, of course, only to be expected on such sums as I shall place in your hands previous to arrival of returns in exchange for first consignment of goods, or say within four months from the date of such consignment.

3. I propose to pay you a commission of 2½% on amount of invoices of all goods consigned to me, and a commission of 2½%

[11]Irvine and Woodward were established as West Africa merchants in Liverpool during 1864. They failed in 1881 but James Irvine continued on his own account. See Wharton, unpublished mss., 173; and F. Pedler, *The Lion and the Unicorn in Africa. The United African Company, 1787-1931* (London, 1974), 140-141 and 284.

on the nett proceeds of all produce, Bills, Specie, or other remittance which I may make you in payment of the amounts of your invoices.

4. That interest at the rate of 5% per annum be charged on the amounts of all invoices from the date when such become payable for cash, and a similar rate of interest be allowed on the nett proceeds of remittances as they become due.

5. That the discount allowed for cash be in all cases allowed me, but it is understood that this does not apply when not having funds to my credit you find it necessary to give bills. In this case I only look for interest to be charged against me from the time when such bills fall due.

6. That I execute a deed giving you a preference over all other creditors so as to enable you to protect yourselves in the event of it ever unfortunately becoming necessary for you to do so.

It is with a perfect faith in your ability to do my interests justice and in a firm belief that you will act towards me with candour and integrity that I beg to offer these proposals.

Frankness, good faith, and confidence in each other are necessary to a fair understanding and to make our transactions a pleasure as well as a profit.

Should you be pleased to accept what I now offer from the good opinion I have already formed of you I predict a pleasant business together for some years to come.

I remain, Dear Sirs,
Yours respectfully and truly,
John Holt.

Whilst he was at home another brother, Thomas, approached him with a view to joining him in the business. Thomas Holt, born in 1848, was at that time in the employ of a draper in Hull. John Holt agreed to employ him and made him the following offer in writing, which Thomas accepted, sailing out to Fernando Po in the brigantine *Peep o'Day* on October 26th, 1867.[12]

Burton Stather,
Brigg.

26th September, 1867.

Mr. Thomas Holt Jnr.,
Burton Stather.

Dear Brother,

I am willing to second your desire to enter my employ on the West Coast of Africa, while at the same time no inducement or persuasion shall on my part be used in order to influence your

---

[12]An account of the work of *Peep O'Day* after its arrival at Cape Palmas on 23 November 1867, is provided on pages 191-201.

thoughts. You choose for yourself and are liable for the consequences of the step you propose to take. I only wish to facilitate what you think is for your good, suitable to your tastes, and to which your desires tend. Of your own freewill you have notified to me your desire to join me provided I am agreeable, and we can come to an arrangement as to time and pay.

I have therefore to propose the following which I think will meet your views.

1. I will engage you for a period of three years commencing from the date of your arrival in Fernando Po.

2. I will provide you with a passage out and home, supposing you to remain in my employ until the expiration of the three years engagement. Should you, however, from any cause whatever (sickness excepted) leave my employ before then, the expense of your passage home will have to be defrayed by yourself, and if through neglect, bad behaviour, or any reasonable cause I should be compelled to send you home, I retain to myself the power of stopping the amount of your passage money from the salary hereafter proposed to be paid you.

3. I will provide you with food, lodging, medicine, and medical attendance.

4. I will pay you for the first year the sum of eighty pounds sterling, for the second year the sum of one hundred pounds sterling, and for the third year the sum of one hundred and twenty pounds sterling. The sum of twenty pounds of the first quarter of your first year's salary to be kept to the credit or your account until the expiration of this agreement, the remaining amounts to be paid you quarterly as they become due.

5. I shall expect you to do any kind of work which a white man is capable of and reasonably able to do in that climate and which I may require of you--but more especially to act as salesman in a store, bookkeeper, clerk, and over-looker in any place or places in Fernando Po, or the West Coast of Africa--whenever requested--by night or by day. To be obedient, careful, industrious, honest and attentive, studying my interests as if they were your own, and in fact considering them as such because if I succeed (and my success in a great measure depends upon the conduct, abilities, and exertions of those whom I employ) your welfare is assured.

If these proposals meet with your acceptance I shall require you to sail on or about the 2nd of October next per *Peep o'Day* schooner, from Liverpool. Such acceptance I shall consider binding on both sides and a more formal memorandum of agreement superfluous.

I am, my dear Brother,
Yours fraternally,
John Holt.

With his two brothers now assisting him, John Holt was able to turn his attention to further expansion of his business, and with this object in view commissioned Jonathan to purchase a sailing vessel for him in England.[13]

In December, 1868, Jonathan bought the *Maria*, a two-masted fore and aft 65 ton schooner, built of oak. Her length was 71 feet and breadth 16 feet, and she cost £620. At the time of purchase she was sixteen years old, having been built in 1852, at Plymouth. Jonathan's account of his voyage out in her and his experiences while trading on the Coast form the second part of this volume.

Nothing is known of what eventually happened to the *Maria*, but she remained in John Holt's service until 1877, after which there is no trace of her.

Her figurehead (that of a girl) was for many years attached to the end of the Company's store at Libreville, but in 1908 was brought home and placed in the Company's Board Room.

The diary of John Holt end in 1872, and he finally returned home for good in 1874. On his return he found that his Agents had not managed his affairs to his satisfaction and he was obliged to set up his own offices in Water Street, Liverpool.

On the 25th February, 1875, he married Eliza Longstaff, of Stixwould, in the County of Lincolnshire, and to his fortunate choice he owned much of his success in the ensuing period of his life, since no man could have found a more devoted and helpful companion.[14]

From this time on the story of John Holt and his brothers becomes increasingly merged into the history of the firm they founded, and it is not possible to include this history within the scope of an introduction; it is only possible to say that the brothers steadily expanded their trade and interests until, with the later help of their children and grandchildren, it has developed into the large concern it is to-day.

Jonathan died in 1896. His death was a grievous blow to John, and put a heavy additional burden on him which terminated in an illness in 1910 which compelled him to retire from business altogether. He went to live in Lincolnshire and though he was physically paralysed his mental capacity was not impaired and he continued to take a lively interest in African affairs until he died on the 22nd June, 1915.

Thomas, the youngest of the brothers, died in 1921.

It would be wrong to end this introduction without an appreciation of the character of John Holt. That he was a pioneer is obvious to anyone who reads the pages of his diary. He was also a man of great moral courage, and a stern, uncompromising fighter against injustice and the exploitation of human misery. He was not a man who liked the limelight of publicity, but on the occasions where he conceived it to be his duty he was not afraid to face the full force of public controversy. He was usually eclipsed by his apparently more brilliant and versatile colleague--Alfred Jones (later Sir Alfred

---

[13]Details of the acquisition of *Maria* are provided on pp. 96-97. An account of its subsequent trading is reproduced on pages 137-189.

[14]Details of Holt's marriage and family are provided in the appendix, 203-205.

Jones), but if it was Jones who was the centre and focus of the public eye, it was often John Holt who determined the policy.[15]

His many qualities were displayed at their finest in his fight against the misrule of King Leopold in the Belgian Congo. He had no commercial interests in the Belgian Congo, and by coming out opening in support of the victims of Leopold he drew down on himself the abuse of the many supporters of Leopold and the publicity which he so much disliked. He also came into conflict with his colleague in the Chamber of Commerce--Alfred Jones, who had interests in the Congo State, and who was a formidable enemy. It is interesting that in spite of many clashes between these two men, they retained for each other a very great and real regard to the end of their days.

It was unfortunate in many ways that when the French Government--taking a leaf out of King Leopold's book--adopted a similar system in the French Congo, they directly attacked John Holt's interests and property.[16] He knew that if he fought against injustice when his own interests were closely affected, he would be accused of making a public issue out of his own private quarrel. He knew that the Foreign Office which at that time was trying to negotiate the Entente, would be irritated, and he knew the French Government would be infuriated and would increase their persecution; he was therefore most reluctant to take any public action in the French Congo. He was eventually persuaded to do so only because he realised that the interests of the natives of the whole Congo area were vitally at stake. Very strong pressure was brought to bear to dissuade him from taking this action, but he put that pressure aside and took a bold stand on a great public issue, certain of calumny and misrepresentation, an unsympathetic British Government and the antagonism of the French.

Naturally the interests of his firm suffered severely as a result of the step he took, and the persecution meted out to his employees in the Congo reached heights which provoked protests from some of the French officials themselves. His thoughts at the time are best exemplified by the following extracts from letters he wrote to E.D. Morel,[17] the great fighter for Congo Reform....

> "Your serious note sent me the last day of this year," he wrote "is enough to make me tremble at the thought of the responsibility you would put upon my shoulders; have I power by sacrifice to secure the freedom of the millions of the Congo region from the scourge of European brutality at present being inflicted upon them? So far as I am able to discover, my destiny arranged by Providence is to be a distributor of merchandise. Have I the capacity or mental qualifica-

---

[15]Holt's relationship with Alfred Jones is analysed in Davies, *The Trade Makers*, 112-113 and 138. Their conflict over the activities of King Leopold in the Congo is discussed in *ibid.*, 142-143.

[16]A detailed analysis of Holt's problems with the French administration is in R. Glover, "James Deemin and the Organisation of West African Trade, 1880-1915" (Unpublished MA thesis, University of Liverpool, 1978).

[17]The *Morel* Manuscript Collection is housed at the London School of Economics and Political Science and contains many letters between Holt and Morel. E.E. Morel wrote a large number of books on these topics. See, for example, *The Black Man's Burden* (Manchester, 1920).

> tions for any other role? How can I voice the wrongs of these hopeless millions, and by what means can I bring about their redemption? May God direct you and me in this matter."

His case, once officially put before the Liverpool Chamber of Commerce was irresistible, but the fight--while it lasted--was indeed a bitter one, until finally an aroused and informed public opinion forced the Governments to act.

That was John Holt's contribution to the cause of Congo Reform, and his intervention was one of the turning points in the history of the movement.

To many of his business colleagues and acquaintances John Holt may have seemed to be a hard man; he was brusque and harsh when he might have been genial and kindly, but he had been brought up in a hard school and he believed in saying what he thought, without trimmings, having no patience with the diplomatic and conventional veneer which others affected to use. He was often misunderstood and never took the trouble to remove the misunderstanding.

Underneath this exterior he was a very different man of great kindliness of heart and wide sympathy, and there were very few who genuinely sought his help and came away empty handed.

Among those who in a literal sense have made British trade in West Africa, John Holt's name will always be remembered. He had a grip of West African politics and economics, and of the human problems of the African, which was unequalled among his contemporaries, and as one of the founders of the African Section of the Liverpool Chamber of Commerce he materially helped to give the Chamber the very considerable influence it at one time possessed in the affairs of British West African administration.

Throughout his life he held firmly to the belief that fair, honest, and unfettered trading should be the foundation upon which British influence in the West African colonies should be built; to right the wrongs done to the African by the indifference and short comings of Governments was his constant endeavour and he lost no opportunity, when occasion arose, to make forceful condemnation of bad laws and unjust taxes, condemnations which he supported by a wealth of facts and materials drawn from his great store of experience.

His knowledge of Africa was sought after by Governments and by many influential men and women interested in African problems, and it bought him into all the important controversies on questions relating to Africa and the Africans, such as the Berlin Conference of 1885, which he attended as a member of the British Committee, with Alfred Jones and H.M. Stanley.[18]

Until her untimely death in 1900 he was a staunch friend and admirer of Mary Kingsley, who was a frequent guest at his house in Birkenhead. They kept up a continuous correspondence--at times almost daily--with each other on the African problems of their day. As her many letters to him gratefully acknowledge, it was from John Holt that Miss Kingsley constantly sought advice and guidance when writing many of her articles and books on West African questions, and in her personal contacts with

---

[18] R. Stanley and A. Neame (eds.), *The Exploration Dreams of H.M. Stanley* (London, 1961).

government officials. After her death John Holt took a leading part in the founding and establishing of the Royal African Society in her memory.[19]

He was one of the original founders of the Liverpool School of Tropical Medicine, and his interest and encouragement of Sir Ronald Ross[20] in his fight against malaria resulted in the building by John Holt and Co. of the first mosquito-proof ocean-going steamer ever built.[21]

When illness forced him to retire from active business life he continued his lively interest in African affairs and kept open house to all those, both black and white, who shared his interests.

He was always, to the end of his days, filled with a sincere gratitude towards the West Africans who provided the means of building up his own fortunes, and those of his family. "They made me what I am," he used to say; "their labours, their muscles, their enterprise, have given me everything I possess. I am bound to try and protect them against outrage and injustice," and it was in that spirit throughout his life that he made constant endeavour to discharge the debt which he felt he owed to those who had laid the foundations of his prosperity.

There could be no better ending to this introduction and no more fitting tribute to John Holt's life and work than the words with which Mrs. J.R. Green ended an obituary notice she wrote for the *Journal of the African Society*: "Mr. John Holt had contended both for the material and spiritual side of the British Empire before he was laid to rest. We remember him with honour."

---

[19]Mary Kingsley, *West African Studies* (London, 1899), and *Travels in West Africa* (repr., London, 1976), were her principal works.

[20]Ronald Ross, *Memoirs* (London, 1923) and Liverpool School of Tropical Medicine, *Historical Record, 1898-1920* (Liverpool, 1920). This provides details of Ross' expeditions to West Africa.

[21]*Liverpool Journal of Commerce*, 13 July 1910, gives full details of the *Jonathan Holt*, which had been specially constructed to provide protection against mosquitoes.

The Diary of John Holt

1862

23 June

I have made all preparations for my departure tomorrow in the *Cleopatra* for Fernando Po, and all in one day.[22] I have bought all my clothes; I have had my Carte de Visite taken; I have bade farewell to my friends. I have seen Mr. Lynslager and have got drawn up for his signature a proposal of engagement which is written as a letter and accepted by me. The terms are that I shall engage for 3 years as a clerk, in consideration of which he pays my passage out and gives me board, lodging &c. with £100 per annum.

24 June

Was up at 6 in the morning--a dreary, rainy, drizzly morning, fair type of my own thoughts. Lynslager signed his letter of engagement and gave me instructions. Bade a last farewell to Boyne Hilbon and Henry before leaving old England for so long a time. I might have stayed until next mail but the thought of again enduring the agonies of a second good-bye was enough to deter me from doing so. I am on board and we are off; the die is cast for better or for worse. I trust in Providence. Left Liverpool 10 a.m., Holyhead 6 p.m.

Am not yet sick; it is not very rough. Everything here seems so strange and peculiar; almost all drink; some swear; all idle their time away doing nothing; very different from what I have been accustomed to. There are only some two or three females on board, the rest are men. I expect I shall soon be able to shake off this awful depression of spirits as I get more familiar with my neighbours and the circumstances in which I am situated; at the very time I write, which is evening, my spirits are light compared with what they were this morning.

25 June

We have still splendid weather but since we got from under the lee of the Irish Coast, we have had a nasty roll from the Atlantic which has made me feel a certain peculiarity in the regions of my stomach. Through Mr. Dempster's kindness I have become

---

[22]SS *Cleopatra* (1280 gross registered tons [grt]) was built by Denny in 1852, acquired by the African Steam Ship Company in 1859, and lost at Shebar in August 1862.

acquainted with the Captain and purser.[23] I have also frequently conversed with Mr. Webster the 1st engineer and the mate so that things are now going on a little more pleasantly. In our ship we have a cup of coffee brought by the steward while in bed at about 7 a.m. At 8.30 a.m. we have a good substantial breakfast of tea or coffee, chops, steaks, sausages and other boiled and roasted meats, with bread or biscuits and preserved milk. At 12.30 p.m. lunch is served, composed of cold meats, with potatoes, cold fowls, &c. At 3.30 p.m. we get dinner of roasted and boiled meats and fowls, broth, tarts, puddings, &c.; broth is served first, next the several dishes of meats, after that the tarts and sweet things with cheese, then come oranges, nuts, &c. With lunch and dinner most of the passengers take beer or brandy or some liquor. Tea comes on at 7.30 p.m. and consists of tea or coffee, bread and biscuits, with toast and butter. At 10.15 p.m. a bell rings for the passengers to retire and at 10.30 p.m. the saloon lights are put out and thus we end the day.

26 June

The only people who work on board these vessels are the stewards and, I suppose I may add, the firemen and seamen. The purser does next to nothing and the doctor even less. The Captain and officers have little work, but life at sea is anything but a pleasant existence to me. We have had a fine day again with a slight breeze from the West. Ever since we left Liverpool we have been steaming and since we arrived opposite Holyhead we have had all sail set which however has done us but little good. I was under the impression that when steamers had a pretty good breeze the engines were eased but I have not perceived any reduction of the shake produced by the working of the screws.

27 June

This a strange life; instead of the ceaseless activity to which I have been so long used nothing is to be seen but lazy enjoyments such as gambling, drinking or indolence. The way most of us spend our time is, after breakfast, to commence reading; some, however, walk the decks for a short time enjoying their pipes, after which they read or amuse themselves by gambling, playing with rope quoits, jumping, playing at leap frog, betting without end, raffling, getting up sweepstakes, pitch and toss, trying to walk on a single plank of the deck, and taking the two halves of walnut shells and pushing them together, the one which breaks losing the victory. But with all these things, time appears to hang heavily which predisposes us to think of the homes we are leaving behind us--homes which we never like so much as when we are absent from them; for it is only then we know, or can appreciate, their true value.

28 June

After all, life at sea is not the pleasant life I had pictured to myself when ashore. I find it is difficult to do anything here, because I am so seldom inclined, but even if I am

---

[23]John Holt had become friendly with John Dempster when both were employed by the Lairds; see Davies, *The Trade Makers*, 53. He subsequently became a founder of Elder Dempster and Company.

inclined, there is still difficulty in doing what I wish if it is anything in the shape of writing, on account of the vessel's motion. The sailors say it is not rough but it is rougher than ever I remember to have seen it before. We have had the wind right astern since yesterday morning. As we have been passing through the Bay of Biscay one may reasonably suppose it to be pretty rough as the wind is blowing a good breeze. However, it is not rough enough to make me sick. I certainly have felt particularly delicate in the region of the stomach ever since we left Liverpool.

29 June

I shall never feel the loss of England more than on a Sunday--Sunday at sea--a miserable thought. Alas, how long it must be before I can again enjoy a return of those happy Sundays which I have passed at Oxton.[24] Things are almost the same as usual. People read, but there is very little gambling. Instead of songs we have had psalms, &c. and perhaps to make the day a little different in appearance religious discussion has been indulged in by several.

30 June

This is the last day of my apprenticeship. I write to Mr. Laird thanking him for his kindness and indulgence during my apprenticeship. I also write to most of my relatives and friends in time for our arrival at Madeira. I find great difficulty in concentrating my ideas, this kind of life tends very much to upset one's usual energy and acuteness of thought; my letters I am afraid well read very "boshy."

1 July

Arrived at Madeira and cast anchor off Funchal at about 11 a.m. The town from our anchorage has to me a very foreign appearance. The houses are mostly whitewashed and are situated on the slopes of steep hills. This town, on account of walls enclosing spaces of levelled land, presents a succession of terraces which to my English eyes look very strange. As soon as we are anchored we are surrounded by a shoal of boats manned by Portuguese, to whom the island belongs. The men in each boat endeavour to get the first passenger for the shore who presents himself; this, as may naturally be supposed, is not done without a great deal of jabber and confusion which is increased by lots of boys in boats who show their proficiency in the art of swimming by diving after any piece of silver which their patrons may be inclined to bestow. On going ashore we are at once surrounded by no end of fellows each proffering his service according to his particular vocation. The houses and shops have not the light, airy appearance of our English ones and I should think would not, to us, be so comfortable. The streets are paved all over with stones which are very sharp to our feet and very tiring to our muscles. They are kept very clean and in good order but are comparatively narrow. The flowers are most luxuriant; they hang over the walls in great profusion and at times load the air with their perfume. Potatoes, plantain berries, plums, sugar cane, apples, figs, pears, bananas,

---

[24]Oxton is a residential district of Birkenhead on Merseyside.

cherries, cabbage, tomatoes, grapes, oranges and many other fruits are grown here. The scenery is most magnificent and it would be a glorious winter's retreat. On this day it was very hot, which I , in climbing and coming down the hills, felt severely. I visited the convent and market place. In the latter there are three stalls where I bought apricots, 15 for a penny; peaches were selling at ½d. each and pears equally cheap but these were not ripe. Cherries sold at 2d. per pound--the best. The people are very respectful in their demeanour both towards strangers and each other; they almost invariably take off their hats when meeting another. The whole island I am told is cultivated for the sundries above mentioned; little corn or maize however appears to be grown and from our ship the mountains looked very bare compared with English hills there being very little grass, except in the valleys where water is plentiful. This water is used by the millers to irrigate their fields of Indian corn. The island is well worth visiting.

2 July

We left Madeira last evening. I have not felt very well all day, I suppose in consequence of the quantity of fruit I ate. However I have found myself better towards night and have exerted myself sufficiently to write up my journal since Sunday.

3 July

Arrived at Santa Cruz, Teneriffe, early in the morning. The appearance of this island from the sea is more bare, bold and rugged than Madeira. It looks very majestic and its celebrated peak, which I only saw indistinctly, on account of the hazy atmosphere, as we were leaving, looked magnificent and rises to an immense height, about 12,170 feet. The inhabitants are chiefly Spanish and are not near so respectful as the Portuguese I saw at Madeira. At this place, I saw prettier women, some of whom wear men's "wide awakes" with a square yard or so of cotton, or rather I should say calico, attached. It was too hot for me to see much of the place but from what I learn from other passengers who say a good deal of it I am inclined to think it is not to be compared in any way with our last port. At both places the only mode of conveyance is by a kind of sledge drawn by oxen. Horses do not appear to be used except for riding. At Teneriffe, I am told, camels are also turned to good account. I noticed that the shops had no windows; in some, doors were the means by which light was introduced; in others, besides the door, the shop is made so that the whole (or nearly so) of the side is made of board which is likewise opened. Most of the houses have too, a kind of court open to the street into which the other apartments lead. In many houses there is also a square which contains plants, shrubs and flowers, and around which are galleries. The rooms are high but the hotel in which I saw all this was but poorly furnished and looked very commonplace. I went into the shops for the purpose of examining or purchasing something native, but I saw nothing. Most of the articles bore LONDON in plain English capitals and I did not want them when I could buy the same things for half the value at home. I did however get something made on the island--a glass of wine for which I paid 3d. While ashore I could not help thinking of Nelson's unfortunate attack on this place where he lost his arm and particularly so when I was passing the church in which are kept the flags which were taken from him by the Spanish on that occasion. It is said they are much prized by the natives.

Figure 1: John Holt, Prior to Sailing from Liverpool, 23 June 1862

Source: The John Holt Group, Courtesy of D.J. Holt.

5 July

I am thinking not of the beauties of a tropical sea but of Saturdays past and gone in which I looked with a longing desire for the following day of rest. I must now class this with the things that are past. I have only to do with the present. Sorrow for the past is unavailing; I must look forward, my motto "Excelsior, spero meliora."[25] The other

[25] *Excelsior, spero meloria* literally means "Higher, I hope for better things." It should perhaps be translated as "I aspire and hope for higher and better things."

night I had a beautiful view of the setting sun, it is a sublime sight to see this at sea; a pleasure from which one's heart naturally turns in admiration of the world's Creator.

6 July

I am sorry we have no service on board; everything goes on as usual in the saloon but I believe the Captain and sailors make it as much a day of rest as possible.

7 July

The atmosphere is much clearer here than in more northern latitudes, at least I should judge so from the appearance of the moon and stars which seem more brilliant than they do in England. We also see something else not seen in our seas at home, the flying fish; to-day I have seen many, sometimes alone, sometimes in numbers; at a distance it is hard to distinguish from a bird but the other day one flew on board; its size was about that of a herring with large wings a little beyond the head. The cause of their flying is that a dolphin is in hot chase anxious no doubt for a meal, and I suppose they have little chance of escape from their cannibal foe, when once he begins his race, as they cannot fly far before becoming "fagged." I never see them flying without a feeling of pity for their fall which from the nature of their remorseless enemy is almost certain death.

8 July

Sighted Africa at about 2 o'clock p.m. and arrived at Bathurst at 4 p.m., this being the first time of my seeing this continent which is to be my future home for the next three years. As might be expected I take a lively interest in its belongings and was anxious to get a view of it as soon as possible. At the time we approached the atmosphere was hazy so that we only saw land when we were within a few miles of it, particularly as the land lies very low. This place is considered very unhealthy although the ground is of dry sand. For my own part I was disappointed with its appearance; instead of the disgusting country which one expected to find judging from its notorious climate, I saw nothing striking but the lowness of the land. In fact it resembles very much my own dear Garthorpe or rather Isle of Axholme--low land with trees of good size dotted here and there, fine large buildings and in the harbour some 20 vessels of different sizes, chiefly French, waiting for cargoes of ground nuts. A good many passengers went ashore. I stayed on board watching the "niggers," who are inveterate traders, ply their trade.

Thermometer under ship's awning 98° Fahr., in the sun 128°. I felt this heat fearfully, broiling from morning to night. Had a walk ashore early in the morning. The natives are clean people but their dress and appearance would not please a fastidious person. The market place and barracks are the chief buildings and there are many well built shops and houses of brick or stone. The natives principally inhabit huts built of wood, mud or bamboo, enclosed in a palisading of matted bamboo, which form the streets. There are many idling about doing nothing. The most industrious appear to be the women, some of whom I saw carrying on their heads bags of ground nuts. This ground nut trade, I am told, is principally in the hands of French, although the settlement itself is British. Boats continued to come alongside until 2 o'clock and must have carried a good deal of things ashore from the steamer. A sea breeze blows here from morn to sunset and a land breeze the remainder of the day and night. I believe, from what I can recollect, that this is the case all along the Coast. The odour of these blacks is most offensive when in a state of perspiration. They appear to feel the effects of heat, being in a state of almost continuous perspiration. I could buy nothing useful of native manufacture--almost everything, except food, is brought here for sale from Europe.

10 July

This heat is awful; it interferes sadly with one's comfort day and night. Our passengers may be seen lying about all over the place; some on deck, some on the saloon floor or on the sofas; a few in their berths and all in a state of tremendous perspiration. To-day I assisted the purser to collect passage money from a number of Mandingoes (a people from the interior, of large stature). We has a tedious job of it. They keep their money in all sorts of places--in curious looking bags, in the corners of their handkerchiefs, in little bags kept in strange places. It is brought from somewhere under their clothes, as if by magic. They make all sorts of protestations but of no use--they have to pay. Our chief officer says they are going to Sierra Leone on a trading expedition and that they always try the same game although they well know the amount of passage money; but I suppose they love the talk and squabbling, although I am inclined to think their purses suffer for it as the collectors are not particular about taking a little more than the true amount. The sun was blazing hot on our poor heads while collecting and made us sweat. We passed a great many porpoise and shark to-day. Some of the passengers amused themselves by having a shot at them. Many porpoise leap a great height out of the water and dive down again head first, some follow one after the other and the sight is most amusing.

11 July

Yesterday at dinner I was the innocent cause of a great deal of contention. I had unintentionally taken the seat of a Captain White, who is going out to Bonny as Tobins' chief trader.[26] He commenced enlarging upon my "impertinence" but as I said nothing in return another passenger took up my part, said I had been bullied and as much as offered a challenge. Of course all was done or rather said in harsh and loud language sufficiently so as to disturb the equanimity of the rest of the passengers and make a regular hubbub.

Arrived at Sierra Leone before daybreak. It has a very pretty appearance being surrounded by hills which are clothed with verdure to the tops, the valleys being luxuriant. No vegetation of the usual kind that one finds in the tropics. On going ashore I was very pleased with the town, Freetown, which must contain a population of thousands. Pretty as it certainly appears, it is said to be one of the most unhealthy parts of this deadly Coast: is it not awful and sorrowful to think that in such loveliness, death finds its surest lurking place? The natives have been civil enough to me but they have

[26]The Tobins were an old Liverpool family. John Tobin retired from the sea in 1803, established himself as a West Africa merchant, and became Mayor of Liverpool in 1819. His brother Thomas joined him in 1810 and later became a partner with Charles Horsfall; their joint company dominated the palm oil trade for many years. See Wharton, unpublished mss., 182-183.

generally a bad name, caused chiefly by their means of claiming in their courts of law, justice, perhaps in an elastic sense, for wrongs inflicted by whites. They sue for damage on the most trivial occasions and such is their sense of the distinctions of colour that they usually declare in favour of their own countrymen; cases are tried by a jury composed of blacks. In the case of a person I know who struck a negro on the face, the "darkey" sued him for damages and £60 was awarded. It sounds queer to a white man that he may half kill his own countryman in England and only have to pay a fine of £5, while by thrashing an African who can get the case tried at Sierra Leone, he has to pay £60 for his trouble. The price of bananas sold by retail is three a half-penny, of pine apples one penny each, oranges and other fruit in like proportion; but fruit eaten here, being grown in the country, is far more palatable than the same eaten in England.

13 July

In the morning I went ashore to church; never did a service give me more pleasure than this; lost things are doubly dear; a pity such should be. This is Mr. Train, the purser's, birthday and such a day; eating and drinking, talking, shouting and singing, as if Sundays were made for sprees. These things would be all very well if done in moderation but when people turn blessings into curses by going into extremes, it is decidedly wrong.

14 July

As I expected, those who made so free with their drinking yesterday have to suffer for it this morning. Left Sierra Leone last night. Took on board a quantity of Kroomen;[27] they are a set of merry workers, singing, to tunes peculiar to themselves, when at work and sometimes keeping time to them with their feet. These men are considered invaluable in such a climate as this where Englishmen are not able to work hard without endangering their health, but they appear fit for nothing but hard work and that of the simplest description. They can pull a rope or carry weights as well as white men but for anything else that requires an exercise of something besides brute power they are next to useless. I don't say they are incapable of being taught because I have seen very well-educated and enlightened black men at Sierra Leone, but I speak of them as I find them.

15 July

On waking this morning I found our vessel pitching about rather too emphatically for my stomach for I could eat but little breakfast and on going on deck I soon found myself compelled to vomit. This relieved me for a time but I felt very unwell all day. I however experienced a great difference in the effects of this sickness from what I felt when at sea when only 15 years old. Although I found it to-day very unpleasant it did not make me half so ill and miserable as my former trial.

16 July

---

[27]An account of the life and recruitment of Kroomen is provided on p. 69.

Arrived at Cape Palmas at 5 o'clock and departed at 10. I feel somewhat better to-day but anything but well. We expected to meet the *Athenian* here but she has not arrived.[28] Kroomen were engaged here by passengers for working the oil trade in the rivers, as they can be had much cheaper than at Sierra Leone; they do not, however, trouble themselves with so many clothes as at the latter. Our vessel was surrounded by a fleet of canoes with cargoes of these boys who came on board and kicked up such a bedlam as is never heard in England I'll warrant. They are indeed a curious lot of fellows; they belong to Liberia and are I suppose the descendants of the liberated slaves of America who have here been freed and have formed a republic on the principle of the Yankee constitution. Some of them wear ivory on their ankles and wrists; some prefer steel or beads, while round their necks they also wear beads. Some shave their heads in all kinds of modes, sometimes with a little hair left on each side of the head, sometimes with only the crown bare. Their skins are also very marked, some are dyed with a line running on the top of the nose. How astonished they would be in England if we were to land there instead of Africa. They would stare at our boys, but what is there to stare at? One is so used to think of a black man as being next to naked that, when we really see one we are not much shocked or surprised at his appearance; it seems natural to find him so. It would be very different if they were white but only so because it would be an unusual thing to see them in such a state. If we knew them to be so, we should feel no more repugnance or surprise. But whether white or black, I think they look much better with clothes on; but a black man might think differently and who shall say which has the best taste. It is merely a matter of opinion and I suppose everyone has a right to his own so long as it affects himself alone.

17 July

The purser finds himself a gentleman now I am doing all his work, so far as writing goes, and I am glad to have the opportunity of doing so as there is no knowing how soon I may want it. I forgot to enter on 7th that I wrote home to friends in England which will soon be near 5,000 miles from me. Beloved England, no Swiss ever loved his native mountains more than I love thee, my country. I have missed the bag my friends at Jersey Cottage made me. I do not wish to wrong anyone but I suppose someone has taken a particular fancy to it. I would far rather they had taken anything else but it is a fancy thing and would sell well here.

18 July

I don't feel at all well, perhaps it may be the effects of sea sickness or it may be change of climate; anyhow it is a particularly uncomfortable feeling. I am disinclined for work and afflicted with lassitude as if I were fit for and could do nothing but sit and idly waste away time. None of the energy or desire for employment (or at all events very little of it) which I felt in England. The way we mark the flight of time is by the ringing of the bells every half hour; thus for 12-30 one bell is struck, for 1 p.m. two bells and so one

---

[28] SS *Athenian* (1107 grt), built by Smith in 1854 for the African Steam Ship Company, was sold in 1871.

every half hour until 4 o'clock, when it commences again with one bell at 4-30 and continues changing from eight bells to one bell every four hours. The purser and chief officer could not agree to-day. As we approached Cape Coast the purser with several of the passengers went on the bridge; it appears the chief officer told them to leave it, but the purser not choosing to comply with his request, the chief officer, after the ship was moored, commenced lecturing him on the subject and told him that he was his master. After a good many words on both sides it ended by the purser calling him a liar upon which the chief officer seized him by the collar and raising his fist threatened to thrash him. The purser no doubt having great faith in the old adage "He who fights and runs away" or "Discretion is the better part of valour," retreated to his berth.

19 July

Arrived at Cape Coast last night; people from shore bring sad news. The fever at Bonny continues unabated and, worse still, it has infected Fernando Po. This looks bad and bids fair to put a stop to my ambitious dreams; however, I will hear more before I decide upon my future course. Mr. Fell has offered me a month's hospitality at Lagos if I like to accept it but I think I will go as far as Fernando Po. If I find matters so very bad I will take advantage of his offer and return. It is enough to make one wish he had never left England but then why should I; Heaven has it purposes in the shaping of a man's life and if it has pleased God to send me out here ought I not to trust in providence, to go where duty calls me and to hope for the best? This is a serious matter, one which affects the dearest of earthly ties, my life; and although it would make an imperceptible difference to the world if I were to lose my life, still there are some who would deeply feel the loss and none are less desirous of the end than myself; life is dear to me. I am young and full of hope and ambition, perhaps the time may come when I shall think but little of this world, its joys, its hopes, its cares or sorrows, but experience and sad experience must work the change. May God help and guide me in doing what may be best for me; I am as a child, helpless, and can only look to Him for guidance and support not only for the present evil but for time and eternity.

The news I heard at Cape Coast is confirmed from what I have heard ashore to-day. The yellow fever is raging in Fernando Po and the rivers continue unhealthy. I did not see much of Accra.[29] The earthquake has knocked down several houses and cracked many but I hear only one person has been killed. This is a healthy looking place with mountains in the distance, the most prevalent diseases being I hear dysentery and the guinea worm which is supposed to be caused by the bad water. I, with the captain and several others, dined at the house of a native. The house proper was built over the shop and consisted of one large room, considered here perhaps well furnished, it had no windows but folding doors answered their purpose; on one side these doors lead on to a plastered ground supported beneath by walls; from this a flight of steps lead to the yard and in the yard was situated the water tank, some depth in the earth, which looked more like a duck pond walled in than a supply of drinkable water. We had a good dinner of soups and turkeys, &c. and a dessert of pine apples, ground nuts and grapes. Most of the houses belonging to the natives are of mud and but few Europeans, I think, live here.

[29]Accra was the principal town of the Gold Coast and subsequently became the capital of Ghana.

Indeed on all this coast there are comparatively very few white men resident. I did not go ashore at Cape Coast but I may state here that it is situated on elevated ground and looks healthy enough but I understand it has the same faults as to water, &c. as Accra. The purser obtained a summons for Sampson at Cape Coast Castle. Sunday is past, how sadly different from what I have been accustomed to.

21 July

Cast anchor off Badagry at dark, the Captain being under the impression that it was Lagos. I suppose the Captain was misled by the number of ships at anchor there; it was also very dark at the time and I am told he was unable to take the sun's altitude but I can't see how such a mistake could occur if the log had been thrown overboard and the time of our departure from Accra noted. Both the Captain and officers it appears were astonished that we should have arrived at the supposed Lagos so soon; the mate said that he made the distance, according to his calculation, 20 miles off.

22 July

Arrived at Lagos this morning between 6 and 7 having left Badagry at 2 p.m. and with a strong wind and the greatest sea I have yet felt. Lagos from where we are anchored, outside the bar, cannot be seen. The breakers appear to stretch quite across the mouth of the lagoon in which Lagos is situated. None but vessels of light draught can cross this and cargo has to be sent to ships outside in canoes. This must necessarily greatly increase the expenses on goods exported or imported but in spite of these hindrances to commerce Lagos has a pretty active trade in palm oil, &c.[30] A tug is kept here by a Lagos house to tow in such vessels as can cross the bar for which they charge 5/-per tow. Yesterday the purser asked me if I would return in this ship as purser, if wanted; I don't yet know his reasons for asking such a question but the bare idea of returning home in three months instead of three years has risen my spirits from zero to blood heat. I have also had another hint from a Dr. McMath who is going out as supercargo up the Benin; his promises are fair. Some of these Bonny traders, young fellows who have got their initiating term of servitude over, speak indifferently of my situation at Fernando Po. I don't know how far they may be correct. If a person has health and a fair share of sense he may soon get to be a supercargo and some of these boys after an absence from England of three or four years are known to take their £10,000 or £15,000 home with them.[31] Such salaries as these can only be obtained where there is but little competition and I suppose the want of that, to the extent we see it in England, is on account of the climate the sickly nature of which I see more striking proofs daily.

---

[30] Despite the bar at its entrance, Lagos rapidly became the most important port on the coast. See Davies, *The Trade Makers*, 116.

[31] For an example of high mercantile earnings, see P.N. Davies (ed.), *Trading in West Africa* (London, 1976), 178-179.

23 July

Still outside Lagos until the afternoon. Some of our passengers at almost every calling place are like sailors just arrived home, in for a spree. A young officer from ashore who stayed with us all night, a fast young man, very talkative and rather intoxicated, commenced chaffing with one of our passengers, a Dr. Davey, a man very similar, with the utmost confidence in the strength of his arm which makes him partake of a good deal of boasting as to what his capabilities are and continuing this until they had well nigh quarrelled. The "sojer boy" had ultimately to be requested to leave the ship.

24 July

Arrived off the mouth of Benin River early this morning. Have been taking in palm oil all day from a schooner anchored some 100 yards or so from us. The casks were thrown overboard with a rope attached by which they were hauled alongside. This is a very tedious process. We took on board a Dr. Henry who a short time ago lost his wife. I am informed that through the persuasion of Mrs. Henry her husband was induced to flog a native chief for some misdemeanour which he had committed. Some time afterwards when Dr. Henry was absent this chief, with a number of men, broke into his house with the supposed intention of taking revenge on his wife. She however managed to escape from the house, which they ransacked, and hid herself in the bush for a night. She was attacked with fever shortly afterwards which eventually killed her. Some chief and men also came and took all his goods, worth a great deal of money, and walked off with them. Indeed from what I have heard him say he has lost from £10,000 to £18,000 in one year. He has been unable to obtain assistance from the men-of-war here cruising or the British Governor at Lagos. He is now going to first lay his case before the British consul at Fernando Po, having in the meantime written to the Foreign Office, and if nothing can be done there for him I believe he intends to prosecute the affair in England.

25 July

We left Benin this morning and have been coasting along shore all afternoon and I can distinguish nothing on shore but trees which appear as if growing in the sea. I should fancy from what I have read that these trees must be the mangrove. Yesterday was an awfully drunken day; I never saw such a waste of wine. Several passengers were leaving us and of course must take a parting cup. I am more used to this kind of life than when I first came on board and cannot view it or think of it with the same feelings of annoyance and pity. At first whenever I saw people gambling, swearing and drinking I was sorry and annoyed, for on the outbreak of every curse I could not help noticing it. Now, however, it having been so often repeated and having become so usual, I have grown familiar to the sounds and did not always notice the error of so doing. Of course I have the same dislike of such evils when I think of them, but I can almost imagine a person who by so constantly hearing people swear may unconsciously take to it himself merely through habit.

26 July

Arrived at Bonny which if ever a place merited the name of "the white man's grave," it does. The yellow fever has left hardly any white men there. I had expected to have seen more ships as it is the best palm oil river on the Coast. At present the trade must be a monopoly. The river is wide and has a good channel; it is also buoyed. On both sides of the river is a profusion of vegetation but the land is low. A sea breeze generally prevails here and it is generally considered the healthiest river on the Coast. I have been in the habit of playing a game at cards with the engineers, who are nice fellows, particularly the chief engineer, Mr. Webster. We drank a glass to our wives, bairns and sweethearts, this being Saturday night. It appears this is a custom at sea of which I was not aware until I came on board this vessel. Another wrinkle.

27 July

Left the *Cleopatra* this noon. Another tie broken. I have become so intimate with the crew of this vessel and have been such a long time with them that I regret their loss. This is human. We make friends and take to liking things familiar and when we part from them we feel their loss and grieve.

28 July

Arrived at Fernando Po, my destination, the place whence it has pleased God to send me.[32] It has a beautiful appearance being completely covered with trees as far as can be seen but I must leave my description of it until I become better acquainted with it. Wrote home to parents and friends. A little yellow fever is still stirring here, but having been advised by my fellow-passengers, among others by Dr. Henry, to stay here I have resolved to do so instead of going back to Lagos. In doing the latter I should have to go through Bonny waters and it is thought by some that the fever is little better there. I delivered my letter of introduction to Mrs. Lynslager who was glad to hear news of her husband's good health and then wrote Mr. Lynslager advising him of my arrival. I am now on Spanish ground and have bade farewell to my present personal connection to things English, although in heart and mind I am a Briton still and, like every true one, proud of my country and my home. May God grant I may ever remain so.

29 July

Of all the hissings and tumultuous rows that ever I heard this beats all. I have been used to the working of a screw for the last month but it is not to be compared with the uproar caused by what I am told are lizards and cockroaches. They commence their hissing at sunset and continue until I fall asleep while ants and other "animals" unknown to my foreign senses gambol and fly all over. There is one blessing, however, mosquitos "no live here." I have done nothing to-day in the way of business but have been employed

---

[32]Fernando Po was the original terminus of the African Steam Ship Company and the most southerly point that could take advantage of regular sailings to Liverpool. See Davies, *The Trade Makers*, 43.

assisting Dr. Henry with his correspondence relating to the affair up Benin River and looking about the premises with the clerk. At some part of the day I have not felt well, a dizziness and swimming in the head on moving it. I suppose this however is the effect of the climate; I cannot expect to be freed from the evils which must attend such a sudden and marvellous change, a change the very opposite to what I have been accustomed. I am undergoing a sort of regeneration not only in body but in things outwards. How extraordinary to English people would appear the inside arrangements and comforts of an African abode with all its accompaniments of negro and every peculiarity the very opposite to their own, if they could be for a time transported into England. It would almost be worth one's while to attempt something of the kind if only for the novelty of the thing.

30 July

Busy the greater part of the day helping Dr. Henry who is going to have his correspondence on the Benin River affair published in England. I feel very strange and awkward with my duties here. To-day Mrs. Lynslager wanted to know the prices of some goods sent from England by last mail. I added 75% to the invoice price but Mrs. Lynslager seems very much inclined to doubt the accuracy of my calculations. This is novel work, my present experiences are of a ship keeping nature. I must try to show a little more courage before these fair blacks. To-day one wanted to know the price of petticoats, a nice question to ask a bachelor, and on looking over the list I came across chemises. What would my feelings have been had she asked how I sold them; I ought to have been a draper or grocer but not having had the privilege of learning the duties belonging to that class of society I am at a loss. I do not find a great variety in our dishes here. At 9 a.m. we have breakfast of fowls, coffee, pork, &c. and at dinner at 4 p.m. we have the same with the exception of coffee. These two meals are the only ones each day.

31 July

It was my intention to have taken stock to-day but being very unwell I was obliged to postpone it. Mrs. Lynslager has also been unwell all day. My afflictions are pains in the bowels, a little in the back and head but I suppose it is the change of climate and food &c., indeed an almost total change. When I first went to Liverpool the change was sufficient to cause an attack of diarrhoea, therefore the fact that this should be again repeated when coming to Africa is not to be wondered at. This however makes it little the less difficult to bear.

1 August

I am much better this morning, indeed I suppose as well as I can expect to be. I have been busy all day taking an account of all the things in both shops so as to enable me to commence a new set of books; this I am obliged to do as I cannot make either head or tail of the books which have lately been kept here and I should likewise prefer to commence a system of mine own. Dr. Henry has this day departed in the *Bloodhound* with Consul Burton for the purpose of obtaining satisfaction against the people of Benin River for the injuries done him. I feel his loss, now that he is gone I am a total stranger here for although I have only become acquainted with him since we left Benin together in the mail steamer we have become very intimate for so short an acquaintance. Captain Roberts of H.M.S. *Wyl*, another nice old gent from what I have seen of him, has also left to-day. I have therefore none but English residents to whom I have any affinity, for at present I believe there is but one English ship in the harbour of whom I know nothing and ashore I only know two Englishmen in Laughland's office and they do not appear to care much for any society if I may judge from the frequency of their visits.

2 August

Yesterday I made a regular clearance in the shop under our house. I have taken stock of the goods in it and instead of leaving a lot of servant girls to attend I have put a black clerk in it whom I have told that I shall hold him responsible for all the goods under his charge and of which he must give an account. I have told him how to do this by putting down on a slate all money received during the day and for what received, if on credit for house use to make a note of it and to enter all these in a day book provided for the purpose. In this book I also enter an account of all cash received, from which at certain intervals I intend to journalise. I am sadly bothered how to arrange the nominal accounts. Mr. Lynslager has two shops, a farm, is agent for coaling Government vessels and men of war, sells and buys poultry, and has lots of traders all over the country who have got goods in hand as well as palm oil. To commence properly I should have a knowledge of every halfpenny he is worth, I could then make a correct capital account; as it is I can only take and account of the goods and make of them a capital account, this will be omitting the greater part of his capital but I can see no help for it; had he just been commencing business instead of having his money and goods all over the world my duties would have been much less onerous.

3 August

The most extraordinary Sunday that ever I passed in my life. Nothing but my own thoughts and the company of my black friends, with whom I as yet converse but little, to pass the time away. I may often think of home and the past during week days when I have work to do, but on Sundays I shall ever feel its loss most deeply. This place being Spanish, none but the Roman belief is openly allowed. There is only service once on Sunday at 8 a.m.; the rest of the day is as each one pleases. The street before our house, which faces the sea, is the favourite fashionable promenade, the Bold Street of Fernando Po on Sundays when the beaux and belles of the place dress themselves in their finest and most brilliant feathers and strut and mince up and down like our own fashionables.[33] Some of the belles are dressed quite in the English style, crinoline flounces and all, while others dressed according to native fashion, and some preferred a combination of both. I was much amused at my good lady to-day whom I saw in an American four-wheeled spring conveyance drawn by Krooboys, it looked so odd and strange.

---

[33] "Bold Street" was the centre of fashion in Liverpool.

Figure 2: James Lynslager (1810-1864), Governor of Fernando Po, c. 1858

Source: See Figure 1.

4 August

Mr. Wilson a clerk of Laughland's was supposed to be lost on Saturday, a party was sent in search of him by the Governor and he was found on Sunday, trying to find himself, after having been without food some 24 hours.[34] He had been on an excursion up the mountain and lost himself in the labyrinth of paths by which it is intersected.

[34]Taylor, Laughland and Company were an important West African merchant firm in Glasgow. See Wharton, unpublished mss., 181.

5 August

A Boobee marriage party came to our house to-day. These Boobees are the natives of the island and are a dirty lazy lot of beings. The bridegroom had matting plaited round his arms and legs with a rum looking hat, beads and other absurd looking things. The bride was dressed in a similar style, her head-dress was very high and consisted of a goat's skin from which was suspended tassels hanging over the face; she had beads and matting likewise. They were attended by people dressed more ludicrous if possible. I was unable to find which was the bride until told. They, it appears, make a practice of visiting on these occasions for the purpose of getting presents. After sitting and squatting in our house for a short time the female part of the party favoured us with a dance, the bride taking part in the performance. A very dull dance it was, no spirit in it whatever, a simple shuffle and twist of the body with a low mumbling, an unceasing grumble of the voice. I was so little interested in it that I was not sorry to see them walk.

6 August

Yesterday I went to report myself to the Governor as, this being a Spanish settlement, such is the order of things. I felt my lack of his language, no doubt he equally felt his lack of mine. I could only make my bow and stare at him while the interpreter was talking something which appeared to relate to me. I was told that the Governor was much obliged for my visit and so I made another bow and retired. Thus ended this most important visit which to me and my view of matters was totally unnecessary and tended to nothing; but this may be because I was unable to hold conversation with him; had it been otherwise, I might have enjoyed it.

7 August

A soaking wet day. Still busy with the stock and as the transport, which lately brought some emigrants from Havana, is leaving on Saturday I am writing to Mr. Lynslager. Regarding these emigrants I understand that the Spanish Government is anxious to eradicate everything English on this island and to make it an exclusively Spanish colony. At present the inhabitants of this place speak the English language, believe in their religion and more or less are used to English customs but the Spaniards wish to change all this and in its place to plant things Spanish. This is the reason of their emigrating their West Indian slaves but not this only, they also wish to cultivate and colonise this island which is believed capable of growing almost everything the world can produce as it has so great a variety of climate. They are to serve either in the army or as labourers for about seven years, after that time they are to have land to commence on their own account, being at the same time free men. As soon as possible I hear the Governor intends to construct a road up the mountain with these men and at certain intervals to have stations along the road at which as they become free they will be housed.

8 August

This house in which I live is made of wood and of an oblong shape. It has two stories, the bottom one is used as a shop and store, the upper one is the house proper and is reached by a wooden flight of steps in the front and back parts of the building. In the front these steps lead on to the balcony which extends along one side of the house, the shop being underneath. Six pairs of folding doors form the entrances into the rooms; the inside is divided into two unequal parts by a wooden partition extending as far as the eaves where a second floor is laid; above the partition is a wooden palisading three or four feet high, behind which is hung, for half its height; a netted screen. This apartment is also used as a store for light goods, underneath it are two rooms, one well furnished, as either a drawing room or bedroom if a stranger stays. A sofa is put in this room and the sofa is so made that it can be used as a bed. The other room is the private sanctum of our good lady and her husband. These two rooms communicate by doors with the largest room; this is the room into which we first enter when coming into the house; four pairs of folding doors admit you, inside are two large tables, sideboard, sofas, chairs &c.; it is hung with pictures on the partitions. In this room we dine, eat, drink, live, receive visitors &c. It is the grand room, a room of rooms. Although not the best furnished, its top is the roof of the house and on its furthest side and facing the back is my office and bedroom which are divided from each other by a wooden partition: they in turn are divided from the main room by another partition of the same material which rises a distance of about 10 feet from the floor and is open at the top. At each end of the house shutters are made which in the day are propped open with pieces of wood, these, with jalousies which are also opened every morning, compose the whole end of the house to a height of several feet, so that when all are opened there remains but the props which support the building. In this house the folding doors have panes of glass inserted as in England, some have jaloused doors. the house is covered with bamboo matting fastened on the top by long pieces of wood laid on the roof and extending over the balcony. The apartments at the back have only glass windows, no jalousies or shutters; these are thrown back and fastened during the day, at night time all is closed. The entrance to the retail shop is through the yard to one end of the house, at the front. A door leads from the little garden to the store. As high as the first story the house is barred [tarred], above that it is painted. Inside it is in some parts painted, in others varnished. The upright and cross parts of the panelled partition being painted, the inside of these varnished.

11 August

Yesterday I tried to write a description of our house but omitted to say that such a one is worth £1,000. And now for the invariable accompaniments of a house. Attached is a garden, which would not be considered well kept in England but which is almost so compared with other gardens here. In the garden stands an alligator pear tree, an orange tree, a mango tree and a lemon besides sundry flower trees whose names are unknown to me; while in it also are grown cocco, a something in the shape of a kidney potato with a rough skin, which I have not tasted, cabbages, sweet potatoes, &c. Our premises must altogether cover more than half an acre of ground and in it, besides the house and garden, is a small unoccupied piece of land in which grows a bread tree and here the cooking house stands with sleeping room attached and a place for empties and rubbish. The rubbish heap is full of filth and everything in it is upside down: the goats are fastened here at night so that its cleanliness and sweetness may readily be imagined. The cook house is something similar; on one side is a shelf, on which the cook operates; the floor is used for a hearth as there are no fire places and wood is burnt for fuel. The smoke has to find its way through the roof, door or a window, there being no chimney for that purpose. This of course makes the place as black as a smithy. The sleeping place attached is for the cook and other men who belong to the house. The sleeping arrangements are very simple, a mattress thrown over a raised platform serves each man for his nap. I had almost forgotten the fowl house; our good lady keeps ducks, fowls, guinea fowls, geese, turkeys, goats and she has also a cow. These things are very necessary as it is principally on these that we have lived since I came here.

13 August

To-day I went with Capt. Mulligan as far as the head of the southern point of Clarence Cove and was surprised at the numbers of guavas we met with. Many of them were ripe and the ground was covered with the trees on which they grow. They are wild and the quantity which I saw was astonishing; I came back with three dozen besides what I had eaten. Every other yard the Captain would draw my attention to a nice one and I, agreeing with him on the point, went on pulling them and filling my pockets until I could hold no more and was obliged to turn my longing eyes away. On this point is erected a monument to the memory of those who died in the Niger Expedition in 1841 and at another part of it is one which was intended to be erected to the memory of the late Governor Beecroft having been subscribed for by the residents here. It has been purchased and brought out to the very place where it is to be erected but for want of someone to look after the affair it lays covered with grass and guava trees. Such things as these are a proof of the want of energy or else the procrastination of these people. It has been purchased at a great expense and now that it is at the very spot where it should be erected it is left to go to ruin, a memorial of the evaporating character of a negro's gratitude. I saw a cannon left there by the English and a well also dug by them for the purpose, I am told, of getting fresh water but I don't see how they could expect this when the well is only some few feet from the sea.

14 August

Our establishment consists of Mr. and Mrs. Lynslager, a son of the late Governor Beecroft, for whom Mr. Lynslager is guardian, nine wenches, three boys and myself. These sleep in the house, outside is a cook and two or three men. Besides these, we have a clerk in the house ship whose assistant is one of the above girls and in the other shop, in another part of the town, two girls, also some 18 Kroomen who do any kind of labour. The girls who live in the house are too thick by half; they do nothing but wash clothes, look after the three bedrooms and wait on Mrs. Lynslager except when Mr. Lynslager is at home when, I am told, it is usual for them to lend him a hand in his bath and dressing. This seemed rather too delicate for me but although Beecroft cannot get into this room when the "old man" is dressing, the girls have a free passage and have to wash him all over. They sleep in the same room with Mr. and Mrs. Lynslager but it appears to be nothing thought of. The three boys are for the purpose of cleaning the large room and office and for waiting at table, &c. If I had an establishment of this kind I fancy I should make about a third of our number of girls and boys do for me; however, I suppose it must be fashionable here, perhaps it may be a sign of aristocracy as our powdered flunkies are at home.

Figure 3: Clarence Cove, Santa Isabel, Fernando Po. Based on a photograph taken in the 1870s.

Source: See Figure 1.

15 August

Mrs. Lynslager has been at her farm since Monday, she took most of the girls and Krooboys to work there so that we have had a little peace. This evening I went there by boat. It must be from four to five miles and is situate[d] on a projecting point of land N.W. from this place from which it can be plainly seen as it is on the eastern side of this point. This was a strange looking farm compared with ours at home; instead of a cleared space with dykes and hedges, corn, potatoes, &c., &c., it was covered with trees and the roots of trees, planted with yams, plantains, bananas, coffee trees, cocoa trees, pine apples, sugar canes, &c., placed in a very higgledy piggledy sort of way. The farm is intersected by footpaths in no particular direction, the grass and weeds grow very quickly and she is busy with her men and wenches clearing it away: this is done with knives with which the grass is cut, put on a heap and when dry, burned. Mrs. Lynslager has charge of this, she only visits it occasionally to help those whom she keeps on the place to look after it during her absence. She has a fellow there who like nearly all who have the chance prefer making an easy time of it rather than exerting himself to keep things in order. Out here people don't know the meaning of that word, nothing has a proper place, they are the most careless, wasteful beings I ever saw; this proceeds from nothing but laziness.

16 August

To-day I took a walk as far as Coal Bay which is the place where English and other steamers take their coal from stocks kept by Mr. Lynslager as agent for the English and American governments. He has cleared a road from Clarence or, as the Spaniards call it, Santa Isabel to this place which is distant about a mile. It must not be imagined that this road is anything like what is called a road in England; there it is understood to be a paved or stoned highway fit for drawing vehicles over but here things are different, the roads are not paved, they are simply land which has been cleared of bush. Stone roads are not required where everything is carried by men. The road is lined with a great many trees and bush with grass, &c. Some of the trees are remarkably high such as I never saw before. If the wood which grows here could only be for a few years in England until its peculiar use was known, and some must certainly be very valuable, there would very probably be a good timber trade established. It seems a pity to see nature so lavish in its development and to be passed by without a notice or without being cared for, or made use of by man while where its blessing may be said to be less abundant it is properly appreciated. But plenty will induce laziness and carelessness and ease while necessity promotes industry, activity and energy. Not being anything of a botanist which I much regret, I know nothing of the trees which I saw save the palm tree of which there were a great number.

17 August

This morning a bird of the owl kind was caught on the balcony; these people say it is a witch bird and Mrs. Lynslager had the poor thing tied and put in a covering with straw inside and burnt to death. I had thought the intercourse with the English which they have had would have removed these superstitions which happily are little believed in England but it appears I have been mistaken in such supposition.

31 August

To-day there has been a great deal of marrying and giving in marriage. The Spaniards have married a lot of these Cubans by wholesale. I should think there can be little liking on either side in such matches as these. I don't know whether they like it or not but it seems strange to one who has always thought of exercising his own judgement and having a little bit of his own way when this shall occur to him.

1 September

To-day I was attacked by the African fever. I did not at any period of to-day think that such was the case believing that I had caught a little cold which was the cause of my present slight headache. At night I took measures to give me a perspiration; this however seemed to have little effect for on rising the following morning I found myself as bad as ever. All to-day I lived on about 2 ounces of yam, towards nine o'clock I felt worse with headache, a peculiar dullness and had a rather dry, hot skin. I thought however that this was nothing to be afraid of so I took my old Inverness and wrapping myself in it, lay down on the sofa. Mrs. Lynslager wished to send for the doctor but I assured her that it was only a temporary headache which required no medicine for a cure--towards noon, feeling myself worse, I went to bed but before doing so I took a few spoonfuls of arrowroot (not having tasted anything at breakfast) with a little brandy in it. After I had done this I felt my head growing hotter and hotter with a dry skin, the heat likewise extended over the whole of the trunk but my feet were very cold. I did not like this so sent for the doctor, meanwhile the fever (for there was no mistaking it now) continued until it was very painful. At length, sometime in the afternoon, I felt something different, my hands were a little wet at first, I felt other parts of my body and they also appeared to feel damp. I fancied that the fever was over now so I thought I would give it a lift off by a gentle exertion of the muscles of the legs and arms. I soon produced a good perspiration; this would have been hastened if I could have got hold of a cup of hot tea which I asked for directly I felt the turn but this was only brought after I had got into a state of good perspiration. The doctor came and said that all was well, gave me nothing for the present but ordered me some mustard plasters for my forehead. These through inattention were never applied. On Wednesday I felt very weak, took some quinine pills, had tea and toasted bread in water for drinks and nothing to eat. The doctor called morning and evening reporting progress towards recovery. On Thursday I took castor oil which did its work effectually and in a short time, this is the first opening medicine given my by the doctor. On Friday and Saturday all went on the same; no physic, no medicine, very little to eat and on the latter part of Saturday I was able by great exertion to dress myself and toddle into the room. I am greatly weakened but the folks here say it is only a slight attack. It may have been such but it was quite enough; I never in my life had anything half so serious and it is a most disagreeable thing to have even in its simplest form. I pity all the more those who may have had more serious attacks, mine was enough to be very painful, to lay me up for a week and to make me so weak that it will take several weeks to see me as I was before the fever touched me. I am sorry to have to notice the neglect of the doctor and of the people under whose care I live. The doctor instead of coming when sent for only came when the fever was going and the greatest danger over. The servants would not obey my wishes when I wanted anything, I had to first ask Mrs. Lynslager and then patiently wait for they are never in a hurry. Mrs. Lynslager may be kind but she did not anticipate my wants or make the servants attend to me as I could have desired. Indeed I am of opinion that a person dangerously ill out here would stand a much less chance of recovery than another person with the same degree of illness would in England on account of insufficient attention to his wants. These blacks are deficient both of activity and sympathy, both of which are necessary in a nurse.

I could not help contrasting my present attentions with what I should receive if in the same condition at home, how every wish would be anticipated, how every want attended to, how friends would come and endeavour to amuse and sympathise with me, none of which I now know. I was lonely and felt lonely as if cared for by no one near me but thank God it is past and I may never have another such sickness amongst my African friends. I suppose I must have had another slight touch sometime during last week but if so I scarcely felt it. I don't know how to account for this, I have been most careful in adopting the measures recommended by Hutchinson for the prevention of fever. I have taken quinine daily;[35] I have been very little exposed to the night air or the sun; at the time of the fever my bowels were open sufficiently; I have been careful in my food and have drunk scarcely any spirits or wine. I have risen early in the morning and gone to bed early at night and a fever is the result whatever Hutchunson's experience may have been to the contrary. To-day I am better than I have felt since the attack except for an occasional pang in the spine and a little dizziness in my head. My hollow eyes and prominent nose are however telling facts that the ravages of the fever are not yet repaired. To-day it is hotter than I have before felt it. The weather is merging into the dry season, lately the thermometer has been standing in the morning at 75° and increasing towards noon to 80°, where it has stood until late on at night. This morning it was 75° as usual, at noon it was 83°.

11 September

Thermometer for the greater part of the day about 78°. A rainy day--I may here mention that my thermometer is Fahrenheit. The *Retriever* came in to-day, she is taking in coals after which she proceeds southwards in search of cargo.[36] If she is successful in finding any it is expected she will continue to go to Loanda, Gaboon, &c. monthly. This will be a great advantage to those living south if it is only carried out. I hope she will find sufficient cargo to give them encouragement.

12 September

Thermometer at 78°: wet drizzly day. Had breakfast on board the *Retriever*. This is a treat, we are so used to the same food on shore that a change is very welcome. We had some capital cocoa to breakfast. I mention this because I have tried to get it ashore but the stuff they brought me for cocoa was not fit to be drunk. I have very little to do now but read and study. I am endeavouring to get an insight into Spanish; whether I shall succeed or not remains to be seen. In the evening I went to see Jane, a black girl who came out at the same time I did, she has changed her English dress for the native costume and to my mind she looks much better and more natural in her present one. She is as nice a girl as I have met out here and having been in Glasgow some time she is a more interesting person to converse with than others of her sex brought up here. She is taking quinine and has been doing so ever since her return. Thermometer 78° and 79°. Cloudy but fair with strong breeze for a few hours at noon.

15 September

Thermometer 78° to 80°. I am in trouble again. To-day Mammy came from the farm and it appears the cook had kept half a fowl for dinner and gave the other half to myself and

---

[35]Quinine was used to help prevent the onset of malaria and also to assist in its treatment. See C. Lloyd, *The Navy and the Slave Trade* (London, 1949), 137-138.

[36]SS *Retriever* (329 grt) was built by Denny for the African Steam Ship Company in 1854 and was sold in 1867.

Beecroft. I did not like this so I told the cook to bring up the other half; he would not do it so I took it myself. He told me it was for Mammy but these fellows have so little sense and are such hypocrites that I took no notice of him--Mammy however was hungry and she did not like my proceedings. In the evening I went to the consulate to see Capt. Thompson who is ill there and on returning home at 9.30 p.m. I found the place locked up. On finding this I immediately returned to the Consulate and said to Capt. Thompson that I was locked out. Mr. Wilson, the Vice-Consul, was absent so I took off my coat and laid down on the sofa as Capt. Thompson was going to bed and I felt very sleepy. Some time afterwards I awoke and found Mr. Wilson and Capt. Thompson in the room. I immediately told Mr. Wilson that I had been locked out and had come to seek a bed at the Consulate. He made some remark about it and afterwards went to bed. In the morning a black man came into the room with a lot of Kroomen asking who I was, what business I had there and said that he was the steward of the house and that it was a great piece of impudence on my part to go and sleep in the room without saying anything to anyone about it and threatened to send me to the quartel. I immediately appealed to Mr. Wilson when to my great astonishment he very unkindly said he knew nothing about me: I never had his permission to stay there and instead of assisting me was against me and made matters worse than ever. I was sorry to hear Mr. Wilson say this, I had thought him a friend as we were on very good terms previously and I don't think any friend would have done this. Had he come into my house for a night's rest even under any circumstances I would never have allowed anyone to ask him what business he had there or threaten to put him into the hands of a lot of Kroomen and send him to court. Mr. Wilson is a great stickler on propriety I suppose, or he perhaps does not wish to encourage my friendship. I had calculated on his friendship as he had previously shown himself disposed to companionship and had always been kind and polite; perhaps this was only politeness, an artificial friendship, an outward profession of what never really existed; perhaps not having had much experience amongst strangers I have mistaken politeness for friendship. However this may be I was placed in a very awkward situation, it appeared as if I had gone into the house of a stranger and had made myself at home by taking my night's rest in it. I felt Mr. Wilson's unkindness very much and felt very grieved on that account. I explained to the man how matters were, told him that had I known him to have possession of the house I should never have thought for one moment of going inside it without asking his permission. I said that I had spoken to Mr. Wilson and had thought that I was no intruder. This pacified him and before I left he was as polite and amiable as any black man could be. On my return in the morning I asked Mrs. Lynslager why she had locked me out and wished her to tell me a time when she closed her doors at which I would always endeavour to be in. I also spoke to her about the dinner. It was soon explained, the boy had fastened the gate without her orders but then she never called him to account for it and of course this only serves to encourage them to do as they like with me. I wish Mr. Lynslager was at home so that I might understand my position and if not satisfied, return home. These disputes unsettle my mind and make me very unhappy, but I suppose I have yet to learn what life is and must prepare myself to bear its trials. If I give way to some men I may be run over and thought nothing of, quiet people are generally worse treated than those who love strife or who return kick for kick with their neighbours.

19 September

Thermometer from 75° to 80°. I do not know whether this climate will agree with me but I have not felt its effects so much of late. When I first came I was troubled with giddiness and a peculiarly languid sleepy feeling. Although not altogether without these now, I feel on the whole somewhat better and if I could have an easier mind it would I have no doubt tend to make me more healthy. The annoyances with which I have to put up with at present gave me constant trouble at first but I am gradually getting to make no trouble of them.

20 September

The *Retriever* arrived last night from the south. I can see she has got little if anything in her as I cannot perceive any difference in her trim. None of the officers have favoured me with a call so that I am not certain of the result of her visit.

21 September

Sunday is not the day of rest it used to be with me; my body may be pretty easy but my mind is not. Sunday is indeed a boon where it is properly appreciated. I make it a point of duty to go through the Church of England Service every Sunday. It recalls to memory the past when I used to join my prayers with those who meet at Oxton Church though, I am ashamed to confess, it was at times more like reading a book than praying. Now that the opportunity is lost, I feel its loss most deeply and could wish most earnestly that it might be again renewed, but here it cannot at present be. I think I never felt a greater pleasure in going to Church than I did at Sierra Leone on my way hither. Although the principal part of the congregation were black, still the service was the same and as I knew that it would be the last opportunity of joining in prayer with Christian people of my creed before my return, I felt the greatest pleasure in being there. There was only one white lady in the church at the time, a very precious jewel to be found on the verge of civilisation.

22 September

Mammy is having a long stay at the farm, she occasionally sends a "good day" and inquires after my health. To-day she sent me some alligator pears but I cannot say I like them; my taste is rather for things sweet or sour but any fruit which has neither of these qualities will not suit me. I am very fond of ripe bananas which are beautiful. These I am inclined to think would make good pies or preserves. I may mention as I am now speaking of pies, that on my voyage out I had some pumpkin pie to dinner which I mistook for apple. It tasted very good, I have since learnt that as the pumpkin has the appearance of fruit without any particular taste it can be the addition of particular essences be made to taste as the particular individual manipulating it may desire. A very useful vegetable the pumpkin, I should think. I wonder it does not become more generally used in England.

23 September

Thermometer 6 a.m. 70°, at noon 82°, 7 p.m. 79°. Although this has been a hot day I have not felt very uncomfortable--I suppose this must be on account of the dryness of the atmosphere for at the time I write (7 p.m.) when the air is cooling and the earth radiating heat which of course will increase the dampness of the atmosphere, I feel the perspiration on my skin much more than during the heat of the day. When I first came I felt the perspiration at evening most oppressive but this trouble appears to be gradually wearing off.

24 September

A very rainy day, Mammy came home from farm. The *Bloodhound* comes with a good deal of sickness on board. I am told it is yellow fever. On Sunday last I took a walk of about two to three miles up the road being made by the Cubans. I should hardly say road for in an English sense it is not one. The bush is only cleared and a pathway made through it, this will always require a good deal of keeping clear as it soon becomes overgrown. In wet weather a road which is not macadamised must always be very dirty.

25 September

While I was writing a letter to-day a winged insect lit on my paper when immediately its wings dropped off and of course it could no longer fly. It appears this insect is an ant, I am told that at a certain period of their existence nature has furnished them with wings for the purpose of emigrating. At this time they are led by a sort of Queen who while she continues to fly in an upward direction or in a straight line is safe but immediately she attempts to descend her wings drop and as the others continue to follow her movements of course they meet with the same fate, thus the whole of the company drop on one spot where they form a colony. In some parts of Africa ants are to be found in prodigious numbers, ant-hills will sometimes be found to cover a large extent of ground. Is it not a wise provision of nature to endow them with wings to emigrate for the purpose of preventing their becoming too numerous in one place. On Sunday, in taking a walk, I met with several lines of ants crossing my path, they bore underground, say, an inch deep and continually break through their tunnel. I can't understand why they should do this, why do they trouble themselves with making a tunnel when they continually expose themselves by breaking through it? I have read of African travellers who have watched a line of ants passing them for many hours. When I returned an hour afterwards the lines were continuing their courses just as when I saw them at first. The number of ants in this place must be enormous for they may be seen all over and everywhere; they are very useful as scavengers for I am told if they come upon a carcase they make short work of it in a very little time. Mr. Wilson told me that he once slept with a friend in some house in the interior of Sierra Leone and in the morning when they awoke his friend could find nothing but the buttons of his trousers; it appeared they had been hung up and had unfortunately been in the way of an emigrating colony of ants who fell to and soon devoured all but the buttons which were probably too hard for them. I have read of African travellers who have been in the track of an army of ants and of course were attacked by them and to get rid of them they had either to strip as soon as possible or plunge into water but before this could be accomplished they generally found themselves very much bitten.

27 September

Busy most of the day writing and wishing the mail would come in to-day; she did not however arrive until Sunday and such a Sunday I never spent before unless it was when I used to go to sea but to-day my head and hands were as full of business as they almost could be. This vessel brings news of the loss of the *Cleopatra*,[37] the vessel I came out in. It is said that the Captain is entirely to blame. The only loss was that of poor Webster, the first engineer, a very nice fellow and my most intimate chum and companion coming out. The Consul of the place near where the steamer was lost attempted to go off to her but his boat upset and himself and Kroomen all perished. I hear everything on board is lost, even the mails.

29 September

I have had touches of the fever during the last two or three days; yesterday it was so bad that I had the greatest difficulty in writing; to-day I am almost laid up with it. These Boobies are a dirty set. They come by six or seven sometimes with a basket of native make filled either with palm oil or yams; they, after unloading themselves of their burdens, squat down on the ground and make themselves quite at home. These are generally women who appear to have the larger share of hard work, it is very common to see them, when so squatted, spit on their hands and lest such a precious ointment should be lost they rub it on their dirty bodies. The women are generally of a peculiar twisted form, some of them fat and out of shape and have anything but a nice appearance--their breasts have none of the beautiful rotundity of form natural to our Venuses at home but hang down a shrivelled dried bag of flesh. They fill their hair with a kind of red earth and rub their bodies all over with the same. The men wear hats of native make stuck all over with feathers which is cocked on the head and fastened to the hair by a piece of stick running through the small crown of the hat; they are generally indeed almost altogether without clothing, perhaps a small piece of some kind of cloth round their waists but although they have little the women have less. The men are generally accompanied by a knife tied to the arm which is used for all sorts of purposes, from scratching their dirty bodies to cutting their yams. The women have very often a sort of plaited straw around each arm above the elbow and also under each knee, these are made to fit pretty tight but why they should wear such things I cannot imagine. The only things they wear of European manufacture are beads tied round the neck and the aforesaid thin piece of string for the purpose of covering their nakedness. It is very common to see ulcers and disease of the skin and flesh of their legs, I should fancy their dirty way of living has a great deal to do with this.

---

[37]Davies, *The Trade Makers*, 50.

3 October

To-day the thermometer was as high as 85°. My fever is about gone I think, it has not been so severe as the last. I only learnt the other day that we had an hotel on the island; such is however a fact although perhaps not so generally known. An enterprising trader, Captain Townsend, who has been on the coast 27 years, is the proprietor of this establishment; he has also built a shop in the town which is a great step in advance of all others there but I do not consider it well situated.

5 October

A thorough wet, rainy day. It was so thoroughly dull and quiet in the house that we all fell asleep. We took our meals very irregularly to-day, 10 o'clock breakfast and at noon Mammy brought out some alligator pears and biscuits (these taken together are not bad), some roasted ground nuts, then some roasted plantain and butter and to crown all some port wine and hot water. Dinner came on at about 4 p.m., it is usual to have dinner at 2 p.m. on Sundays to let the lads off for a stroll.

6 October

Mammy is having the house painted; I don't know how this will agree with me; I was ill at night with headache and sensations of fever. Some folks from the town and our wenches had a dance to-night and I went to look at them. The dancing consists of a shuffling step and a twisting of the body as much as possible. This is done to a chorus and solo of common time consisting of a few bars. The chorus commences with clapping of hands to mark time, this is slightly varied by the soloist who commences when the chorus finishes and they in turn take it up when he finishes. Both solo and chorus are composed of four or five words which are continually repeated. Of course there are a variety of both words and tunes. A Krooman with two sticks made a drum of a bench; when they can have a proper drum I should fancy they think it grand. To them their dances are as our English dances are to English people, each appears to feel the desire to have a step when dancing is going on but the miserable shuffle and the clapping, drumming and singing such as are to be met with here would look very absurd in an English drawing room. There is to me so little spirit in their dancing, no activity, no romping, tearing and wild excitement as one sees in a galop or polka, but it is all a difference of opinion. Their shuffling may be as sensible and to them as exciting as any galop or other dance is to my own country people.

8 October

I write this on Monday 20th for from this date until then I have been for the most part ill--this I think has been occasioned by our painting of the house to-day. I did not feel well on Thursday I was worse with fever and slept on board the hulk *William Mooney*.[38] On Friday I went to see the doctor and meeting him in the street we went together into the shop of a Spanish friend where I became worse, vomited and was finally put to bed. I continued at intervals to vomit when a quantity of blood was each time discharged. At night or rather in the evening I was removed very ill indeed, vomiting, as I was leaving the ship, a quantity of black stuff. By the aid of two friends I was taken to the house of a native and put to bed; the vomiting now ceased and I soon fell asleep. In the morning I felt better and in a few days I was able to get out of bed again. I did not visit the house again before Wednesday up to which time I had continued to improve. Since then I have had two attacks of vomiting and purging but I do not know whether these have proceeded from the effects of the paint or the food which I have eaten. The doctor says my first ailing was caused by the paint. I felt awfully bad at the time and am weaker after it than I was when I had the fever a month or so ago. It takes a longer time to pull up my strength and flesh. I never was stout at any time but I am now hardly anything but skin and bone with a face that would frighten my mother if she saw it and it is not a false index of my state of health for I have scarcely strength to move about. One would think that with such experience as this, it is anything but safe for me to remain here. I am anxious for the arrival of Mr. Lynslager in order that I may first properly arrange his books and then if it is thought that I endanger life by remaining I must see about going away. Providence has placed me in my present circumstances and I must wait its all-wise workings with patience. It has pleased God to bring me here for a purpose, and to Him and not to me is it known what my future is to be. The native with whom I am living is a joiner and has got a very nice house with many European comforts inside and I am very comfortable with him. He is also an invalid, having ulcers on his legs and hands, but is fast recovering. He is an intelligent person but like many more of his countrymen is given to drink. One can seldom gain an acquaintance without gaining information; my host tells me that his trade is a very good one and one in which a great deal of money may be made; he considers his trade should be worth from £200 to £300 a year. I can readily believe him when I know that for the building alone of a house, without anything but the actual labour of putting the wood together and fastening it, he gets from £100 to £200. I must not omit to state in justice to him that out of this sum he has to pay his assistants from 4/- to 5/- per day. Unlike our builders in England a builder here does not contract for the material. The person who wants a house must find the wood as best he can (and although this island is covered with it there appears to be no little difficulty in doing that) and then make his contract with the joiner. When I was sick for the first time I heard a tornado; it was night and all of a sudden it began to blow and rain in a manner sufficient to astonish me. It blew a gale for the short time it lasted and, except for the temperature, I might have fancied myself in the midst of a March gale in England. The elements appeared to have gone wild, they stormed and raged so furiously. It only lasted for a few hours when all became as calm as ever except a continuation of the rain which lasted most of the next day. It is no uncommon thing for a storm to come on suddenly, but not so severely as the one I mention and it often happens that a strong breeze

---

[38] *William Mooney* (835 grt) was built at Calcutta in 1820. A teak-built "East Indiaman," the vessel served as a hulk at Bonny before moving to Fernando Po where its timbers were used for a coal jetty (see p. 88). Further details are available in Wharton, unpublished mss., 142.

suddenly sets in, generally from the sea; but for the most part all these are only for a few hours. I love to watch the sheet lightning which I think looks extremely beautiful and is very bright and large; sometimes for a moment it will look like sunset, it is so brilliant. Thunder too is very common, it may, at times, be heard at intervals the whole day or night. The weather is becoming hotter but we have still frequent rainy days and showers. I think this climate and sickness, or something else, is making me quite stupid. The energy so apparent amongst my own country men at home and of which I used to think I possessed a fair share, seems to be gradually diminishing in me and I can fancy myself growing lazy, listless and apathetic as a black man. Perhaps it is a peculiarity of the climate where everybody and everything appears to take matters so "coolly," although one would think it is hot enough to make them different but I suppose the heat is the cause of their apathy. When my mind is unemployed, as for instance when I am sick, I muse and build all sorts of castles; I plan and arrange as would amuse folks if they only knew. I think and plan how I am to make money for I make up my mind that if I had a certain sum I should soon find myself quartered in a snug little house on the banks of the Trent which I think is the "Abode of love;" and then I think of the happy days when I used to go a boating on its waters, of when I used to go to school and when I used to go to grandmother's for a week to help her with the wheat or potatoes or what not. I think how happy those days were contrasted with the present. I think of the good cakes and butter, the berry pie and cream and the many other good things which appear better than ever now that I know I cannot have them. I think of my mother's love and of my happy condition when at home and could almost wish to throw my arms around her and desire to live with her for life. I think of the providence which has brought me here and I plan as to how I can arrange to make this land supply me with a living while I myself may be 5,000 miles away from it and I long to go back to England and to my home but, with all these thinkings and plannings, all is the same. I know that if I want to fulfil my dream of a house on the banks of the Trent I shall have to wait and work; that the cakes and good things of yore, the very thoughts of which make my mouth water, must be forgone; that instead of living by my mother's side I have a destiny to fulfil. Such is life, I could not remain at home for ever and in spite of the cuffs of my fellowmen and the buffeting and battling of life I must do something for myself. I must wage a competition against all mankind for the attainment of my end and I must work hard and fight well or I cannot succeed. I must also have patience and hope. This constant battle for existence seems hard lines but then one must do something for one's self. I ask myself, could I not do battle nearer home? I could wish to do so. Oh gladly would I work and work hard if I could there obtain my ends but I am here and here I must try to make the best of it. I will endeavour to be happy and do my duty in that state of life to which it hath pleased God to call me. If I cannot remain here and am to go back to England I shall still hope for the best and by God's blessing do my duty and be preserved from want. It is a curious fact too that during my sickness I continually dreamt of home, its associations and the happiness to be met with there.

23 October

Mammy is building a new store down at the beach in which palm oil is to be manipulated and goods kept until wanted for sale. For the building of the store, which will be of wood, the builder will receive £60; the length of the place to be 100 feet, breadth 30 feet. This shows how extravagantly high prices are paid for building houses. For building a good sized dwelling house the cost would not be less than £200, the owner providing all material. Everything but yams is dear; the price of labour particularly so.

24 October

There are other objections to this climate besides that of sickness, not least are those of the dampness of the atmosphere and the tremendous number of insects. The former spoils everything in the shape of iron or leather, it also makes black clothes mouldy. There is also a continual liability to catch cold in changing clothes. The damp is worst at night and in rainy weather, on rising in a morning and feeling the clothes taken off the previous evening, there is no mistaking the damp heavy sensation produced. Cotton clothes feel particularly wet or damp if shut up any length of time. I frequently give my outer clothes an airing or I am afraid they would soon spoil but its effects are most apparent on my boots. A person out here should if possible have but one pair and they should be of patent leather so that they may be cleaned without much trouble for the "boots" here is a lazy thing and although we have three lads to wait on table and do other odd jobs I have the greatest difficulty in getting a pair of clean boots above once a fortnight. A novel sight to one who has never seen it is the washing of our large dining room floor. This effort is accomplished at various intervals, sometimes once a week, fortnight, three weeks, or month and was done this morning (Saturday). Imagine half a dozen girls and boys in line, each provided with a piece of cocoa nut shell, down on their knees and the floor having been previously wetted, scrubbing and advancing keeping time with each knee. This business will last them from two to three hours. If done by an English servant in her own way in England I am sure it would be done in half the time.

27 October

The mail ship did not turn up this morning as usual but arrived shortly after 3 o'clock p.m. In consequence of an attack of fever I was unable to go off to her, being very weak and ill. I, with great difficulty, managed to read the letters. Mammy was expecting the "old man" and had made every preparation for his reception. The house was put in order, clean covers were put on the sofas, best table covers were spread, the doors of the best room flew open and Mammy looked her best. A splendid palanquin to carry him up the hill was made ready. Her own gig, newly painted, with awning and everything complete to bring him ashore was brought out and all was hope and anxious expectation. Alas that they should be met by frowning disappointment; the messenger returns--the news arrives he's not on board--no Daddy comes this month. Mammy is vexed but waits with patience for his letter and listens to the news--he will return next month--or the month after--this is beyond all patience. Next month or the month after, yes Mammy, you're doomed to another and perhaps another repetition of your labour; your hope, expectation, disappointment and vexation may all again recur. I hope not, I trust your desires may be fulfilled next month but, as you wish it, I will write to him and urge him to return; I will tell him of your troubles but even if this letter should be seen by him yourself cannot see him before the end of January, '63. Poor Mammy, I hope he will never see it for your sake, but as the sending of it will give your relief it shall go. Moore, the purser of the *Retriever*, very stupidly forgot to give my parcel last month to the purser of the *Armenian* so that my letters for two months go together. I had to see Moore on Tuesday night but he not being on board, I awaited his arrival until about midnight. The vessel was full of passengers, several of whom I knew. The Consul of this place Capt. Burton has gone this mail to Madeira. His consulship at any rate is a sinecure, he is seldom here. Mr. Wilson acts in his absence. On board was an awful scene of drunkenness and confusion, fighting, cursing and shouting; it was worse I think than anything I saw on board the *Cleopatra*. I felt myself much better on Tuesday but being out until after midnight is not good. These young fellows who come out here, drink, smoke and get drunk at all hours and still live, many of them well, while I, who endeavour to avoid all excesses, am ill.

31 October

To-day is my birthday, I mean the anniversary of my birthday and not only that but I am of age. It will pass off without notice, only one person in the world has reminded me of it and that one is Getty (singular); even the old feast of spiced bread &c. to tea at home must and will be dispensed with and in the eye of the law I become a man, unconscious of the change. Such a thing as this which to most people is an occasion of joy and merry-making is nothing to me; I am nobody or at least a drop in the ocean of human life, unknowing and unknown; none of the occurrences in my life have affected, or will affect the world, events to me are unknown to it; my birth, my coming of age, my marriage or my death produce no impression on society or are taken note of by it but for all that I am one and a number of ones make society; and so, in my own way of reasoning, I will conclude that to myself I am as much as anyone else but that everybody else will not own it or I should be somebody instead of nobody. Some Boobie traders came from some part of the island a good way off. These were a different lot from any I have previously seen. The Chief or headman wore a bladder of goats lard, suspended by a string tied round his neck and his companions had a quantity of small sea shells strung together and plaited about them and very few beads. Their hats were plaited and ornamented with feathers and some kind of dried leaves. One man had taken a fancy to a string of large pearl coat buttons. Each had a wooden bell with a wooden tongue attached to his right arm and when they walked these beautiful pieces of music would have charmed the finest ear. They certainly have a most lunatic appearance dressed up as such guys.

3 November

I feel much better now. I am gradually gaining strength and I think, improving in appearance although I have been told that I look very seedy and at times I suppose I do look so. I have lately been more exposed to the sun than I could have wished but as Mammy is building a store it requires a good deal of my attention which necessarily involves my being exposed at times to that luminary. I have not, however, experienced any ill effects from such exposure except the unpleasantness arising from excessive perspiration. The store is "getting on" pretty well but there are a great many hands to it; seven carpenters with so many people to wait upon and assist them, why as many English men would build such a house in a week while these men will take a month to do it. It is annoying to observe the careless, lazy way in which they go about their work seemingly as if they were only waiting for six o'clock. They sing, laugh, talk and squabble over it and besides, when it is done, it is a miserable attempt at anything like good workmanship. I let Mammy have all her own way now and do so without feeling at all annoyed, she gets gradually more aggressive while I find I have more indulgences thereby. When I first came I and Beecroft (a ward of Mr. Lynslager's) always had our victuals by ourselves in the large hall. By degrees as Mammy became more familiar she takes the head of the table and has introduced thereto others of her black countrymen: I am not fastidious and have no absurd objection to treat black folks as men provided they have commonsense and manners as some whites have, besides I find our living is much better. I have the privilege of more dainties--tit bits--and, unfortunately, I am fond of nice things; previously we often had only yams and fowls, or fish and yams, or rice, while now we can have pork, fowl in two or three varieties, fish the same, scouse, plantains, boiled and fried, with several country dishes. This makes me glad of Mammy's company at our meals although I know she is never seen at our table when the "old man" is at home. She at times annoys me and I feel at the moment inclined to "burst forth" but I have hitherto restrained myself and so we on the whole "get on" very well together. Indeed the same is the case with the girls; since I have given up my dictatorial and master-like conduct towards them we have gradually inclined towards each other and I am now treated occasionally to a roasted plantain (ripe), or one boiled in palm oil, both are very nice and are extras which I should miss but for the girls. I can see if I were desirous I could make friends with these girls and by their means do almost anything I might wish. They are very dishonest and although Daddy has purchased their freedom and done great things for them, they would rob him of any amount to satisfy their own fancy and to make presents to their "sweethearts." This is universally the case with the girls who have been liberated and although Mammy thrashes them tremendously on finding out their misdemeanours, they are not at all improved by her castigations but would rob her again without any apparent compunction the first opportunity. I tell Mammy that it is plain that the less girls she has the more profitable for her, she knows it too but I verily believe she would have more if she could easily obtain them.

10 November

Mammy has gone to the farm again this week. She went to-day saying that she should return on Wednesday. Wednesday, Thursday and Friday, but no Mammy comes; she sends word of her intention to return on Monday next but I don't expect her before the middle of the week. As Mammy would not support my previous policy towards the girls I have therefore adopted a different course; instead of being reserved I am free with them and by doing so I am often supplied with, what I consider, little luxuries which I should otherwise have missed. When Mrs. Lynslager is away I honour the head-girl with a name of Mammy, this she takes as a great compliment as it appears to be as pleasing to her to be called this as it is to an English girl to be called Miss. With a vanity common to her sex (and not only to her sex) she is thus easily flattered and this little word removes mountains of difficulties, it is easily said and I am soon afterwards sensible of its effects while at the same time I enjoy an amusing experiment. The girls have almost all their own way now; they do as they like or the next thing to it, shout, sing, laugh, dance, run all over the house, shop and town, "sweetheart a bit" and live as well again as when Mammy is at home. I have heard Mammy say that the last clerk was always glad when she returned from the farm as he found great difficulty in quieting the "conscience of an empty stomach" during her absence. Thus was the case with me when I first came and when I was at war with the girls, but as I am now reconciled to them and have gained a better knowledge of country dishes I have no difficulty in living well. Instead of roast fowl and yams, I have lobscouse, palaver sauce made of palm oil, fowl, onions, pepper and occia (a herb or fruit) which is very good, fish, boiled and roasted plantains, and foo-foo (beaten yam). The scouse and fish are sometimes cooked with palm oil, at others with butter. This does not look like pining. When I first came I found everything tasting of palm oil was nauseous, but now I have become exceedingly fond of it. After meals I generally have an orange or some bananas; when Mammy is here she keeps these at a distance, giving as a reason that they are bad for me. They may be, but for all that I am very fond of them. When she comes back I fancy she will observe a slight different in the appearance of her orange trees, these girls and boys about the place devour enormous quantities of them. Oranges here are very good and very plentiful but like everything else here they are dear, a dollar per 100, equal ½ penny each. Pineapples sell at 10d. or 1/- each, while in Sierra Leone they can be bought at 1d.[39] I often think Mammy is rather stingy with the produce of her farm, she seldom gives me any of it. During her absence last month I had a bottle of port wine and a bottle of vinegar. I also gave the Consul and a friend who called on business, some lemonade; this I find she has heard of and told the shop clerk to charge it to me. Had I known, or imagined, there to have been any doubt as to who should stand the cost of these I should have mentioned it myself; as it is, I shall let it remain until the return of Mr. Lynslager. I think it is usual for people in the same position here as myself to have wine to dinner; this I was provided with at first, but as I did not, I suppose, use much it has gradually been put a stop to. I say nothing, I think I must naturally be of a quiet easy temperament or I should not suffer this to pass without a word; however I wish to avoid any unpleasantness with Mrs. Lynslager and with the exception of one very little huff about the half fowl which the cook refused to give me and which I took from the kitchen shelf in spite of his declaring it was for Mammy, we have gone on pretty smoothly. I think it was hardly fair to expect two to dine out of half a fowl and I had so often been bamboozled before by such protestations which I knew, or strongly supposed, to be lies that I was determined to have the other half. Mammy has lately become more confidential with me and she tells me that the young fellows who are always in the house, smoking, eating, or drinking, are her countrymen. Now when she is at home and has her meals with me, her friends and all sit at the same table. I know some white people would object to sit with blacks unless they had some interest in doing so but if they only conduct themselves with propriety and good manners I am not fastidious on such matters. I believe I have mentioned about this elsewhere and also that when the "old man" is at home such is not the case.

---

[39]P.N. Davies, "The British Contribution to the Economic Development of the Canary Islands with Special Reference to the Nineteenth Century" (Unpublished paper presented to the Coloquio de Historia Canario-American, Las Palmas, October 1984); Davies, "Edward Wathen Fyffe," *Dictionary of Business Biography* (2 vols., London, 1984).

Figure 4: Thomas Holt (1848-1921), brother of John Holt.

Source: See Figure 1.

17 November

Since my attack of fever last month I have gradually improved in health. I think I have as much flesh on me as I ever had but for all that I have not the same strength, nor desire for work, as I had when at home. This week, however, with exception of Wednesday, I have been busy enough with the store and looking after the starting of palm oil; this latter ought to be done by our shop clerk but he is not very well and so remains in the shop and I have been in the habit of going to it three or four times a day and the road being up and down hill it is equal to four miles a day on level ground. Oranges are now well ripened and are very good but, so far as my experience and taste go, I like ripe bananas the best, they are delicious. I have tasted of many different kinds of fruit here and am told of many more which I have not tasted. I wish my friends in England could share my enjoyment but the fruit would not keep the length of time required for its transportation. I must also mention that I am warned by Mammy against the eating of too much fruit as it is said to be anything but good for us whites out here. This to some extent restrains me or I could almost live on it in some form or other-ripe, boiled, or roasted. On Wednesday the Queen of Spain's birthday was kept and at night three or four of the principal houses were illuminated. The new Church was opened and at it were the Governor, the Spanish officers and soldiers stationed here (all in uniform), Mammy and others, the building being crowded with people. Mammy like, no doubt, many others went for the sake of seeing, being seen, and getting into favour with the Governor and the priests. She laughs at the service which, of course, she cannot understand and appears to look at it more in the light of a show than of devotion, indeed I do not believe she had such a thing as prayer in her mind all the time she was there. The head padre intimated his intention of preaching in English every Sunday afternoon. The ships, one English gunboat and one Spanish hulk, exchanged salutes and, first thing in the morning, the Spanish ship fired a salute, I suppose, in honour of the day. There was nothing going on until the illumination at night; the Spanish barracks and the Governor's home were pretty but there were no fireworks. Our own, Townsend's, and the English Consul's were the only private houses illuminated. I think ours was the best being illuminated by lights on the railing and floor of the piazza in tumblers, and coloured glass bowls with five old ship lamps hung outside. Inside the house were ten candles and three lamplights. The Governor and officers called to express their thanks for the demonstration of good-feeling towards Her Majesty, expressing their opinion that it was very nice, and then went to Miss Matthews, who was having a dance outside her house. I am told they all enjoyed themselves there, dancing in the hall and drinking champagne like water. The English gunboat fired rockets and burnt blue lights during the evening, which compliment pleased the Governor very much and which, to my eyes, was also very much to the shame of the Spanish hulk and gunboat who made no demonstration whatever at night. I think I am not a little humbugged about here after all. Mammy tells the men to do one thing at the store and as I suppose I have the matter altogether in my hands, I tell them another. The consequence is that there is a great deal of confusion; often when I give an order it is stopped or altered by her. This interference annoys me but, as not I but she loses by it, I let her have her own way for the sake of harmony although I often feel riled at it. She is a woman who likes to be a great deal thought of, and tries to be important; she is jolly good-natured and loves, excessively, table gossip and play. She is passionate and, when thoroughly vexed, I hear people say she is a devil. I frequently hear her say to anyone who has done or said something to vex her--"Mind! Don't get my devil up!" This she will say in a passionate manner and then, immediately afterwards, burst out with laughter. She is grasping and never knows when she has charged high enough for her goods but withal, kind and charitable. She is very fond of her husband whom I believe she sincerely loves. At times she is prompt and decisive, at others fickle and unsteady. Her character changes according to the mood she is in. The women in this place spend their time in a way which would disgust such people as my own mother. They laugh and gossip and chat and give orders, and themselves do nothing. I can hardly recollect ever seeing my mother sitting to talk to anyone without something with which to employ her hands.

27 November

Expecting the mail ship all day on a sick bed, with fever which got better in the latter part of the afternoon. It is peculiar that the fever should always attack me about the time when the mail arrives.

Friday has come, so has the mail, but no Daddy with it. Mammy is, of course, very vexed and down-hearted as greater preparations had been made by her this month than last. She not altogether sorrows for the "old man's" absence but also for the money which he necessarily is spending to a great extent, and the way he has been living during the eight months he will have been absent, if he comes next mail, will take a long time to earn. We have a great deal of cargo and plenty of correspondence but I worked hard and got done by 8 o'clock. Capt. Walker, "Old White" of Bonny and the doctor of the *Cleopatra* were going the rounds. I was not a little astonished to see the first of these; he had been two years away up the Niger and only stayed four months at home; besides I had not heard of it being his intention to come out here any more. Laird Fletcher & Co. had started another Niger Expedition intending to send out Walker in charge but it has been a failure. He has now come out for F. Huth & Co. in the Brass River. "Old White" I only know through having come out with him and the doctor the same.

1 December

The way people till their gardens is to make high beds by means of a hoe (they don't use spades as I suppose they could not do so on account of not wearing shoes), upon which they sow seed in rows. This is the way Mammy has done with her garden, and now that the different seeds are up they appear in irregular lines with large spaces between. This is her way of doing it and, as by shewing any other plan I should only be troubling myself, I say nothing for "Where ignorance is bliss 'tis folly to be wise." Many useful eatables may be grown here which also grow in England, radishes, lettuce, cabbage, turnips, beans, peas, cucumbers flourish but, as with everything else, the laziness of the black is such that he will not put himself to the trouble of cultivating them; the consequence is that vegetables, livestock and everything else except fruit which grows wild and yams which are got by trading, are scarcely to be had, either for love or money, in a place where they ought to be cheap and plentiful. The Spaniards are most anxious to buy fowls just now but they cannot get sufficient for their use. Some of them have lately been known to go a-shooting, in places likely to have fowls, for their game and I have no doubt they bag a good many. I see them on the road which goes to Coal

Bay and which leads past one or two Boobie villages. On this road, which I often have to use to the bay to look after the coals, I often see fowls and could easily shoot them. I don't like the Spaniards to do so for the Boobies are sure to know of it and some one may have to suffer for their folly. I often fancy I should be all the safer with a revolver in my pocket when I go along this road and if the Spaniards do not give over shooting the Boobies' fowls I shall not relish going along this road unarmed.

15 December

The *Retriever* has come for some cargo which she left on board the hulk last month. I hear she returns in a week. Moore is sick and is going to-day to Townsend's until the 28th. Hemmingway Senr. is there and Cheetham has come to recruit his health here for a week.

20 December

The *Retriever* has gone and left the Captain and Moore at Townsend's sick. Miss Matthews has gone to Bonny with Cheetham.

21 December

Sad news--Ablett is dead--I only learnt this at 5 p.m. although he died at 10 this morning. Poor fellow, it is only a few months since I first knew him strong and hale when he told me that he did not think the Coast was so bad as represented but thought it rather the fault of those who come out here drinking too much; but he drank little and has nevertheless died after a three days illness. I had no idea when the *Retriever* sailed that it was any serious sickness that had attacked him or I should certainly have gone to see him. An hour after I heard of his death I attended his funeral. I am told that the supposed cause of this was his going with a Capt. Bragg to the brook, bathing a long time in the sun, and also walking in the heat of the day. Anyhow the next morning, Thursday, they both complained of violent headaches. The Spanish doctor attended him but without any perceptible benefit for he became insensible on Saturday evening and vomited black matter until he died. Townsend says it was yellow fever and had the body removed under his house and then fumigated his room. The *Retriever* ought not to have gone on Saturday as Thompson had no good reason for going except that the Captain had ordered him to do so but it is said the Captain was delirious at the time.

25 December

Xmas day. To-day I was invited to dinner at Capt. Townsend's. There were ten black women and myself, Wilson, Townsend and Captain Thomas. The girls were ill at ease during dinner, particularly at first, but after taking one or two glasses of wine their tongues were loosened. How amused would our folks at home have been could they have seen us as we sat together. They were dressed well in light clothes. On ordinary days they are very differently dressed. On going to dinner the gentlemen politely offered their arms but what a farce it all was for they have not got a bit of lady about them in the sense that word is generally understood; they may play at ladies but will never be made them. We had a capital dinner and in real Old English Style; actually roast beef and plum pudding amongst many other things. The "ladies" or the greater part of them left immediately after dinner; they indeed might be said to have come for their dinners. We had a little chat with those left but a lot of the townspeople having been allowed to come in with drums to dance, our little party soon broke up. The noise of these dancers continued until most of them were drunk and left, I suppose it would be, near twelve o'clock. I went home about 9 p.m. but finding myself locked out I returned to Townsend's and slept there. The next day I waited at home for my breakfast until 2 p.m. and then being out of all patience asked Mrs. Lynslager if she intended me to go without food upon which she replied that she thought I was perhaps going out to dine. After a very few remarks I walked out and went to call on Captain Mulligan where I got something to eat and stayed with him and Captain and Mrs. Hogg on board the *Copeland Isle* until 8 o'clock having spent a very pleasant afternoon and evening.

It appears Mammy was offended at my not saying to her that I was going to dine out on Xmas day. She knew that I intended to do so because I was present at the time she dined, but because I did not formally inform her of my intentions she adopted this way of punishing me. I have always tried to please her and let her have as much of her own way as possible; I keep myself steady and indoors and this is the result. She tries to play the tyrant but I will not stand this show of power any longer. She is not my master and that she will soon have to learn.

1863

1 June

A fire broke out in a shed at the back of Laughland's shop used for the purpose of boiling palm oil in but it was put out in a few minutes and before any material damage was done. A great many people were there.

2 June

The Governor is very energetic in improving the Colony; he has built a house up the mountain at Basilte and cleared a space there of not less than 100 acres. At Santa Isabel he has much improved the land round Horsfall Bay and on the road going to Coal Bay he has cleared and partly planted about eight acres. he is also contemplating building a jetty and a market place. I believe he is anxious to improve and advance the Colony to the utmost of his power and he appears particularly interested in his eight acre farm of cotton, cocoa and coffee. Every morning and evening he is looking after his business there and his efforts presage a happy result.

4 June

Corpus Christi. To-day a procession took place from the Catholic Church round the quartel and back and each person taking part therein had a candle to carry lighted. Daddy was there with the Governor. Everybody walked with hats off and any one meeting the procession had to do the same. Opposite the quartel was erected an altar before which the priests knelt and sang something, what, I cannot tell. The head padre carried what

I took for a crucifix before his face while four or six men suspended a covering over his head by means of poles.

12 June

The rainy season may now be said to have fairly set in, for this morning it came down in torrents for several hours, and continued more or less all day. Last night I was dreaming of being in England, I don't place much faith in dreams, but the Governor having already hinted that if I don't keep better health I shall have to bid adieu to Africa, it is not altogether improbable that this one may come to pass. At present, however, I feel no particular desire to go to England; I certainly should like to see my friends, but having entered on my present prospects, why should I wish to give them up until I find them unsatisfactory?

27 June

Murray (Hamilton & Co.'s agent at Calabar) and Gregg are waiting here for the mail to go home. Murray is a very jolly fellow; I was up at the Consulate with him and a few others last night and we had a merry evening of it singing and dancing.

9 July

Poor Obon the younger died to-day. He was a good-hearted soul. This morning, I am told, he was comparatively well but at 3 o'clock he was dead--poor fellow, I liked him very much and expected anything but death to him. At the time I was very sick of a bilious fever, such an attack as I have not had before, vomiting a large quantity of blood and bile and suffering a great deal, while to add to my horrors poor Obon died and during the whole time of my sickness the general conversation has been upon the death of people I know. Very consoling it certainly was for a sick man. We had news of Watts of Cameroons the other day that he was burnt and had to jump overboard and so get drowned; this also occurred at the commencement of my illness and I am almost afraid to stay longer at this place. My last attack was such a caution that I do not wish to receive another like it for which I may have to pay with my life; however, all's well that ends well, and we shall see what will come.

28 July

The mail did not arrive this month before the 29th on account of a fog at Bonny.[40] To-day Daddy has been talking to young Babington about my situation but he is afraid the young man is too delicate and not likely to live long, however, he has invited him to come over for a month to try how my work and climate agree with him. I wanted him to commence work at once and asked Daddy about it; he at once began enlarging upon the great expenses of sending me home and when I told him that I would find my own passage home, he then said that I had made an agreement for three years which I ought

---

[40]The diaries do not say when Lynslager returned to Fernando Po.

to fulfil. I replied that I though I had sufficient sickness to make my request a reasonable one and that he had now an opportunity of procuring my successor without being put to any expense. He then said I must understand that I could not be allowed to come out again for another party as after having made an agreement of three years duration with him would not be satisfactory to see me coming out for some other person in a few months. He was by this time getting excited and mentioned that he had heard it reported that I was going to Smith.[41] On retiring to his bedroom with Mammy they had a loud conversation on the subject in which I suppose further facts were brought forward relative to my going to Smith, for after a short time I heard Daddy tell Beecroft to ask Mr. Smith to step over. When Smith came they both went into the drawing-room and with closed doors; Mr. Smith, I believe, was questioned as to the truth of the report, for Daddy afterwards informed me that he had asked Mr. Smith on his honour as a gentleman if I was intending to go to him, upon which Smith replied that I had several times applied to him; it appears Smith has told him in such a way as to excuse himself of all blame for to me he was the theme of Daddy's admiration. After asking me several questions at to what I was dissatisfied with, he said I was to write to Laird Fletcher & Co. to send out my successor which has accordingly been done. Now the fact of the matter is this although there are many things in Daddy's house which are unpleasant, annoying and unsatisfactory, still they would not induce me to wish to leave him for on some points I should feel much more comfortable with him than with Smith but, when I consider that in three years my being with Smith would make a difference to me of £150 (which I think would fully compensate for all other drawbacks) and I should also get a better idea of trade and have a better chance of getting on in life, I must confess I could wish to change situation. Since Daddy commenced to talk of sending me home I have spoken to Smith about by probably having to leave and the first time I mentioned it was when Henry said I was wasting my time with Daddy Jim, advised me to invalid home and promised to recommend me to some first rate firms for a berth in the Rivers. I told Smith that I did not like the Rivers and would prefer a situation out of them upon which he at once offered me a place for two years at £150 to £200. When I first came out, thinking I was not comfortable with Mrs. Lynslager, he told me that if I wanted to change I had only to apply to him but at that time I had no intention of doing so although her conduct towards me was anything but what I had expected. Later, however, since Daddy spoke to me about going away on account of ill health, I had intended to go home if I found myself sufficiently ill, but if in the meantime a successor had been appointed and during the three months which it takes to get one out from England my health should have improved I then should have gone to Smith. During the time I have been out I have had a fever to every month and the last a most severe attack, therefore I think Mr. Lynslager would not have exceeded what was right if he had sent for another person to take my place on that account. He appears to think I have done something dishonourable in the affair and is very ill pleased with me. I feel very uncomfortable in consequence for I like the "old man" and he has been very kind to me. I almost think it would have been better to have told him of my wish to go the Smith, as it would have looked more straightforward and I think he would not have stood in my way. Only the other day he gave me a month's salary so as to make the year end on the 30th June and I have

[41] This refers to E.I. Smith, but it is unclear which company he represented.

received other proofs of his regard but this transaction has sadly thrown me down in his appreciation of my work. I trust the change will not harm him and I shall always be glad to be of use to him. If he gets Bayne, whom I have advised to apply for the situation, I do not think he will suffer from my leaving him and I hope Bayne will come out for I am sure he will find a good, kind and generous-hearted master.

6 August

To-day I had another severe attack of fever and ague; it was the sharpest ague I have ever had but the fever and other symptoms such as vomiting were not so bad as formerly. My attacks appear to be quite systematic in their return, every month as regularly as the moon. Since my last attack to the present one is about twenty-eight days, for the one coming next month I intend to provide a good dose of quinine beforehand. I think if this does succeed a change will be the best plan to break the regularity of these attacks which, if successful, may then disappear altogether.

7 August

I went on board the *True Briton* this evening to see Mr. and Mrs. Bushnell and Miss Green, persons belonging to the American Mission at Gaboon to which place they are now on their way, also to hear Miss Green's performances on her harmonium and her singing. It was a reminiscence of old times, and old sensations and feelings were again revived. She sings and plays very well and although I heard but little of either I was very much pleased. It was indeed pleasant to listen again to what were once such familiar sounds and I thought at the time that if I could add these enjoyments, these luxuries, to my present comforts, I might soon be led to think Santa Isabel a much more pleasant place to live in than I do at present.

9 August

The Governor went over to the farm to see Mammy who is staying there. Miss Meyer went on board the *True Briton* to see the Missionaries. She is, and has been "off and on" for the last two months, very unwell of fever, ague and general debility and having had an invitation from Mr. and Mrs. Bushnell she talks about going to see them the first opportunity at Gaboon. I was therefore a bachelor along all the day but I managed to amuse myself pretty well by reading, eating and fiddling around and I think I fared as well as my absent friends. I had a capital breakfast and, as a luxury to my fowl and green peas for dinner, I set to work with my coffee machine to make a pudding. According to full directions on Brown & Polson's packets of corn flour (for making blanc mange) I took four table spoonfuls and mixed it with sugar and three eggs well beaten up, and a few drips of essence of almonds. I boiled some hot water to add to these and then put the mixture in the bottom part of my machine, placed it upon the top of three ink bottles and applied the spirit lamp underneath. In a few minutes I had a first rate successor to my "first course" for after being placed in a tub of water to cool I had it served up with jam and my word didn't I lick my lips. It was first rate and was relished all the more by the knowledge that I myself had made it. I almost think I ought to have been made a cook instead of a clerk. My abilities certainly incline to that art more than to any other and indicate in a manner visible to anyone with half an eye what my employment should have been. I am afraid my worthy parents must have been rather short of discriminating faculties not to have observed the bent of my genius.

A musical-box, which Daddy won last Sunday by the investment of a dollar in a lottery or raffle for it, is all the rage with us now. His favourite air is "Home, Sweet Home," which is one of the tunes played by the instrument, but unfortunately he does not know the words and can only sing "Home sweet home, there's no place like home, there is no place like home, my boys, there is no place like home."

13 August

Mammy is at the farm still. Mr. and Mrs. Bushnell and Miss Green have gone to Gaboon in Laughland's schooner. Miss Meyer is getting well again and has given up all her ideas about going to Gaboon now. She talks of going up to Basili but as she and the Governor are not making any arrangements preparatory to going up, I suppose this scheme like the other will not be effected until it becomes absolutely necessary for Miss Meyer to have a change, or continue sick. Half of what the Governor proposes is simply small talk.

14 August

Daddy got into a great rage with me to-day on account of my not having answered some question of his to his taste. I had omitted the 'sir' and he thought it was my duty to put a handle to my sentences when speaking to him. Talking to George Beecroft on the subject in a tone made high that it might reach my ears he said I had been deceitful but that God would reward such people and he prayed that the curse of God might follow them, that I should yet leave my bones in Fernando Po, that what he said always came to pass, and that he knew God would listen to his prayer.

15/16 August

To-day I went to Pellon's house at Basili, or rather I went as far as Banafa tonight, and went to Basili on Sunday morning. J. Laughland is up there. Dr. Paterson came up in the forenoon of Sunday. Aldama and three other Spaniards were staying at the Governor's house. They went up on horses. Sunday was a rainy day, and it was not so pleasant as I could have wished it; however, I was in good spirits all day in spite of clouds and rain by both of which we were surrounded. I had a bath at the brook close by and was very much refreshed by it, it was so beautifully cool and nourishing. Late last night, Selina, one of the girls, got very severely burnt by her clothes coming in contact with the palm oil light when asleep. This light is placed on the floor of the place where the girls sleep and being unprotected by any covering it is not at all strange that such an accident should occur. The girl on finding herself in flames lost all presence of mind and rushed frantically into Miss Meyer's bedroom screaming the while. Had not Mrs. Lynslager on hearing the girl's screams at once got out of bed and torn off her clothes by sheer strength the accident might have ended much more seriously, particularly when it is known that under the same room there is about 100 lbs. of gun-powder.

Figure 5: Jonathan Cockin Holt (1844-1896), brother of John Holt.

Source: See Figure 1.

25 August

A man named Meol of Sierra Leone has lately been condemned to hard labour for three years for having stolen a great deal of property while in Laughland's shop, in the capacity of shopman. He has been carrying on this game for a long time but like most thieves he has been caught at last. He is the man who was to have married Chin Cherry.[42] This scoundrel has met with the greatest sympathy from his countrymen and the Spaniards foolishly allow them to feed him while serving the time of his sentence in chains. They are a great deal too lenient with the blacks. If a man is found out to be a thief and is sentenced to hard labour, that hard labour consists of easy work, for a black man is put over him and of course he does next to nothing; thus stealing is very rife in the Colony and unless the Governor adopts measures more severe it will no doubt increase. There are continual complaints made that oil is stolen in Boobie. This, however, is for the most part "dog robbing dog." To steal or cheat a white man out of anything, the blacks think a fair game. Daddy Jim tells me of a man who murdered a cook of his when he was Governor; he was kept two years in prison waiting orders for his disposal from Spain, which not coming, he was set at liberty and sent out of the Colony, but before going he had great sympathy from the people of his colour. Although he was known to be a murderer they looked upon him as an injured fellow creature.

28 August

To-day I got my letters and was glad to learn that my relatives and friends were all well. Jonathan writes and encloses his "carte de visite." He tells me of his return home after his very long voyage and of his having succeeded in passing the Board for a second mate. Getty has been so greatly offended at something I have said in one of my letters that she declines writing to me at present. Thus does she chastise me for my offences. While I now think of her kindness my mind wanders from England to Fernando Po, a place of gossip and scandal. It is here reported that Miss Meyer and Wilson are going to be married, that Miss Meyer and Fanny are going home, that S------ is a great deal too friendly with Helen M------, as the Administrator is with her sister, and that I have a sweetheart in Jane. By the bye, sweethearts are plentiful here, any quantity may be had for a trifle, but unfortunately I have got no trifle to throw away on them and their charms. I came out from England with Jane and have often gone to see her since but I have not the least intention of having any connexion with the blacks although nothing is easier. They have a fashion of calling people Daddy when they find such fools enough to "dash" them something.

20 September

Went with Gazulla and Armengol to the farm and spent the day in eating, drinking, singing, dancing, shooting and boating. This, I am afraid, is hardly the right way of conducting oneself on a Sunday but then one has no place of worship to go to and if one

---

[42]Jane Beckley came out from England on the same vessel as John Holt (see p. 35). Her African name was Chin Cherry and she eventually became the mistress of E.I. Smith (see p. 82).

were to stay at home moping over some book, talking gossip and looking serious all day long, I question whether that would be any better. It is certainly generally made a day of rest in the true sense of the word for we scarcely ever stir out of the house and in it mostly talk of things secular and loll about all day long as if we did not know what to do with ourselves.

21 October

The Captain of the *Strang* managed to let our two boats sink last night with a lot of coal in them. A nice how do you do this is.

22 October

Busy all day and part of the night at the boats. Brownsworth and his boys are helping us. Got one boat up. The Captain of the *Strang* is giving us no assistance whatever. Daddy Jim, I hear, has been pitching into him well and the Captain is very humble about it; Daddy came down to the scene of action this morning in his carriage and was in an awful rage with the Captain.

23 October

Slept on board the *Wm. Money* last night but I got no more than three hours sleep. We managed to get up the other boat to-day, or rather to-night, for I did not get home before half past nine. I'm glad it's over.

24 October

Griffon came in with the Consul who is going to the King of Dahomey as Minister Plenipotentiary to His Majesty. Daddy Jim thinks this all humbug and wonders what Burton can do after the Commodore has been. He says a good army of Indians would be the most likely minister to persuade him to leave off his slave trade and murderous atrocities and the best civilizing agent that could be employed and I think he is not far from the mark.

8 November

Went with Daddy Jim in his carriage drawn by eleven Krooboys to Banassa, a Boobie town about three miles off and about five hundred feet higher than Santa Isabel. We had some difficulty in getting there as the road is bad and in some places very steep. We had to cross three brooks, one without a bridge, which we had to ford, the water just reaching to the bottom of the carriage. We stayed only a short time at Banassa, just long enough to get a bit of luncheon and give the boys some food, grog, tobacco and rest. We also called on the Spanish padre there who appears a very jolly, stout, middle-aged man and in good health. He had some tobacco plants in his garden which appeared in a thriving condition but not sufficiently large to cut. This padre has been (he tells us) two years in Banassa and has had very good health but during the four months he was at Santa Isabel he was three sick. This station is the only one which the Jesuit Mission have got amongst the natives and from what I can learn they have made but little progress. The padre speaks Boobie very well. We are the first persons who have ever been so far, so high, or to the same place in a carriage. How peculiar we should have looked in the eyes of our friends in England could they have seen us. I also went to the judge's "house warming" where I met a number of Spanish friends and Wilson. I think we almost drank the judge dry, for we kept up the "warming" until near five o'clock in the evening.

10 November

Poor Armengol, the successor of the late younger Obon, who died during my last serious illness, departed this life at 2 o'clock a.m. The sickness of which he has died was the first he has had since his arrival here some nine months ago. He has only been sick some five days and a few hours before he died it is reported that he was comparatively well and no one had the least anticipation of what followed. His fever became delirious which soon killed him. Daddy swears at the Spanish doctors and says it is their fault and amongst many other similar remarks that he would not have one to attend his dog. It does seem strange that so many Spaniards die of fever whilst the death of an Englishman is a rare occurrence but then I suppose there are twenty times as many Spaniards as English in the Colony. It also seems strange that two out of the same house should have died with the same symptoms. Daddy says had calomel been administered the man would have lived. It is sad to think that so young a man should have been cut off so soon in life; I suppose he would be about twenty-five years old. He was a really kind-hearted and amiable friend, one whom I esteemed as much as I do any Spaniard in the Colony, and that is saying a good deal for I like some of them very well. I attended my poor friends's funeral with most of the Spaniards and three other Englishmen and buried him in the Spanish burying ground according to the rites of his Church. Thus do we part with friends for ever. How soon will he be forgotten by those who on earth were his best and dearest friends.

The Major and Reilan are both sick with fever. They are my English pupils and of course I am greatly interested in their welfare. We have spent many pleasant evenings together and hold very friendly relations towards each other. The Major is a particularly good-hearted soul, a real gentleman in sentiment and character. The town is sickly now, it being the change from the wet season to the dry; I hear several carpenters are in hospital and not expected to recover.

19 November

The Queen of Spain's birthday was celebrated in great style to-day. Three salutes were fired from the Isabel at 6, 12 and 6 o'clock. The Governor gave a spread to the heads of each department who appeared in full uniform at his table. Daddy was there and also the Consul. Most of the Spaniards came to our house to see Daddy and the show of Fernando Po products which he had collected in his house for the occasion, and were astonished and pleased with the idea and the number of fruits, vegetables &c. which they saw. The collection was composed chiefly of oranges, pines, bananas, yams, plantains, custard apples, palm nuts, palm oil, the seed of the bamboo, the croton oil and castor oil berries, coffee, cocoa, cocco, honey, calabash with topi, arrow root, beans, sage and Indian corn. The different varieties of some products caused astonishment. The palm oil made for eating was much admired for its clearness and pure smell. In the evening, the whole of the Governor's house and the quartel had the lights enclosed with variously coloured cloths and the houses decorated with branches very nicely. Our own house had about a hundred lights lit. There was a plentiful supply of wine and it was freely indulged in both by our guests and those of the Governor. The illumination and the spreeing was kept up until early next morning by the Spaniards, who after we had all gone to bed made us open the house again and with their music and dancing kept all awake but me until about 1 o'clock. I did not turn out to partake of their jollity and how I managed to go to sleep with the noise they made is a mystery.

22 November

Yesterday I went on board the *Torch* to breakfast with Captain Smith, R.N., during my stay the Commandant of the Spanish Station visited him and I was victimized as an interpreter.

28 November

The *Retriever* arrived early this morning and brought with her my successor, Mr. R. G. Tomlinson.[43] Brown, who had been previously appointed and was expected out, showed the white feather.

2 December

The Governor tells me Wilson has been popping the question. Of course Miss Meyer will not object but when the event is to come off I cannot imagine, unless Wilson has got funds in Scotland at his disposal to buy his bird a cage to feather her nest with and to keep themselves in clover.

28 December

Bad news from home this mail, my old dear friend Polly Porter has gone to a better home. How often we have sung and played together in our school days. It is sad to think of. How little I ever dreamed of this when I last saw her. Dear Polly, most vividly do the past scenes of life in which we took a part return at this moment when thinking that you are no more. What will Ness Field House look like without your sweet face to welcome one. Mrs. Dempster is also dead.[44] How hard it must be for poor Dempster thus soon to lose his young wife. May God support him and the dear parents of my lost friend Polly in their deep affliction.

---

[43]R.G. Tomlinson was sent in response to Holt's letter to Laird, Fletcher and Company referred to on pp. 51-52. He later proved unsatisfactory (pp. 71-72) and left for a position at Elobey.

[44]She was the wife of John Dempster.

1864

14 January

Received news of poor Watson's death in Calabar.

7 March

Embarked on board the *Isabel*, Captain Argimon, chartered by Messrs. Lynslager, Coco Obon y Co. and Gazulla to bring Krooboys and live stock from the Windward Coast under my direction. I left the shore soon after eleven and am sorry I did not sleep there for the ship did not set sail until six o'clock the following day. I was surprised to find that Gazulla had arranged with the Government to send thirty-five kegs of gunpowder by this ship. I think he might have said something about it before I came off; such a thing as this is not safe in a sailing vessel without a powder magazine and it is anything but pleasant to contemplate the possibility of being landed on "the other side of Jordan" like a flash of lightning.

8 March

We set sail early this morning and very slowly crept out of the harbour. There is always a sympathy in me with what I am accustomed to and although I have been longing for this change I could not but feel a sort of regret at leaving Fernando Po even for so short a time. I saw Mrs. Lynslager going to the farm and I think that was about all I did see until night for I had an attack of ague which laid me up all day and my misery was aggravated by the feelings of sea sickness. After we rounded Cape Bullen we had a strong W.S.W. wind all day and kept standing towards the Coast until 6 o'clock p.m. at which hour the ship was put about, the Captain expecting to clear the Island on this tack, but a tornado from the N.W. came on, preceded by most vivid, continual and blinding flashes of lightning for several hours. It blew very hard; all sails were taken in but the topsails and I believe they were afterwards taken in, but I went to bed and saw no more of it. However, I heard enough for it blew and rained and thundered tremendously. The thunder was very near and had a very peculiar sound, very like the report of an Armstrong gun, with none of the deep-toned rolling sound one generally hears. In consequence of this tornado we lost ground and to-day are becalmed about thirty miles from Santa Isabel, making little or no headway at all but the ship appears to be doing her best to make up in rolling what she loses in headway. To-day I am a good deal better but for the most part keep to my bed. I have been able to take some "sweet oil" to-day with the rest of the Spaniards and I dare say bye and bye when I become used to it I shall not feel the present great dislike I have for it.

10 March

We are still within sight of the Island and when we are going to be anything else I can't tell for the Captain appears to be trying to get to Bonny instead of round the Island. He is awfully nervous when it blows a little, at least not nervous, but frightened either of his ship or his sails. The latter are very old and are no more fit to stand a good breeze than an old woman's apron would be if put in the same place. Not very well still; afflicted with debility, lassitude, feverishness and a touch of sea-sickness; anything but comfortable; could wish myself anywhere but on board this ship.

11 March

At noon to-day we were about twenty-five or thirty miles west of N.W. Bay. The Captain appears to want to get to the westward rather than south. To-day I am better but very weak yet. The change has, so far, injured me instead of doing me good. The cabin is a most miserable place to sleep in; I am hot to suffocation, tormented by mosquitoes, bored and nibbled at by goodness knows how many cockroaches, and half poisoned by the stench of the rotten water in the hold. It is enough to make one go mad. I should think it would be pleasant and amusing for a person to watch my pranks with the cockroaches; sometimes I find one eating my hair or nibbling at my cheek and am fortunate enough to hear him crack against the opposite boards from the headway I have given him but it more often happens that I miss the fellow altogether (and how can a fellow take aim when he is asleep), or if I am not careful feel my hand come unpleasantly against a harder substance than I had bargained for.

12 March

About forty-five miles S.W. of Fernando Po. We shall get near Cape Palmas about Christmas if I am not too sanguine. However, not being very well, I'll make an allowance for any error which that might cause and give us until New Year's day.

13 March

Captain sick of fever. Very unlike Sunday. Making little progress towards our destination. I managed to work out our latitude to-day by Norie's "Epitome."[45] We are in 20° 53' N. I suppose Wilson will have returned from Batanga by this time and is no doubt enjoying himself with Miss Meyer. How jolly it must be for two people who like each other to be so often together. But for her health's sake I could be so selfish as to wish for the same felicity with someone I know.

14 March

Captain still sick with fever. Had good breeze all day and got well to the S.W. I get on with these Spaniards much better than I expected. They have some very good dishes and live better or at least have a greater variety of food than our English ships. What I have never before seen on board a ship is here in plenty--eggs preserved in lime. I am becoming quite Spanish. I speak Spanish and with the others take my coffee first thing in the morning, my breakfast at 11 a.m. and dinner at 5.30 p.m. Two meals a day would not do for an English sailor but the Spaniards are quite contented with them. Like the Spaniards too, I wear old clothes, loll about the deck or sleep in the cabin, am too lazy to tie my shoe strings, sit down on deck to my victuals and wash my face once a week.

---

[45]John William Norie, *Complete Epitome of Practical Navigation* (London, various eds., 1805-1896).

15 March

Captain next thing to all right. He appears to have lost all patience with the baffling winds we have had. This morning we were becalmed but as it looked very black to windward the Captain had the ship put under topsails and jib. It happened to be only a good breeze and of course all the sails had to be set again. He is either a very prudent or a timid man. Up to twelve o'clock we have done very well–made about 60 miles S.W. This blessed old ship goes so precious slow on a wind. The Captain says she will go her nine knots but I don't think she will do it while I am in her. He says he has not got ballast enough but if he had much more the hold would be full of casks of oil and water; about this latter he is anxious as he fears he has not sufficient on board to last us.

16 March

Have made very little progress during the last twelve hours. Last night the stupid "piloto" (mate) fearing by the lightning that a tornado was coming, put the ship under topsails. I don't well see how he could expect a tornado without thunder. Of course there was nothing and when it became his turn to go below his successor put on all sail as before. This "piloto" is a perfect gentleman unlike our English mates he does nothing but navigate the ship on his watch and in the daytime take his observations, eats, drinks, smokes, talks and sleeps. In the latter accomplishment he is quite an example and in his duties he may be equally so if they are those of what I should call a vice-Captain. The Captain not quite better; cook too has been laid up with fever the last few days; myself only middling.

17 March

Had a capital breeze all last night and to-day. Ship has been making a W. by S. or W.S.W. course of four knots during that time. Captain is all right again, so am I. Cook sick still. In consequence of some of our casks of water having turned bad we are pestered by mosquitos. On account of these, the cockroaches, heat, &c. in the cabin, I slept on deck all night. We have been busy making balls and cartridges for the old flint-lock muskets which are on board. Bad as they are, we expect with them and my double-barrelled gun and six-barrelled revolver to be able to put down any disposition the Kroomen may show to take charge of the ship.

18 March

I have just learnt that on her last voyage this ship called at Cape Palmas for the purpose of taking Kroomen to Fernando Po on account of the owners but that the Captain was unable to induce any of them to trust themselves under the Spanish flag and in consequence he had of course to go without. Now if this should occur in the present instance, it will place me in a "nice kettle of fish." My only plan will then be to give the boys "books" to go down by next steamer and do the best I can with the goods I have on board in purchasing stock, &c.[46] We have had a very good S.S.W. wind to-day, which with yesterday's good work has put the Captain in better humour and spirits. I hope we shall arrive at Cape Palmas in five or six days.

19 March

I slept last night on deck but early in the morning I had to bolt on account of rain. We have had a good breeze right aft with incessant rain from 8 to 3 and from 3 to 6 p.m. During the night we have had a splendid breeze for the most part about four points free. The "contra-maestre" (bosun) and the "piloto" had a little fight last night about the changing of the watches, one complaining of the other not coming on deck when called. They did not hurt each other but made plenty of noise over it.

20 March

I am still anything but well, very weak and languid. I have neither strength nor inclination to move a step. If this voyage is to do me any good it has yet to come. Pains about the liver with low spirits. We are doing very well with the ship now, making our hundred miles a day in spite of the frequent calms we have.

21 March

Weather fine; not much wind but making our usual day's work. At sea it appears to be the Spanish custom to live almost entirely on salt codfish and beans. The sailors usually have these with biscuits. In the morning first thing they have coffee and biscuit, at eleven they have breakfast consisting of the above--but at present varied by fowl and yams with soup, at 5 or 6 o'clock dinner of the same. They eat with wooden forks out of tin dishes. Aft we are favoured with plates, knives and forks, &c. and generally have soup, fowl and yams stewed with some kind of force-meat in which is, I fancy, a good share of bacon, salt codfish with onions, cheese, raisins and coffee for breakfast. Dinner with exception of the soup and the addition of beans is the same. But both breakfast and dinner are occasionally diversified by omelets, a little salt beef (eaten raw with onions and vinegar), sardines, salt fish differently cooked, nuts, almonds and figs. The wine has gone sour but for all that the Spaniards seem to like it as much as an Englishman does his beer. The wine I refer to is what we call "Black Strap"; the Spaniards call it "Vino Tinto." It seemed very strange to me at first to see them bring the beans without meat--they make a separate dish of it and eat fish or meat with biscuit. I am very fond of their beans, particularly so when browned; they are an excellent vegetable. Occasionally we have a little sweet pastry which is also generally very good to my sweet mouth.

22 March

Captain down with fever again. Ship making no headway in calm sea.

---

[46] Any letter of recommendation or record of employment was referred to as a "book."

23 March

Still calm; Captain worse than ever; very sick all day; vomiting and purging.

24 March

Captain somewhat better but still very weak and cannot eat anything. I have been trying to get something made that he would relish but these Spaniards will persist in giving him all sorts of drink and greasy broth and soup. We had a splendid tornado this morning and our "contra-maestre" kept the ship to it like a good one. It was very pleasant to see us going through the water so fast after the calms we have had. Many of the sailors were in the whole of the storm in their usual dress and of course go well drenched. In such times as this a sailor's life is anything but a pleasant one.

25 March

Captain getting better; myself very unwell. I know nothing about the ship except that we had squally weather. This "piloto" of ours is as much use in the ship as an old woman would be, when he sees the chance of a breeze he takes in sail like a madman, but when there is no wind he puts on all he can. In the tornado yesterday it really did one good to see the "contra-maestre" lay her so nicely as he did but this other stupid beggar is of no use for anything.

26 March

(I write this on Monday). Yesterday and to-day I have had severe attacks of fever and am very low and miserable. I have been ailing ever since I left Fernando Po or rather I should say since I left England. Confound it, I wish I was anywhere but where I am. Good health with a crust at home would be better than bad health and a feast out here in this sickly climate. When I am going to get strong again is a puzzle to me for our ship has only two or three fowls left and on salt provisions it is not easy to grow stout.

28 March

I don't know when we are going to arrive at Cape Palmas--we are about 120 miles off the Coast and 60° to leeward of the parallel of longitude of Cape Palmas. We have been trying to be too quick and instead of gaining, we shall lose. Had we made our proper longitude when we had the help of the current, we should not have had to turn to windward as we are doing and fight our way against wind and tide. I suppose this latter mistake will humbug us to the extent of a week and the Captain will be bothering me on the coast and hurrying me to get back in the time wished by his employers (forty days). How he is going to comply with their wishes I cannot see when I know that he will have to fill all our casks with fresh water in addition to the time I shall require for my business.

29 March

At noon to-day we were about sixty-three miles off Cape Palmas and if our present breeze continues we shall reach it to-morrow morning, that is, supposing the chronometer to be correct. We are now steering about north-west and this course allowing for the set of the current on our bow should bring us well to windward of our port. The Captain ashore and on board are different persons. Ashore he is all smiles and talk and tries to be respectable but aboard ship he is dirty, grumpy, and an awful tyrant. I have not seen our Captain smile or, excepting the few days when we had made good work, heard him speak a pleasant word since we left Fernando Po. He tries to make himself and everybody about him miserable and is swearing everlastingly at what would not have been, had he been wise enough to adopt the advice of those who know this coast better than himself and have gone to the southwards of the line and to westward of his port before he tried to make it.

30 March

We saw a fine looking vessel early this morning standing away to the eastward, a merchantman, we thought, but by degrees she came nearer and nearer, almost head to wind; all sail set, as if driven by some mysterious power behind; at midday she saluted us with a gun at the same time running up the Blue Ensign and not wishing to show any want of courtesy we returned the compliment with our Spanish merchant's flag. A boat then was sent alongside us to make friendly enquiries as to where we had come from, where we were going to, and what was the object of our voyage, and being hard of belief they searched our ship and mustered our men to prove the truth of our replies and then left us, taking our papers to show the Chief of what proved to be H.M.S. *Rattlesnake* under Commodore Wilmot whom I thought was at Fernando Po, and about whose arrival there during my absence I have been grumbling so much, thinking I should miss the good spree they expected to have.[47] The Commodore having satisfied himself that we were pursuing our voyage with honest intentions sent back our papers, dipped his ensign and after our having returned the compliment we parted company. The officers of the *Rattlesnake* were kind enough to give us their latitude and longitude by which we find our distance from Cape Palmas in N.E. 38 miles and that the difference of longitude between that shown by our chronometer and that given by the Rattlesnake is 24 miles. Thus we have run past our port a good distance and had we not been fortunate enough to see the Commodore we should have had no little difficulty in finding it.

31 March

Arrived in Cape Palmas after a passage of 23½ days, anchored at about 4 p.m. Our Chief could not convince himself that the point we were steering for early in the morning

[47]HMS *Rattlesnake* (2431 grt) was a single-screw, wooden corvette of seventeen guns. Built at Chatham in 1861, by 1864 it was the flagship of the West African and Cape of Good Hope Station. See J.G. Cox, *Cox and the Ju Coast* (St. Helier, 1968), 74 and photograph opposite 52. Further details are in Conway's *All the World's Fighting Ships, 1860-1905* (London, 1979), 48.

was the Cape until an adventurous Krooman came off to us when we were about 10 miles distant from land and convinced him of his being right and guided him clear of some rocks which but for his help might have become dangerously near.

On our arrival I went on shore, saw the Captain of Artillery, and arranged with a Mr. McGill where to get the water from. This is a most dangerous place to land and I got very wet going ashore in a surf boat. The ship's boat sent ashore for me was capsized in the surf.

1 April

Examined our casks and found we had only some eight or nine of good water, the remainder are all bad or empty. The Captain and I had some few words as to upon whom the palaver of water is to fall. I consider that it is his duty to see after getting fresh water and shall let some gentlemen in Fernando Po know it on my arrival there. I don't see why I should be exposing myself to the dangers of sun and sea while the Captain, mate and all sit down on board. However, I have been ashore again to-day and have had the water casks sent ashore to be filled; some casks need repairs. The canoes and Kroomen have all to be hired and the water has to be paid for. Who is to pay for all this will be seen hereafter. Water is scarce, it being the dry season and will have to be brought from some distance.

2 April

Nothing done with regard to water. The wells near the town are all dry, consequently the water has to be fetched from a distance of two miles up the river. The man who is getting the water has promised to have all the casks and the firewood alongside on Monday without fail.

3 April

I should have like to have gone to church to-day but I understand that there is only one service which commences at our breakfast hour 11 o'clock. I have engaged a few men at an advance of $2½.

4 April

Up to-night I have engaged thirty-three boys. The Captain of Artillery, instead of shipping some seventy here, has only got about thirty and in consequence will have to get the remainder at the places I had intended to obtain them. This makes it very awkward for me as he gives an advance of $4 per man and I am afraid I shall have to do the same. The Captain has been greatly imposed upon in Cape Palmas and very stupidly has paid Russwurn for the wood and water $50½, along with his own account. I went ashore upon learning this and remonstrated with the man, but what was the use after he had received his money? This water has cost an awful lot whoever has to pay for it and I cannot get these people to fill up their tanks now that the water in the casks is good nor can I get them to put a little lime in to prevent the water becoming bad. I am afraid they will all become putrid.

5 April

In the affair of water and also in all my own arrangements I have been so horribly bored by these people that I could almost wish I knew nothing of their language. Advising me to do things and then questioning if I had done, or said, or arranged the very things that I had accomplished. They might, one would think, either arrange these things themselves, or let me arrange them without interference. The last lot of water came alongside at 8 a.m. and we have had a good sea breeze all day, but the Captain is not well and instead of trying to get to Cavally we have been lying here all day doing nothing but losing time.

6 April

The very small breeze we had being fair, the Captain was obliging enough to set sail first thing this morning. I had a severe attack of ague in the forenoon but upon reaching Cavally and hearing the Captain of Artillery hard at work bargaining for Krooboys, and having got over my sweating, I went on deck and made some few cask sales but was not able to get any Krooboys. It is very annoying to have another person in competition with me in the same ship and apparently also in competition with the interests of the persons I have come to serve. It was expected that the Governor's boys would all be shipped at Cape Palmas, but in fact there has not been more than half shipped at that point.

7 April

Got some fifteen boys at Cavally; the Captain has got about twelve. The boys we have taken here are in general better than those we got at Cape Palmas and I have paid each an advance of $3. We now have about half our quantity on board. We left Cavally about noon and having a good breeze right aft, we soon reached Taboo but I was disappointed at not seeing more boys come on board. However, we are promised what the Kroomen call "plenty" to-morrow. There are five or six villages about and one would therefore think that there should be Kroomen somewhere.

8 April

Had another severe attack of ague today but at the time of writing this (7 p.m.) I feel better. In spite of my fit of shivering, I managed by the aid of a tumbler of rum with hot water and sugar (there was no brandy at Cape Palmas) to secure five or six boys. In all I have got eight to-day and Captain about the same number. I was obliged to give in at last and leave the selling of rum and tobacco to our "contra-maestre." It is my firm belief that we are not near Taboo (in the Spanish Chart this part is called so), but in the English one which is larger and called "Tafon," and "Taboo" or "Grand Taboo" is some six miles distant. The Captain has thus been misled by his chart and by an impudent beast of a fellow who has come with us from Cape Palmas as pilot and guide.

9 April

I was led to understand in Fernando Po that in Taboo, that is Grand Taboo, to which place we have come this afternoon, I should get any quantity of boys; I have got four. I am now getting anxious to obtain what boys I can; we have been a long time from Fernando Po and I cannot reasonably detain the ship much longer on the Coast. At 12 o'clock we moved down to Basha but got nothing but promises for to-morrow morning.

10 April

I have done pretty well at this place having got ten men. Aznar went ashore last night and saw about his boys; he has got nine here which finishes his number. I am very glad of this as I shall sooner complete my own but I have great fears of being unable to obtain the number I first intended to take. At noon we left Basha for Half Bereby at which place we arrived at about 5 p.m., and as usual were visited by a lot of headmen who, while screwing rum out of me, made great promises for to-morrow.

11 April

This Half Bereby is full of people but for all that I have not been able to get more than three boys here. We were beset with lots of canoes with maize, fowls, ducks, plantains, carada &c., much of which was bought by the ship. The King of the place came on board expecting no doubt to get something. I gave him a half tumbler of rum but His Majesty was not too well pleased with the treatment he received, I fancy. We moved down to Grand Bereby in the afternoon and as usual we had lots of headmen with "books" and brass plates making all sorts of false promises for the sake of a little rum. I want to get some canoes here if I can but am afraid I shall not succeed as Townsend's schooner is here for the same object. At Half Bereby I could not get any. I wish this voyage was finished; I am worried to death with anxiety and thought; I never had so much trouble over anything in my life.

12 April

I have only got five Kroomen here. King Tom came on board in grand style this morning; in his canoe he had some thirty or forty men, with a flag at the bow, and himself (a fine looking fellow) standing up in the middle dressed in a shirt, grey coat of last century and a beaver hat. They came alongside singing, paddled round the ship once, splashing the water up above them as they paddled and making the canoe go through the water at a great speed. Of course he required rum for himself and headmen, and biscuits having been offered, he asked for beef also which he did not get. I tried to buy his canoe which was a very large one but we could not come to terms. He sold it to Townsend's Captain. I think it useless to detain the vessel longer for Krooboys as it is not likely I should be able to get more further down the Coast (besides there is the feeding of the Krooboys and the water to be considered) and have directed the Captain to sail for Accra.

13 April

Had a splendid breeze right aft all yesterday afternoon and until 8 o'clock this morning, when we had a pretty strong tornado and afterwards all day calm. The only thing now that I am anxious about is the water which so far is drinkable. I do not expect to buy much in Accra and, as it is desirable to arrive in Fernando Po before the mail, I shall not have time to go down to Jellah Coffee or Popo for stock; besides I question if it would be profitable to do so with the number of boys I have daily to feed. I expect I shall have some little unpleasantness on my arrival in Fernando Po. Some people will no doubt think that I ought to have done more. I have done my best whether I have succeeded or not and no one could be more desirous, anxiously desirous, of furthering the interests of my present employers than I am, but I cannot overrule circumstances.

14 April

A fair wind all day but not much of it. The Captain of Artillery is of the opinion that he has been spending the money of the government rather freely, and from what he has told me I think he is correcting his ideas. He paid for the landing of the boys from the steamer in Cape Palmas where many of the boxes belonging to his boys were seized upon and carried off by the people of that place, under the pretence that they were indebted to them, and to liberate these cases, the Captain paid the demands of the people who detained them, without holding any enquiry before the Superintendent into the justness of their claim. It is a rascally scheme that the people of Cape Palmas should be allowed to carry off the poor Krooboys' property in this manner but the Government of Liberia is a mere sham; they pretend to have certain laws, rules &c., which impose the payment of duties on strangers trading in their ports, and have no power and no money except copper and paper, the real value of the latter being half its nominal value. In Cape Palmas everything is enormously dear, both food and merchandise. After paying the above imposition, the Captain paid for the passages of the Kroomen to their respective towns in a schooner belonging to the place and during the time he remained there, he paid $2 per day for his food and lodging and a commission of $1 upon each boy that his host procured him, besides an imposition of $1 per boy imposed by the ruling powers as a registration fee; half of this latter was returned afterwards with an explanation that the Superintendent has found himself in error in charging his fee of $1. To be in their hands is what Daddy Jim would call being in the hands of the Philistines. The Captain is very desirous that I should not speak of this matter to Daddy Jim as he is afraid of being chaffed by him.

16 April

Arrived off Accra about noon. I went ashore to see Cleaver but he being absent, I made arrangements with his representative to send down by next mail two carpenters for Smith, one for Wilson and a top sawyer for Mr. Lynslager. Stock was scarce and dear. I could have bought some bullocks but having heard that a ship had left Jellah Coffee with 120 for Fernando Po, I thought it useless to take any. To have purchased any quantity of stock, I should have had to wait three or four days. To-morrow being Sunday I should not be able to do anything until the day following, so I have decided not to wait, particularly as the Captain is always fretting about going. I dined with a Spaniard named Curoo who appears a decent enough sort of being.

18 April

We have had a good breeze all yesterday and to-day and have been busy making calculations as to when we are to arrive in Fernando Po, but of course we cannot be sure of arriving at any fixed time as a land squall or a calm will upset the best of calculations. The Kroomen are so far contented, they have been begging rum and tobacco of me but I cannot give them any. However the Captain of Artillery has paid his boys the balance of their first month's advance and they are thus able to ease their minds on this point. I have had my revolver loaded in case the boys should desire to take possession of the ship (as some of their countrymen have lately done with other ships) but they have never showed any inclination to be so ambitious.

19 April

To-day or rather this morning we had a heavy storm which lasted some six hours and being right in our teeth it has driven us back considerably. We ran before it for some time with the jib set and afterwards the helm was put down and the ship's head brought round the wind. This has been the heaviest gale I have ever been at sea in. No accident occurred with the exception of my having slid down to leeward at breakfast time with my plate of soup in my hand and thus peeled my skin against a cask. It is not very pleasant to have one's breakfast on deck in such a storm with the accompaniment of a drizzling rain. Unfortunately, I left my great coat ashore in Accra. These Spaniards appear to have strange ideas of comfort for I can't see why it would not have been equally convenient and much more comfortable to have had our breakfast in the cabin this morning.

20 April

On account of the storm yesterday, our Kroomen made only one meal, each man eating a pound of rice. The sailors caught some ten or twelve large fish. Two of them the Captain gave to the Krooboys. To-day we have had little wind but that has been favourable. Our Krooboys are very happy on board; this is just the sort of life that suits them; nothing to do but eat, drink, smoke and sleep. Their rice is boiled in a very large pot and afterwards emptied into buckets and dishes, each bucket for ten boys. They are allowed 1 lb. of rice each per day; they eat with their hands and the man who can swallow the fastest gets the largest share. It is amusing to see them eat; they lose no time in talking then, but immediately when done they all rush to the water cask and make the greatest possible row--after this comes the pipe and a continual chatter until late at night.

21 April

Had another tornado and afterwards a strong breeze right in our teeth, followed by a calm. In consequence we have driven back some distance. The existence of a Krooman is a strange one; born and brought up in mud huts; used to canoes and water from their childhood, their earliest ambition is, like their forefathers, to "go to sea" as they call it, that is to leave their native country and go to the rivers and towns on the Coast, to work for white men until they can return with guns and flying colours to their home, where they then buy themselves wives and go to sea again until they become rich men possessing plenty of wives. At first they are generally sent to sea by a headman, that is a man who has given up going to sea, a retired gentleman who receives the greater part of the pay they received during their first voyage; afterwards the boy becomes a man for himself and does not require the assistance of a headman. It very often occurs that boys who have been working abroad two years have very little to shew when they arrive at home. They are generally landed by the mail at Cape Palmas where the people greatly impose upon them and if their homes are distant and they have to pass through other towns they frequently have to give up part of their goods at each town. This is what they call eating their goods. I have got two small lads with me and could have got any quantity, they are so anxious to go to sea when young. One little fellow cried so much that it was as much as I could do to refuse him, but I had plenty. In consequence of the tornado yesterday we have had a dead calm all last night and all to-day, and by observations of to-day we find we are 20 miles from our position before the tornado.

23 April

Had a light breeze all day; towards evening it increased and we drove along pleasantly all night.

24 April

Had a fine breeze all day. In the morning we had a great fall of rain and the Captain, fearing that it was wind, took in all sail and stood away, before what little breeze we had. Kroomen as a rule are not selfish amongst themselves; they think it no sin to steal as much as they can from a white man and try to beg as much from him as they possibly can, but with each other they share their tobacco and their rum. Like ourselves the big ones crow over the small ones to no small extent. It is amusing to see them at night sleeping in a row on deck closely packed together with no other covering but their loin cloths, with their legs intertwined and coiled into each other, the body of each forming the latter Z or something very much resembling it.

25 April

Arrived in Santa Isabel. The Captain washed his face to-day, the first time he has done so since he left Fernando Po. The Governor was pleased to see me but, as I expected, disappointed at my not having brought any stock. I was surprised to find Miss Meyer preparing to leave us, she is going away to-night. How fortunate it is that I arrived to-day! A few hours difference, a squall, a calm, and I should not have been ale to say good-bye. She has been very unwell during my absence, and has thus been forced to go. The Governor too has also been very ill; and Ellen Matthews is dead.

26 April

Miss Meyer left us last night and on endeavouring to get out the ship stuck on one of the rocks until high tide. It was quite calm at the time so that she did herself no harm. Miss Meyer goes in the *Elgira* to Calabar where she will embark on board the mail steamer. It is very unpleasant that she should have to make a voyage thus amongst strangers, but the Consul is going to Madeira and perhaps Roy is going home; thus she won't be an unprotected female. I fancy matters have not been so pleasant during my absence, the "old man" has been sick and peevish; Miss Meyer too has been sick, so that there may be other causes than sickness to account for her sudden desire to leave us; she is of too delicate a nature to stand the brusque, tropical manners of the "old man." They are very well with people of good nerves but with people of a sensitive nature they are too abrupt and rude. I wish Miss Meyer every happiness and prosperity, may she meet with better health and more genial society and treatment than she has experienced in the land she now leaves.

3 May

The Spanish transport leaves to-day and I have been very busy ever since the mail left in preparing my business parcel of correspondence to send by her which will arrive sooner by this means than the mail of last month. I have not written any private correspondence since my return but as I told all my correspondents in my last letters that they were to expect nothing from me by the last two mails they will not be disappointed.

The Secretary, Carlos de Rojas, leaves us by the *Consuelo* having been appointed to a four years' post in Porto Rico. He is well liked in the Colony and his departure will be very sincerely regretted by his many friends here. He is a very gentlemanly, cordial and good-natured man.

4 May

Lynslager and Tomlinson having had a quarrel while at breakfast this morning, the "old man" became so irritated that he gave Tomlinson the sack on the spot. They have never agreed with each other. Lynslager says Tomlinson is useless and does not understand what one might expect from a man receiving his salary. He tells Tomlinson that he knows nothing about book-keeping nor is he fit to take charge of the office. I think Daddy is in the main right, as Tomlinson has shown himself very inattentive both with regard to the books and correspondence during my absence, making every allowance for the difficulties of obtaining from Mr. and Mrs. Lynslager the necessary information for properly keeping the books. He is more fit for a shopman than a clerk.

6 May

Poor Morrison one of Laughland's clerks departed this life after only two days illness. Doctor Mullen says that he thinks he died of congestion of the brain.

7 May

Tomlinson wants to go home; Lynslager, in accordance with the terms of his agreement, swears he won't send him. Tomlinson also claims his board and lodging until the mail. Lynslager says he will give him lodging and a month's advance. Nothing is too bad for Tomlinson with the "old man" now. It was the same thing with me when I wanted to leave him; I was fit for nothing except to write letters and keep books (a great exception some would fancy) but soon afterward I was the best of men, without equal. Tomlinson, Lynslager says, has been a dear bargain, a great imposition, having cost him little short of £100 for three months' work.

26 May

Tomlinson has brought his case before the Spanish Governor as British Consul, in the absence of Captain Burton, and after some trouble and a good deal of cursing and swearing on Daddy's part, not of course in Court, for he did not attend. I, however, went as his representative. The Governor decided that Mr. Lynslager must pay Tomlinson's passage home and his board and lodging up to the 28th inst. at the same time stopping any monies which he (Mr. Lynslager) may have in hand due to Tomlinson for salary. This is what the Governor and judge think is meant by the written agreement which Laird Fletcher & Co. made with Tomlinson. Daddy had previously sworn to blow up the place and die a martyr to his conscience and at the same time take revenge on his enemies rather than pay the passage money, but then of course everybody who knows him knows also how to take all such small talk and I was not at all surprised at the cool manner in which he made up his mind to pay his passage money home and, as he said, "send him to the devil out of this and get clear of him for you know he must go home although I defy the Governor to make me send him further than the first British Colony, and that's Lagos."

28 May

I was surprised to see Mr. Tomlinson walk in to-day and instead of claiming his passage home make a cool proposal to treat with the "old man" for a certain sum of money instead. He said that Mr. Townsend had offered him an engagement at Elobey and that he would prefer going there, (he previously stated a few days ago that he had an offer in Fernando Po at £150 but did not want to remain) if Mr. Lynslager would mitigate matters and give him the passage money instead of paying it to the Company. Of course Mr. Lynslager was not going to do this, but he did a good deal more than any sensible man would have done. Had it been me he should have either gone home or remained without a claim after the trouble and annoyance he had give him in taking the matter before the Governor; Daddy, however, though taking a momentary view of the matter in the same light as I should have decided it had it been my affair, at once offered him £15 in settlement of all claims except lodging, and this was finally agreed to after I had written to Laird Fletcher & Co. advising them of his bad "out-turn" and to Campbell of my having drawn on him for the fellow's passage money. So that from first to last he has given me some little trouble. He has been a costly bit of grocery and quill to Daddy, for during the five months he has been in Fernando Po, he has been absent from work three, owing to sickness and other causes, with the Doctor's bill and lodging more than £110.

6 June

The "old man" is very unwell now. He should have gone to Basili this morning as intended, everything had been prepared but he refused to go. There is one thing certain if he does not go somewhere for a change, he will either lose his intellect or die. He drinks a lot of champagne and eats little or nothing. He is continually speaking of things that either have not happened at all, or of which he was at one time perfectly well aware. Indeed he does not appear to be able to retain anything in his memory for he is continually repeating his question. He fancies Miss Meyer is still here and Tomlinson too; he talks of his schooners and vessels (which he had once upon a time), and of his Bimbia Factory; he wants to know where his ships are, where is Cobbin, Tomlinson, Miss Meyer &c., and although I tell him of his being under a mistake he appears ever to forget my replies and goes on everlastingly asking the same questions. At times he talks about bills, wants to know, "where those bills, you know, of mine were sent, didn't Tomlinson take them home with him? I hope they will all be safe," and so he goes on. Of course he fancies that he makes sensible enquiries and it is no use trying to convince him of an error although he acknowledges he is rather light headed. He talks rationally enough and about past things too but still he does not seem to know what has been lately done or what is going on now.

8 June

Wilson went over to Calabar to see Miss Meyer and whilst the steamer was there, they made it up to get married the same evening, and so they were. The next morning saw Mrs. Wilson depart for England and Wilson arrived here to-day to bring us the news. This is what I call "a marriage extraordinary." Wilson says the missionary ladies induced Miss Meyer to marry and his friends in Calabar did the same with him. He protests that he had not the least intention of marrying when he went over to Calabar to see her in accordance with her wishes. The reason for Wilson having hurried the affair is probably because he did not wish her to feel strange amongst his relatives in Scotland which she might have felt as "Miss Meyer" having no exact status.

9 June

This business of ours is carried on under very bad arrangements. I suppose we have £2,000 worth of goods in store (goodness knows when they will be paid for) and most of this is entrusted to the keeping of girls who cannot read or write. Now that Tomlinson is gone, I have to look after the store, sell goods and issue them to the traders, keep books and make out accounts, write the correspondence, gauge oil, look after the coals and the men who are employed down there discharging, in fact I have to do everything and it's most annoying that things should be so. I am sometimes very near losing all patience and was particularly so the other day when the "old man" told both his wife and myself we were liars because we both know contrary to his recollection that he had given the day before a cask of salt to one of the traders. I don't know why I should do the work I am doing and in the bargain be called a liar. I have no interest in staying with him and would not at all hesitate to leave if I knew that he had someone to put in my place. I don't like to put him to any loss or inconvenience but I detest the humbug I have hitherto put up with. There are people in the world who would make an easy time of it in my place by oiling themselves towards the "old man" and letting his affairs mind themselves but I take an interest in his affairs and would gladly do all I can to forward them but I am opposed at every step by his previous arrangements, and by his conservative ideas. He has never been a business man or given his attention thereto. He will never make any money under present arrangements. The cash is never properly balanced; it shows a loss of three hundred or so a year and he and his wife are the cashiers. The goods are at the mercy of untutored and dishonest girls in the stores and he himself spends to the tune of a round sum per annum. I have really no pleasure in working and seeing things go on as they do but I cannot help it--I have tried my best to reform and have to some extent succeeded but I am getting tired of everlasting fighting against prejudice and custom and of working my limbs and head to no purpose and for the interests of a man who neither co-operates with me, nor appreciates my efforts. If my efforts produced a satisfactory result I should be pleased, but the opposition and humbug I encounter, combined with the extravagances before mentioned, and the general mismanagement of affairs make such a thing impossible.

23 June

Daddy has been confined to his bed since the commencement of this month: he does not appear to get better or worse, wanders a good deal in his mind and of course does nothing with the business although he talks all sorts of things about it to me. His principal idea is to pay off his men (he fancies he has got a great many employed) in order to economise. The doctor says that his loss of memory is caused by small globules of water in the brain, and does not think that a change would at all benefit him.

24 June

A great many black people have died of the smallpox in the town and the disease is getting worse instead of better. As yet no white has suffered from it but I suppose if it is unhealthy for the blacks it must be so too for the whites but at present the whites have average health here. At the time of the epidemic amongst the whites in Sierra Leone the blacks died in large numbers from the smallpox.

2 July

The *Whampoa* sailed to-day, or rather this evening. Captain Carter has got a splendid ship and the ship has got a splendid Captain. He is the most gentlemanly, upright, straightforward Captain I have ever met and I deeply regret his departure, for during the time he has been here I have made quite a home of his ship and we have been the greatest of friends. He is an American but in consequence of the war his ship sails under

English colours.[48] I gave him the despatches as he is bound by charter to be in Calloa by the end of August. I say "I" because Daddy was sick and I made the arrangement for him. He pays £55 as compensation for the extra hire of men and boats; of course I do not benefit a single halfpenny by this arrangement, although having done the thing on my own responsibility, I have had a good deal of trouble and anxiety about it. I have been down to the coal shed every day (except when very wet) and exposed myself a good deal to the sun in consequence. I sold some goods for him amounting to £50 upon which I charged commission, apparently for myself, but I had never any intention of making anything on my own account and simply charged it to enable me to pay Captain Carter a difference of £1 8s. od. in the hire of Kroomen (about which we did not agree), a bet of a new hat 13/-, which I lost to the Captain and "dashes" of sundries to the mate &c.; after all was paid I had 1/1 left. The mate is a very dogged, resolute old man who is rather too fond of drink and cursing. He has been quite a terror to the Krooboys and although he never struck them, he frightened them by his looks, shouting and cursing and got more work done by these means than if he had flogged them or had let them do as they liked. I wish them all success and would wish that every Captain and mate were equally to be appreciated. On Monday I saw the *Whampoa* off the point

9 September

Had a big palaver with Mammy: one of the boys having given me some cheek I put myself to the trouble of giving him a knock or two on the head which so offended Mammy that she came out in a rage and said she could not allow that. I told her that I would not put with the impertinence and everlasting humbug of her servants and that if there was to be any trouble about this affair I would leave the house. I fancy she must have been afraid of my doing this so she sent for Mr. Wilson to inform him of the matter and I suppose to get him to be a mediator.

10 September

To-day Daddy signed an addition to his will by which he declared himself a British subject and requests that his will be administered according to English law. The poor "old man" was quite delirious and it was melancholy and affecting to hear him bid us all good-bye as if he were going to die at once. He gave us all his benediction and stretching out his hand to take hold of mine he said "Good-bye thou honest and upright man, may god bless thee." Wilson, Mrs. Lynslager and myself were present. I do not think he can live long now; the doctor says he can do nothing for him.

11 September

I went on board the *Greyhound* to tea with Captain Yates and the American missionaries. There are two gentlemen, Mrs. Clements, Mrs. Nassan and baby, Mrs. Prescott, Mrs. de Heer, the missionaries and Mrs. Yates, the Captain's wife. It is indeed a treat to have the company of some white ladies in this part of the world. They are all very

---

[48]During the US Civil War many Federal ships used foreign flags to avoid southern commerce raiders.

nice people. We spent a very pleasant evening in prayers, hymn singing and conversation--a much more edifying way of spending one's Sunday evenings than the way in which they are generally spent. After seeing nothing but black women's faces for so long a time, those of white ones look strange and peculiar.

13 September

Daddy is much more quite to-day and, I think, seems a little better but he is very weak and his voice is a little husky apparently caused by the shouting of the last few days and nights. Several black women sleep here all night watching with Mammy, a great many more than is really necessary. The "old man" says he has got no pain, he says he feels low and a numbness in the ends of his fingers. This latter is caused I suppose by slow circulation of the blood. It is very melancholy and affecting to see the poor old governor gradually wasting away and sinking into the arms of death. His illness appears to be a gradual failing of his physical powers, a debility, caused no doubt by so long a life in this climate.

14 September

Daddy worse from 3 a.m. At 11 a.m. the shops were shut and all our business suspended and fearing that he is dying I have been to call Wilson to see him before the close. Mammy, fearful of the thievish propensities of not over-conscientious sympathizing friends has had all the things taken off the sideboards and put under lock and key, except those which cannot easily be carried off. I have called Mullins and Dr. Allison of the *Jaseur* but they appear to think that Daddy cannot live many hours. The colour of his face is yellowish, his hands are restless, pulse low, skin hot. Mullins called again in the evening and noticed the enlarging of the pulins; this is a sign that death is near. Mullins says he may live until midnight or morning. He has been all day insensible and has not uttered a word. At times he opens his eyes, but makes no sign whatever, and beyond hard breathing and an occasional groan and a little restlessness of the arms and hands, nothing is perceptible. At ten o'clock I laid down on the sofa for a short nap, awaiting the coming hour which was not then far distant, for at half past twelve he died, and I was aroused by the noise of the servants running off for the tub and water. There was no crying then. Mrs. Lynslager had been crying so much all day that she might not have been able to cry more, or her misery might have been so great that she was unable to ease the aching of her heart by tears. However it might be, everybody seemed to turn their thoughts to the washing and laying out. Thomas Williams, Henry Matthews, Nicol, and others, washed the "old man" and dressed him while I looked on and gave occasional assistance. We put on his cork leg, his drawers, singlet, white shirt, trousers, and waistcoat, with a white cravat. In his shirt were put gold studs, and in his waistcoat gold and onyx buttons. After thus dressing him we carried him into the large room in which a bed had been prepared and laid him upon it, after which I had a lock of his hair and whiskers cut off for Mammy, and then covered his body with a sheet and his face with a piece of lace. And now the mourning commenced. Mammy, with the rest of the women present, and with the servant girls, drew round the bed, and Mammy removing the lace cover said some affectionate words to the corpse and then burst into a paroxysm of grief and tears. All the women present gave vent to their feelings in a similar noisy manner,

Mammy calling out "Oh, my fader, Oh! my moddah, Oh! Oh, my sista, Oh! Oh, my broder Oh!" saying how good a husband he had been to her, that he had never flogged her, and that if he were at times vexed with anything she had done, and used hard words, he would come shortly afterwards to beg her forgiveness. That he had wanted her to go on a visit to her parents and relatives, but that he was father, mother, all, and that she never wanted to leave his side, that she wanted soon to die that she might be with him, and very feelingly told him that he was dressed in white clothes but that she was draped in black ones. This, told in her simple manner, was peculiarly touching. The others cried out that he was their "massa," their only "massa," their father, their mother, their all, asking him why he had thus made fools of them, and sometimes in their grief would give a very peculiar half-laughing cry. Some appeared to lose entire control over themselves, throwing themselves on the floor, and demonstrating in the loudest and most energetic manner their sorrow for the loss of one so dear. At times the crying was done by all together, at other times one was wildly crying by herself, and then sometimes long pauses, and they would commence afresh. We all sat up all night with the body, but several found it too great an exertion, and laying themselves on the softest plank tried to get a short nap. At daybreak a short hymn was sung and one of the women prayed, but spoke so low that I did not know what she said.

Long before daylight the carpenters were at work on the coffin. I gave them fine red wood planks and had it polished outside, and lined with white alpaca within. This was done under the supervision of Thomas Williams, or supposed to be, for I afterwards learned that he was asleep most of the time. I am sorry that either he or Henry Matthews, who have been more or less drunk since the death of the "old man," and who assisted in washing and dressing him, should have been allowed to take any part in this work. Their want of feeling is most disgusting, and is a proof of the little real regret they pretend to feel. Williams wanted two gallons of rum for the carpenters who were making the coffin, but really for those who came to look on at the work, and get drunk, if they could, and this cool request was made with two bottles of brandy for himself and chums. After I had give the carpenters two bottles of rum, and himself one of brandy, I gave him his two bottles of brandy and the carpenters two bottles more of rum, with a half wish that it might poison the lot for the ungrateful, unnatural feeling manifested--a proof that sensuality, the love of drink, is stronger than sentiment in the black man. I sent a note to the Commandant of the Station, Major Osoris, and others, informing them of the death of Mr. Lynslager, and inviting them to the funeral. I also wrote to Captain Grubbe of the *Jaseur*, asking him to read the funeral service, and to invite his officers to attend. Of course, the house was put into mourning by hanging up blue baft, and turning the pictures with the front to the wall. This latter was done by one of the black women a couple of hours before the "ole man" died. The mourning continued all day (Wednesday) the same as the previous night by a great many women. I fixed the hour of interment at four o'clock, and before that time the house was full of people. A little before four, the corpse was put into the coffin and left uncovered for a short time, to give the white men a chance of seeing it. Mammy then took a last look and kiss, and then the coffin was screwed up, and borne to the bier. A cover of white alpaca for the top, and a hanging of black alpaca on the top was crossed with black silk ribbon in the shape of a cross, and on the top of all was thrown the Union Jack lent for the purpose by Captain Grubbe, of H.M.S. *Jaseur*. Then the procession commenced--first the corpse, next Mammy, with Frances, in the carriage, which had been covered with blue baft and with wrappers of the same material, which was drawn by our Krooboys.[49] Next came the servant girls of the house, draped also in blue baft. Next Wilson and myself. After us the black men, then the women, and after them the Englishmen and Spaniards, English naval officers, and Spanish military officers. We slowly moved along to the last resting place of our dear old Daddy in the old burying ground, and by the side of his son William, who is buried close to the Matthews family. The grave of his son had been dug with the head to the North, and we had therefore to dig Daddy's grave the same. Upon reaching the grave Captain Grubbe came forward and read the English burial service, the Union Jack being still spread upon the coffin. Mammy remained in the carriage, and Alice, the wife of Daddy's son, was close to it in a palanquin, she being in a very bad state of health. Captain Grubbe read the service in a very impressive manner and Dr. Mullins threw the soil into the grave on the reading of the passage "earth to earth, ashes to ashes, dust to dust." Jane Barleycorn and others cried loudly on seeing the last of poor Daddy Jim, but Mrs. Lynslager was silent and formed a strange contrast to those who were crying and indeed to herself, a few hours before. I am sure she felt it none the less on that account. There were a great many people present--more black than white, of course, but I do not believe there was absent one Englishman or Spaniard who had known Daddy, and was not prevented from coming through sickness. The arrangements have been left mostly to Mammy's black friends, and in consequence the "old man" has been buried, and the corpse attended to as if he were a black man. In the house there were people very busy with the arrangements who did anything but honour to his remains--people to whom he scarcely ever spoke, and of whom his opinion was so well known that they scarcely ever showed their faces to him when living. Another thing to be found fault with was the showy dress which some of them wore on the occasion, looking more as if they were going to a ball, instead of to a funeral, but I think generally the people who were so finely dressed were those of whom Daddy thought the least. Most of the people accompanied Mrs. Lynslager to the house, and then left. In the evening a good many black men and women came to sing psalms and hymns. They sang very well and on such occurrences as this it is a fitting accompaniment when conducted in a seemly manner, as it has a peculiarly melancholy effect on the mind, but I think it was very unwise to have any singing at this time for Mrs. Lynslager is weakened for want of food, and sleep, and quiet, and nothing could be better for her than to be left with two or three attendants, who would endeavour to soothe and comfort her, and to prepare nourishing food for her use. The singing was kept up until midnight and although I did not remain until that hour, but went and had a night's rest at Wilson's, as I felt very fatigued too, I heard the next morning that one person had to be put out of the house.

It is hard to understand why the Spanish naval officers were not present at the funeral. Mr. Lynslager was always a favourite with them, and I am grieved to think of the want of respect they have shown in not paying the last token of regard which it is possible for us to show each other. It is, however, pleasing to know that their presence would have added no more to the esteem in which his memory is held by all who knew him, than their absence has reduced it. I believe their non-attendance was due to the intervention of the Commandant.

---

[49]Frances was Lynslager's granddaughter. See p. 120 for an account of her subsequent life.

Daddy Jim was born at London, 1st May, 1810, and was consequently 54 years four months and fourteen days old; he has been about 37 years resident in Fernando Po and his death will be regretted by hundreds, for his lively manner, hospitable behaviour, generous and upright conduct are well known and have gained him a great list of friends. He was a particular favourite of the English Navy and throughout the Coast his name has for a long time been inseparable from that of the island in which he has so long and honourable lived. He came here a poor sailor boy and gained his living by making and mending sails, and making hats. He afterwards was put in charge of the government beach stores and by degrees became a merchant, British Consul, and at last Spanish Governor of the Island. In 1858 he was superseded by a Spaniard sent out by the Home Government to whom he gave every assistance and information for the proper conducting of the affairs of the Island. This act showed a fine trait in his character for he was always of a forgiving nature and would be the first to help an enemy.

He was not resentful and always secretly chafed at being on unfriendly terms with a man. His nature was warm and passionate and his passion sometimes led him into grave errors but those who knew him were mostly charitable enough to look over this his one great failing and generally took his angry words at their proper value, well knowing that they had no depth or meaning.

He first began life as a midshipman in the Dutch navy and he has often been heard to say that it was the greatest folly of his life to leave that service. After leaving it he went into the merchant service and was five years in Batavia, shortly afterwards coming to the Coast and staying at Fernando Po. He had been several times ship-wrecked in the course of his life. In Bimbia he was several hours on a bullock's back, liable at any moment to be devoured by sharks and he afterwards got his foot crushed between two vessels. After partly healing it was bitten by a mosquito which eventually made it necessary to have his leg cut off. I have often heard him say that this was his greatest mercy for had he been spared with two legs he would have murdered somebody at one time or another in his anger. In early and middle life he was active, energetic and prompt in action. In Fernando Po, when Governor, he made the people submit to his will. On one occasion a disturbance took place in the town. He took his sword with him and went to the place of contention; one of the peace breakers had the audacity to ask him who he was and his right to interfere and he at once drew his sword and opened the fellow's skull at a stroke. This courageous act so awed the others that they at once became quiet. As British Acting-Consul he blew down Old Town, up the Calabar River, and although this act gave great offence to some people it was fully approved of by the Government. During the time of his Spanish Governorship he never drew a penny from Spain--and although he has made repeated applications to the Government and Queen, he has never so much as received a reply. He had to maintain the duties and expenses of a Governorship with all its details in salaries &c. on what he could make out of import and export dues, the greater part of which he paid on goods imported by himself, while now the Government is spending some $365,000 on the Island with little better result.

During the first period of his residence in Fernando Po he lived with a black woman who bore him a son, whom he ever afterwards acknowledged as such, and educated well in England. This was his only child, who married one of the Miss Matthews--Alice. He died only a few years ago, leaving his wife and two children, William and Francis, the Spanish doctor attending him having given him a tremendous dose of tartar emetic--of course, he said not with the intention of killing him--which, from what I have been able to learn, it certainly did. The latter period of Mr. Lynslager's life has been the busiest, happiest, and most prosperous. An active and busy man, he has always been, but more especially in the last twenty years of his life, during which time he has had the duties of the Consulship, and afterwards that of Spanish Governor to attend to, with those of a merchant. For this latter capacity Mr. Lynslager was ill-fitted. He has had splendid opportunities of realizing a fortune, and no doubt has made several in his lifetime, which he has spent in hospitality, in the expenses of the Island, and in presents, and in liberality. He happened to attach little importance to the value of money, and this is, I believe, often the case with other people who make their money too easily. He cared nothing for business until very lately, when he found too late that it required economy and attention to business to enable him to pay off his debts. His delight was in affairs of the Navy, the Consulship, and of the Government, upon which he was never tired of conversing, and of referring to his experiences in such matters. It must have been a great effort for him to economize these last two or three years, after the years of sumptuous dinners, unbounded hospitality and generosity in his living which had so long been his habit. I have often heard him say--"I will die an honest man if I die a beggar." No doubt he has died an honest man, and he has not died a beggar, although what he is really worth is small compared with what one might expect. He has left by will everything that he possesses to Mrs. Lynslager but I am afraid there will be some trouble about the will as the Spaniards claim him as a Spanish subject, and according to the law of Spain no man has power over his property after death--it must go as directed by the law--but everyone who knew Daddy intimately must have heard him say that he was not a Spaniard, but an Englishman. He was born in England, and he annexed to his will only a few days before his death a statement to the effect that he was an Englishman, and wished his property to be administered according to British law. The Spaniards say that no one but a Spaniard could be Governor of Fernando Po, or sit in the Government Council, as he has done, since the Government left his hands. He married Mrs. Lynslager about twenty-two years ago, and they have always been very fond of each other, and have lived as happily together as most married people do. They have had no offspring. Mr. Lynslager no doubt has been much more extravagant than a white wife would probably have been, as few black people appear to understand the real value of money, but then in a country like this a black woman is much more useful than a white one, and can make a good deal of money by trading, which a white one could not do. By marrying a white woman Daddy might have been a richer man, but perhaps not a happier one, and if a man is happy and contented what more does he require? His death will be a great loss to the black people of this place upon whom he has looked as his children and over whose liberties he has always kept a vigilant guard. Since the Governorship left him he has been of great service to the people by the voice he had in the Council, where his experience was also of great utility to the existing Governor at the time. This house without him is not the same. During his sickness I have been miserable in it and now that he has for ever left it, and as it now is in mourning, with the faces of the pictures to the walls, the effect is most unpleasant.

23 September

Captain Grubbe has given an order to Cutagar--Commander of the *Vindictive*--to take charge of the Coal Depot until an Agent is appointed. Mammy got very little sleep in consequence of the singing last night and is so disgusted with the conduct and insincerity of the people that she has ordered that no singing take place to-night--very sensible of her, I think. How totally lost to respect must people be who come to offer consolation and sympathy to a widow and to show regret for the loss of her departed husband by getting drunk!

24 September

Mammy appears very weak, and no doubt she must be after her trials and anxiety. She has not yet said anything about her intentions with regard to the business. I hear Townsend is making himself very sure about getting the charge of the English coal depot.

26 September

The judge, Wilson, notary, Cutagar, and Aldama were present at the reading of the will to-day. The judge was apparently satisfied on finding that the will was according to English law, and after taking down Wilson's reply to that effect, with the exception of Cutagar and with the addition of myself, they went and read the will before Alice, asking her at the same time if she had any objection to offer. She replied that she had none, and it will, I suppose, only require the certificate of the persons present to that effect to settle the whole affair and give Mrs. Lynslager an indisputable right to everything. Had Alice said that she objected to the statement at the end of the will, by which Mr. Lynslager declared himself a British subject, and wished his will to be administered according to British law--on account of its having been signed by Mr. Lynslager only a few days before his death, and at a time when he was unable to comprehend or to be responsible for his actions, there would no doubt have been a tremendous palaver. I'm glad it has been done so quickly.

On Friday I told Mrs. Lynslager that I considered my engagement with the house was now finished and that I should expect a different arrangement if she intended to retain me. She said she would speak to Wilson about it and so after having a talk with him he informed me that she was ready to enter into a new engagement and he asked me what I had to propose. After a good deal of talk about the premature termination of my agreement being due to mere accident, about my better position, and prospects, and about the thoughts of other people in case I should leave the house, I made a proposal that I should remain for twelve months and should be put in entire charge of the business having my own servants, food, and £200, which proposal I asked him to take to Mrs. Lynslager. He afterwards told me that he had mentioned the matter to Mrs. Lynslager and that she perfectly agreed. In consequence I am now very busy writing circulars to the correspondents of the business, advising them of the death of Mr. Lynslager and of Mrs. Lynslager's intention to continue his affairs under my management. I have written to the Storekeeper General of the Navy, to John Lenthall, Chief of Bureau of Construction in New York, applying for the vacancies of coal agent and to the African S.S. Co. applying for the vacant agency of that company.

29 September

After the hard work of the few past days, I feel somewhat lazy to-day. Had a visit from Mr. Hewett of St. Paul de Loanda, who in case of obtaining the agency for the coal depot, promised to give me any hints I might think useful if it was his power to do so.

30 September

Busy taking stock. Had the Captain of H.M.S. *Snipe* making purchases. Had a good day's receipts of cash in consequence.

1 October

Still busy with the stock. Bessy and Joe at the small shop live like a cat and dog together, and the shop in consequence of their mutual fight for mastership, and their continual squabbling, it in a most filthy state and one of the two ought certainly to be removed.

3 October

I have got a subscription up towards a testimonial to be presented to Wilson on the occasion of his marriage. Only his oldest friends were admitted to the list consisting of the following:--

	$
Robert Kirkwood	25
Townsend	30
E. I. Smith	30
Dr. Mullins	20
Knight	25
Gordon	25

	155
John Holt	20
	175--£37 18s. 4d.

Having been appointed treasurer by the subscribers I have obtained a bill for £38 for Wilson on John Laughland which I have sent to him with a note asking him to purchase as good a silver tea service as he can for the money. The origin of this subscription list arose in a desire of mine to make Wilson a marriage present. I thought about a silver cup to himself and another to his wife, but as that was more than I could afford I thought of a subscription list by which the best part of his old friends might show their regard unitedly and with more economy to each than if they had made presents separately. Having hinted the matter to Kirkwood he at once agreed with my suggestion, and thought that his friends only required to know of it, when they would only be too happy to subscribe to a testimonial intended to be presented to one so much appreciated by them. He also thought with me that it would be better to confine the list within the names of those who have really subscribed, not one of those whom I invited having refused to do so.

17 October

Chin Cherry or rather Jane B-----y, the black girl who came out from England with me, has, like every other girl in the place (with very rare exceptions) gone the way of all flesh. She is now the mistress of S-----[50]and thinks so little of herself in consequence of the honour and patronage conferred by so distinguished a lover. I hear she has had an offer of marriage from a black in Lagos and is going by the next mail to that port in order to get married. I would not mind laying my old pen to anybody's old penholder that if S----comes out this month as reported, she does nothing of the sort. It is an awful pity that the black girls are so led astray. There is hardly more than one virtuous girl to be found in the place and in spite of their constant depravity, a child and more especially a mulatto child is scarcely ever born. The black men find it so easy to gratify their passions and have so little faith in the virtue of the girls that scarcely a marriage ever takes place and the children that ought to be born perish through the effects of medicine taken for the purpose, both of producing abortion and preventing conception; whereby they do themselves also great bodily injury and I have good reason to believe a good many die from this cause. They are a most deeply demoralized set and would sell themselves to the devil for fine clothes or would exchange the jewel without price for the paltry things of fashion and appetite.

Mammy has gone to the farm to-day. It is now four months since she has been there and I am again left in charge under circumstances similar to those of two years ago. She was going to leave the cook and another girl but, having told her that I wanted neither, she has happily left me in single blessedness with the boys. The house deprived of both its masters seems very lonely and it was only by means of indulging in the solace of a pipe, that I got rid of the uncomfortable feeling caused thereby. I saw poor Mammy crying as she was going away, no doubt she was thinking of how differently she departed when she last went to the farm. Poor old woman, I heartily pity her; her tears and moaning make me feel miserable.

26 October

Mammy came back to-day.

28 October

Mail arrived in the morning and had on board Mr. Saker, wife and family. In the forenoon I was surprised to hear of a prospect of a marriage on board the *Retriever*, John Showers and Bessy being unable to contain themselves any longer are going to be married or I should now say have been this day married along with two other couples by Mr. Saker. I wish they had waited for the arrival of the *Rattlesnake* as I should then

---

[50]This presumably refers to E.I. Smith.

have been able to take part in the ceremony but it is impossible longer to restrain their wishes.

29 October

Went to a dinner given by Mammy Showers with the help of Mrs. Lynslager and friends. There were a good many people present both white and black. The latter colour of course predominated. I enjoyed the seat of the right hand of the bride, the husband being opposite us at the other end of the table. Very little daintiness was shown by the ladies in their mode of eating; I could not carve enough for them and it was a very noisy dinner, a perfect succession of shouts. I proposed the united long life and happiness of the bride and bridegroom, which was followed by three cheers or rather three times three--by the company present and afterwards responded to by the bridegroom who made a speech which he must certainly have made up from an irrelevant mixture of the contents of some Scotch novel, the most striking part of it having reference to scientific gentlemen and bonnie lassies, of which no doubt the company was principally composed. After dinner, Mammy Showers got nicely quit of us by sending us up to Townsend's for a dance. I must confess to being a little merry when I left Showers but I became all right at Townsend's by dancing like a madman and drinking nothing but water--the girls did not much fancy my high spirits and so I had to get male partners. I left Townsend's a little after one (a.m.) and slept at the Consulate which I did not leave until Sunday evening. Mrs. Lynslager thinking something was the matter had sent all over the town on Sunday to seek me.

31 October

I placed the corner post of our new shop which is to be built in the garden facing the square.

Nobody at home appears to have anticipated the coming anniversary of my birthday. I have received no congratulations from England and as Africa is ignorant of the event no blame is attached to her.

Mr. John Holt--In lieu of all other congratulations I have this day the sincere and heartfelt pleasure to wish you many happy returns, hoping that the future may have in store for you a realization of your most sanguine dreams of happiness, and worldly prosperity. May each successive year add to your grace and your share of this world's comforts as well as to your age, and may you (in a good old age) find perfection in the world to come. Mr. Holt, I wish you joy on the completion of your 23rd year.

1 November

I have to-day learnt that Bessy was found a virgin pure. In Fernando Po this is a virtue almost unknown and she has of course gained a good name amongst the men and an awful amount of envy and ill-feeling among the women. She is a Bimbia girl and consequently the Fernando Po girls are taunted by the men with her being better than they are, at which they are very annoyed and are not at all careful of hiding their chagrin and vexation at it.

7 November

Wilson and Smith returned from Calabar yesterday and report the death of Paterson the purser of the *Retriever*, poor fellow. He came out with me in the *Cleopatra* as doctor, like my own case, his first African voyage. He had an attack of bilious fever here on the 28th October, and on the sailing of the vessel was carried down to the beach in a palanquin. He seemed to be improving, they tell me after he left this, until he reached Calabar when the fever attacked his head and affected his brain sufficiently to kill him. A good kind-hearted soul he was and I am sincerely sorry to lose a friend so much esteemed by all who knew him. Captain Davis was by the advice of the doctors left in Calabar and the *Retriever* went on under the charge of Captain Mullans, one of the Calabar supercargos.

A screw ship named the *St. Patrick* of Glasgow chartered by the Portuguese Government to carry convicts, cargo and passengers to their possessions on this Coast, put into this port having burst one of her boilers during her passage out and being consequently unable to steam. Strathern and Middleton, under the impression that she was one of Hamilton's ships, put off to her and Cotter, Hamilton's beach-store-man, also went with them. The ship had her "jack" flying for a pilot until the party arrived on board but five minutes afterwards she hauled it down thus signifying that the pilot was on board. And so it appears, for Mr. Cotter took charge of the vessel and steered direct for the reef upon which he at length placed her most beautifully at high water mark, a more stupid piece of business I never heard of. Had the Captain been left to himself he would certainly have steered a midway course which was all that was required to bring his ship safely into the harbour but by the officious meddling of busy fools a fine vessel and a great deal of property has been endangered. Fortunately the ship was got off the next high water with the assistance of H.M.S. *Wye* apparently none the worse. But the ship had a most narrow escape and it is a piece of good fortune that she was got off so easily, she might as easily have gone to pieces where she lay had not fortune been so favourable. Strathern and Cotter are very much to blame and it seems very strange that they who have been here some time should have shewn such great ignorance and stupidity. The Captain promises to do this best to punish them.

15 November

I went on board the *St. Patrick* with McCormack and had a look at the large black and lustrous eyes of several Portuguese lady passengers. They have certainly got splendid eyes and hair, but their faces cannot be compared with their English rivals.

19 November

To-day is the Queen of Spain's Saint-day. The Governor, his officers and soldiers attended mass this morning in full dress. In the evening we had a grand illumination: the quartel and Governor's house being tastefully decorated with palm branches and coloured lamps. In consequence of our recent loss, this house made no show (how different last year!). In the evening a ball was held at the Governor's, open to all respectable people, and at it I enjoyed myself very much although I did not dance. The white Portuguese ladies from the English ship which struck on the point the other day were there. Of itself this would be sufficient attraction to most white men who had been any length of time in Africa.

20 November

Two holidays together. This Sunday has an unnatural appearance. The Spanish officers had a dress ball this evening at the Government house. I, having been invited, went with Renilein and enjoyed myself of course, although without dancing a step. The white ladies were again present and a great many white men. The black girls who understand our dancing and who generally attend the balls at Townsend's were, most of them, there. I had hoped that no black girls would have been admitted but I suppose those who had the getting up of the affair, finding themselves short of partners, had no alternative but to send for them. I would not risk much on the chastity of any black girl in the town and these "ball-going" girls are notorious for their deviations from the path of virtue on ball-nights. It is a great pity that there are no distinctions in favour of virtuous society here. As it is--prostitution meets you everywhere with the smile and mien of virtue, dressed up to the eyes and indeed forming a sort of aristocracy by its fine appearance and connection with its white patron who, for his pains, is uncared for when his patronage is withdrawn. It is not the white man that a black woman likes; it is his money and the distinction of the connection.

21 November

I went this evening to another ball, at Townsend's. This was given at the expense of those who liked to take a part in its eating and drinking additionals; the others of the last two nights were of course free. I enjoyed myself very well and danced a good deal. A great many people were there and I was again surprised to see the white ladies. I fancied the fact of having to associate with such mixed company would have deterred them from coming. It was kept up to a very late hour on Thursday morning.

24 November

Chin Cherry came up this morning to tell Mrs. Lynslager that she and S[mith] were going to be married in the forenoon. I was rather surprised at this and at first felt much annoyed at the idea of his committing so foolish an act but after thinking over this piece of information I soon felt convinced that he was not so great an ass. I cannot well divine his object in going with her to the *Vindictive* and to have his likeness taken and then on his return proclaiming her Mrs. S[mith]. It is so well known that he has been for some time keeping the girl as his mistress and it seems strange that he should adopt such a foolish plan of trying to make people believe that she is his wife for the purpose of transferring her from her home to his. Anyhow the transfer has been made, an act much more easy of accomplishing than that of persuading people to believe her his lawful wife.

25 November

S[mith] gave a ball to-night at which were present the white ladies, the black dancing girls and a great many Portuguese, Spaniards and English. The house was very tastefully decorated with palm branches and the dancing was enjoyed although the room was not large enough for the dancers at times. Chin Cherry kept herself very quiet all the evening and did not look at all like "Mrs." S[mith]. The music came from the *Lee* (now in port) whose performers managed their duties very well. I went in pretty freely for the dancing as well as for the many good and enjoyable eatables. Company left at half-past twelve. I think it is almost time to put an end to the balls until Xmas, four in the course of a week is enough for the most dissipated.

Figure 6: John Holt, Fernando Po, 28 July 1868.

Source: See Figure 1.

19 December

Yesterday the Commodore came in and gave orders at once that the *Vindictive* should be ready to go away at 4 p.m. to-day.[51] He is going to tow her up to Jellah Coffee with the *Lee* as convoy.[52] To-day I went on board to see him and asked if I was to have the pleasure of receiving his orders respecting the coal depot on behalf of Mrs. Lynslager. He replied "You know I must give it to Wilson, he is Acting-Consul. We shall see what turns up." I could get no other reason out of him for thus acting although I told him that from the manifold services rendered to the Government by her late husband Mrs. Lynslager had been led to hope for a continuation of the favours enjoyed by him. Townsend has also applied for it. There is, however, still a chance for us if the appointment is not left to the Commodore. I await with anxiety the coming mail which no doubt will be decisive as I shall then hear from the Storekeeper General. The Commodore is a most eccentric being, the embodiment of perpetual motion, thought and energy. Wilson may have a claim to the agency but it is certainly an inferior one to that of Mrs. Lynslager whose husband has done so much for the navy in his lifetime. His claims no doubt are greater than mine personally but the interest that he will take in the affairs of the depot and his ability to conduct that will certainly not exceed mine.

1869

30 January

8.30 p.m. Left Santa Isabel in company with Lieutenant W. Wiseman and Mr. Robinson, and the Master of the H.M.S. *Danae* in the Consul's gig, with a crew of eight men, on a tour round the Island.[53] At 3.30 a.m. we passed Goat Island. At 7.30 a.m. breakfasted in a small cove beyond Bokoko and about 6 miles North of Cape Badgeley, proceeded at 9.30 a.m. (31st January), at 11 a.m. sounded 12 fathoms a third of a mile off a sandy bay about 2 miles North of Cape Badgeley, and at 11.35 a.m. passed Cape Badgeley. From here to Eureka we passed several beautiful cascades, the land being generally bold and lofty, and although the weather was fine, the breakers were too heavy to admit of our landing anywhere until we reached Eureka at 5.30 p.m. where we anchored and slept. At this place we purchased fish weighing two or three pounds each at the rate of a pipe for one, and a fowl we bought for four leaves of tobacco. We did not see any signs of a town or of palm trees all the day until we concluded that the place was inhabited.

---

[51]HMS *Vindictive* was built in 1813 as a seventy-four-gun "ship of the line." She was cut down in 1832 and served as a store and accommodation vessel. According to the *Diary* (p. 119), Holt purchased it for £20 in 1871 for breaking up. J. Cox, *Cox and the Ju Coast*, xvii, states that "she broke adrift from her moorings in 1881 and became a total wreck." The records at the National Maritime Museum at Greenwich suggest that the latter account is correct.

[52]HMS *Lee* was built in 1860 as a single-screw vessel of 570 tons and served until 1874. See Cox, *Cox and the Ju Coast*, 74; *All the World's Fighting Ships, 1860-1905*, 109.

[53]HMS *Danae* was a single-screw, wooden corvette built at Portsmouth in 1867. See the sources in the previous note.

At 8.58 a.m. 1st February, we left Eureka and at 11.10 a.m. rounded Cape Barrow. From Eureka to this point we saw an abundance of palm trees and on the side of the mountain a pretty large clearing. At Boho we arrived at 1.20 p.m., lunched, and left at 3.10 arriving at Biappa at 5.30 p.m. where we slept, breakfasted, and proceeded at 8 a.m. 2nd February. We touched at Boloko for half an hour to examine a couple of cannon lying on the beach, left there by the first Spanish or Portuguese Colonists, and arrived at Bundahbarli at 10.10 a.m. staying ten minutes to look at the place. We passed Leven Island at 11.10 a.m., Bahow at 12 a.m. and Bahkahki at 1.10 p.m. where we lunched. We started again at 2.10 p.m. passing Baobi, Basakato, Cape Vidal, Basualla, Cupapa, Richards' Wharf, Mrs. John's Wharf, Topi Wharf, we reached Lokhah Wharf at 5.55 p.m., landed and left again at 6. 8 p.m. Arrived at Horatio Island at 7 p.m.--dined and set out again at 8.20 p.m. passing Horatio Point at 8.30 p.m. The Cape was seen from Santa Isabel at 8.50 and we reached Santa Isabel at 11.35 p.m. At Boho the palm trees became more abundant and continued to Leven Island. From this point up to Topi Wharf is almost an unbroken forest of palm trees, and it struck me at the time that a great deal more might be made out of the palm oil trade on this side of the Island than is at present done. I cannot think that even a fifth of what the trees produce is at present collected. What a pity to see so great a waste of the Island's produce!

The trip occupied altogether 75 hours 5 minutes. After deducting stoppages of 37 hours, it appears that we took 38 working hours to go round the Island. The weather was beautifully fine, my companions very agreeable, and thus I made a very pleasant tour. Indeed, we were all healthy, in good spirits, with good appetites, and plenty of good food cooked by ourselves to allay them, and thoroughly enjoyed ourselves. Not an unlucky incident of any kind occurred to mar our joy or comfort, other than a dash or two of salt water, and our enjoyments were in all cases tempered with due moderation.

9 February

Julia Davis departed this life soon after daylight this morning, either of consumption or some other pulmonic disease. She has been more or less sick during the past four months, but not very seriously so until about a month ago. She was considered one of the prettiest girls in Santa Isabel and a better conducted one than most of them.

21 February

One Monday last I commenced a jetty at Coal Bay with two carpenters and ten Krooboys. On Thursday it was finished with the exception of two or three plank ends which required sawing off, and at noon on that day I began coaling the *Terrier* by means of the jetty with hand and wheel barrows. It is amusing to see how the Krooboys stagger along and run off the planks with the latter, but at all events they did more with them than they would have done with bags. On Saturday at noon the *Terrier* was completed, and I estimate that they put on board in the two days they were working at her about sixty tons. This is not bad for Krooboys. Altogether, I consider what with the *Terrier*, jetty, and other work got through, we have done a good week's work. The jetty belongs to the African Steamship Co., is built of the beams and planks of the *William Mooney* and is about sixty feet long and six broad.

Townsend has had the *Edmund* ashore for repairs to forefoot and sternpost, which had become wormed. I expect, however, he has done more harm than good, as he says she has scrubbed some copper off her keel during the time he has had her ashore.

Mr. Wiseman, Lieutenant of the *Danae* who accompanied me on my trip round the Island, has put up a splendid iron shed, or rather house, in Coal Bay, for storing the coal of the British Government. It is a very strong substantial building entirely of iron, and rests on blocks of granite (under each iron pillar) weighing two tons each. This house was put up by Mr. Wiseman, Mr. Barker, engineer and a working party from the *Danae*. The *Danae* was here during the whole of this time and did the commerce of the town considerable benefit. Mr. Wiseman has also put up Beecroft's monument under the large tree on Point William which, to the disgrace of the contributors, had been laying near the grave since 1859 or '60.[54] A part of the inscription has been worn out by having been used as a sharpening stone, and the whole of the stone for the railing has been carried away for the same purpose by the Spaniards and blacks of the town. It is almost certain that if Captain Graham of the *Danae* who knew Beecroft had not thought of erecting this monument, it would have remained on that Point until every bit of it had been used up for the before-named purpose. Beecroft was an Englishman, a Governor of this Island, and British Consul. He explored the Niger and Old Calabar Rivers and during his lifetime did a good deal towards developing the trade of the Bights. He was very much liked by the blacks as their Governor, and by the British as their Consul, and died respected by both, a poor man, after a long residence in Fernando Po, and at a time when money was made without trouble. In his time the first "palm oil ship" opened trade in Bonny, which, up to then, had exported nothing but slaves. Beecroft had the job of concluding treaties with every slave export port in the Bights. People now-a-days refer to these times as the "golden days of old" or the "good old times." Supercargoes could then make their six thousand pounds a year in commission and make yearly fortunes for the Tobins and Horsfalls of that day, and coopers and doctors, after a few years on the coast, could become African Merchants themselves.

6 April

My schooner the *Maria* arrived in charge of my brother Jonathan. She is forty-six days from Liverpool, eight of which have been spent on the Kroo Coast procuring boys, canoes &c. She brings a full cargo from Liverpool, and from the Kroo coast twenty-three Kroomen and three canoes. She has cost me a large sum, £1,200 or thereabouts, exclusive of provisions and wages of crew out to the Coast, and this, and the long delay in sending her out, has been the subject of a little unpleasantness between myself and Irvine & Woodward [John Holt's agents in Liverpool]. She has cost a great deal too much, there is no doubt, and had my brother's advice been taken she would have been

[54]John Beecroft (b. 1790) spent much time at sea before joining the naval settlement at Fernando Po in 1829. After this dispersed he remained and was made Governor by the Spanish in 1843. Six years later he was appointed British Consul, a post he held until his death in 1854. See A.C. Burns, *History of Nigeria* (London, 1942), 102. He was the father of George Beecroft referred to by John Holt on p. 54.

a much cheaper vessel to me.[55] Irvine & Woodward have in my opinion been the victims of Lloyd's Surveyor and the shipbuilders, ship store dealers &c. If ever I have to buy another vessel I shall understand better how to go about it. Great credit is due to my brother Jonathan for his attention to my interests in purchasing, refitting, and bringing her out. He sought and found her, bought her, and was with her in Liverpool away from his friends superintending the alterations being made in her there. He had in consequence little of enjoyment at home. But for his representations there is little doubt she would have cost me a good deal more. She is a yacht and was bought by Jonathan at Cowes, is well fitted, built of oak, sixteen years old, and of sixty-four or sixty-five registered tons. She sails very well and is considered a good serviceable craft by those able to judge. Mr. Coakeley and Mr. Fowler were engaged by Irvine & Woodward as clerks to me, and took a passage out by the *Maria*. The former arrived out safe but the latter unfortunately either fell or walked overboard in the Channel a day or two after she left Liverpool. It was supposed that he was asleep when he walked or fell overboard.[56] This is a slight misfortune for me perhaps, but how much more so for himself and his family, poor fellow. I hope the *Maria* may after all prove a good investment. I intend to open a factory at Bimbia, Bata, and Gaboon, and I have every hope with Jonathan's assistance, to succeed. These factories will be under his especial control and he will receive a commission of five per cent. on the nett proceeds of all the produce he gives me in return for the goods I hand over to his charge. Johnny Thompson has come out with him.

22 May

The *San Francisco de Vorja* has brought from Cuba two hundred and fifty political exiles sent hither by order of Governor General Dulce.[57] They have had a sixty-five days' passage, the engines having broken down on the way, thus causing some delay in Puerto Rico. Twenty or thirty of these exiles are said to be very well off, being composed of merchants, planters, and others. There is one banker named Castillo, said to be very rich. However, as they would not allow him to bring any of his riches with him, they are of little worth to him here. The steward of the steamer that brought them must have made a good thing out of them if what they say is true, as the prices charged for a bit of fowl, ham, pig, or duck were said to be enormous. As a sample, $1 was paid for a bottle of beer and sometimes they had to buy pure water. They appear to have been ill-treated in order to extort money from them. In spite of the restrictions imposed upon them in Havana it is stated that altogether they had on leaving about £20,000 with them. More than half of them are able to provide themselves with food and lodgings. The remainder are on the Government's hands and are allowed one to one and a half pounds of rice and a few ounces of pork or dried beef per day, each. They have been housed in

---

[55]An account of *Maria's* voyage from Liverpool to Fernando Po is provided on pages 126-139.

[56]For a more detailed account of the loss of Mr. Fowler see p. 127.

[57]At this time Cuba was still a Spanish Colony and was embroiled in a ten-year war to secure its independence. *Encyclopaedia Britannica* (11th ed.), VII, 602-605.

the market house, behind the Government stone house, and miserable quarters they must be. Poor devils, I soon expect to hear of the liberty of some of them, for in such a place, and on such food in Fernando Po, even negroes from the West Indies would die. Those who can afford it have taken lodgings all over the town and have caused such a stir in Fernando Po as has not been seen before. Townsend has got thirteen boarding and lodging at his house. Of course, the money they are spending is reviving our late miserable trade, for they must have food and things to cook it with. Poor fellows, how miserable they looked running about in search of lodgings and something to eat during the first day or two. I had a score of them feeding on biscuit, pork, jams, preserved meats &c. just after they had got ashore, and they appeared ravenously hungry. I have two staying in a spare room until they can get other lodgings. One old man, in return for the supper I gave them presented me with his thanks and a handful of splendid cigars such as never passed my lips before. Townsend's house was full of people during the first night or two. They slept on the tables, floor, and even under the house. The town, a few days ago poor and wretched, has suddenly come in possession of a fortune. The women are making money by selling whatever fruit or vegetables they have got, washing clothes, and by other less praiseworthy means. Those who are fortunate to have houses or rooms to let are letting them easily, and at good prices. The Cubans, however, do not spend a great deal in living. A very little suffices them and they appear anxious to take care of whatever money they have got in order to enable them to reach England if they can escape. They live chiefly on vegetables and bread. The thirteen in Townsend's hotel, the richest of the lot, grumble at $2 a day each for board and lodgings. In order to prevent a rise in prices, the Governor in a proclamation referring to the arrival of the Cubans has fixed the prices of the articles of food usually in demand at the same rates as heretofore, and anyone demanding more than the accustomed prices is threatened with severe punishment. Any infringement of the articles of this proclamation will not be decided as usual by the Judge, whose office appears to be dispensed with, but will be summarily disposed of by the Governor, the place being declared under martial law. Poor Cubans! Theirs is a hard fate thus to be taken at a moment's notice, some even out of their beds, sent from their families, homes, and country, to such a place as this. Three fourths of them are married men! Oh! What misery! Poor humanity! And is misery ever to be man's curse on this fair earth, and ever to emanate from himself? There is nothing on this side of death but sin and misery, death is the climax, and yet people say that there is a hell hereafter, that the cup of human wretchedness is not full this side the grave, that death is not in all cases the exit to a happier state. Horrid then must be the destiny of unhappy man. But I am drifting away from my subject. Poor Cubans, I say again. I feel sorry for you, and hatred for the fate and means that have driven you to this unfriendly climate, away from all that is dear to you, perhaps to die thinking of the loved ones you have left behind, they, too, thinking of you and of your sufferings, and yearning in vain for your return. The lot both of yourselves, your friends, your country, is nothing but misery!

24 May

Governor Souza is carrying matters with a high hand. He has ordered me and other importers to present ourselves with our invoices at the Government House, on the arrival of the mail steamer to-morrow. I believe he is afraid of a famine and may possibly give peremptory orders as to the disposal of our provisions.

The Governor's orders and restrictions are giving us no end of trouble. Our boats and canoes have to be numbered, and we cannot send them out of the Bay, or go on board the steamer on business without an order, and this cannot always be obtained, so great is his fear that any of the Cubans should escape. A boat is constantly at the gangway of the steamer from the time of her arrival to her departure, and the Sergeant is charge of her inspects all the permits to go on board, without which no one is allowed to pass. But in spite of all his restrictions, humbug, and vigilance, how easy it would be to take a heap of them away! I could do it well enough with my schooner, but who would repay me for having to abandon my property here, and my future prospects of gain in the place? Nothing that the Cubans have offered, or are likely to offer me, would be a repayment of the sacrifice I should have to make.

20 June

Seventeen Cubans, all who were in Townsend's house, escaped to-day in his cutter. He left yesterday, clearing out for the Cameroons, took the cutter to Horatio Island and anchored her inside. This morning early he came up with his gig and a canoe, and taking them overland to Alburkah Bay, embarked them in his boats, and, after a few hours' pull, in his cutter. He at once got up anchor and set sail for Calabar. The Governor is in a dreadful way about it. He does not know where they have gone. Somebody reported their having gone up the mountain to Basili, and he sent up people to se if it were true. The best of the joke is that one who was staying in his house (Richelieu) escaped. (This man had offered me £400 to get two of them away). Barrenguy, who was staying with Frank Wilson, got an inkling of the intended escape and being on the alert joined the party. They could not but admit him, it was a case of "I go with you or you don't go."

29 June

The *Biafra* arrived and brought us news of the safe arrival of Townsend and the runaway Cubans.[58] Townsend has made between £500 and £600 by the job, but I question if he has not sacrificed more than this by not keeping them at his hotel and selling at his store. He will be unable to come back here for some time, if at all. The Spaniards have taken possession of all the Cuban effects found in his house, and have deposited them in the Governor's house. Townsend's clerk, Hill, and servants have been rigorously examined and the authorities talk of placing an embargo on his property here. The runaways have arranged with Captain Croft of the *Biafra* that on leaving this place to-night he is to proceed to Old Calabar River, up to Parrott Island, where they will await him. They are to pay the usual first class passage to Liverpool and a considerable bonus to the Captain (£1,000).

---

[58]SS *Biafra* (1487 grt) was built by Laird in 1868 for the African Steam Ship Company and sold in 1889.

Figure 7: John Holt (1841-1915), Founder and First Chairman of John Holt and Company (Liverpool) Limited.

Source: See Figure 1.

4 July

The gunboat *Concordia* returned from the Rivers on a fruitless search after the Cubans. She met the *Biafra* in Bonny and knew that they were on board her, but durst not do anything. The Cubans were in a great funk when they saw her.

12 July

It was arranged between Trello, Captain Mercer, of the S.S. *Macgregor Laird*[59] and myself that he should, on leaving to-night, steam round to Cape Horatio and come slow inshore so as to be off Trello's farm at 8 o'clock. Signals were arranged. Trello was to take sixteen Cubans to his farm and for some £30 each--embark them on board the *Macgregor Laird*. The party left as soon as it was dark, with Trello and his Krooboys as guide, but Trello had either miscalculated the time necessary to traverse the distance, or he and his boys took the wrong road, as they did not arrive at his farm until midnight, wet, muddy, tired and miserable. The steamer, of course, had passed and Trello came in to tell me of the accident before sunrise. He had left them in the farm, and as it was known that he was in the town the day before, he thought he would not be suspected of any complicity, if seen there early the next morning. I told him that he should have taken the men somewhere at all hazards, or have brought them back with him to the town. They were soon missed, searched for, and found. They had remained in the house; consequently as scouts were sent on both sides of the town there was very little difficulty in finding them, and on learning where they were, the Governor despatched a boat in charge of his nephew, which soon returned bringing in most of them. One or two ran away into the bush, only to give themselves the trouble of walking to the town, instead of coming in the boat. They were all placed in gaol. Trello was arrested in the quartel. Lauriano, John Phillip and others were also put in gaol, and prevented from communicating with any outsiders. Mrs. Lauriano was threatened with a similar deprivation of her liberties if she did not keep away.

15 July

Trello and the rest of the prisoners are liberated, nothing having been proved against them. I believe Phillip and Lauriano were imprisoned more to shield Trello then for any intention they had to assist anyone to escape, though it is said that Lauriano and Gazulla were maturing a plan of their own. It is certain, however, that they had nothing to do with the intended escape of the sixteen, for which the former has been imprisoned. Trello was a great friend of the officials, and although the whole plan of escape became known, the friendship they had for him, combined with the money given as bribes by the Cubans, effected his release and left him unmolested afterwards. When examined, the questions put by that scoundrel of a custom-house clerk Samson (who had been appointed by Souza as Judge pro tem., the notary having ben displaced) were such as could not implicate or compromise the accused. Questions to the point were not asked him, of

---

[59]SS *Macgregor Laird* (969 grt) was built by Randolph, Elder and Company in 1862 for the African Steam Ship Company and was lost in 1871. For full details see pp. 121-123.

course intentionally. The gold of the Cubans had smoothed the way, even to the report made by the Governor's nephew Hilario Pina. The Cubans, when examined, stated that they had gone out for a walk, but having missed their way, they found themselves in Trello's farm. Trello's Krooboys were not examined as they might have upset the evidence. I believe any or almost every Spanish official would have helped the Cubans away if they could have done it without being caught, supposing them to have been well paid for their trouble, and would as soon have informed against them and have them sent back to prison if they could have made anything extra out of the double transaction.

16 July

The *San Antonio* with Governor Maymo arrived.[60] This Governor is to supersede Souza under the new regulations, placing the Colony under the Naval Department, instead of the Military.

18 July

The Government was this day formally handed over from Souza to Maymo, and the former has gone to a room in the Stone house (where he is nobody and nothing) until the arrival of the first steamer to relieve the place of a great old fool, and tyrant, whose departure with that of all his set will be hailed with pleasure by all who remain behind him. He carries with him the "groans" of the whole colony.

22 August

Governor Maymo died this morning at 10.30 o'clock. He made a very promising commencement as the first of our Naval Governors. His loss is much regretted by most people and all those who have the welfare of the Colony at heart. He shipped by the *San Antonio* at the beginning of August as many Cubans as she could carry (180) to Teneriffe, and the remainder he sent by the *Pinta* (20th August). This latter ship has brought out a number of Spanish men, women and children as colonists, and has taken the greater portion of them back again. By far the more sensible and humane course, I should say. Who but a lot of idiots would ever think of sending white men, women, and children to such a place as this? It is a hard enough fight for life with men and women in such a climate as this. But what are to become of children? They must either die or live to be apologies for men or women. They cannot have the strength and stamina necessary to enable them to become of any use, or to live to any age without frequently being sent for a spell to Europe--and how can poor people afford this, or to give themselves the necessary change? Moreover, at what kind of work are they to earn a livelihood? Not at outdoor work. That would soon kill most of them--and indoors there is no employment to be found except for a very limited number. Here a white man has a constant struggle for existence, and it would be a blessing if there was no necessity for the presence of one on the whole coast. Is it not cruel then, to expose women and

---

[60]*San Antonio*, a 497-ton barque, was built at Sunderland in 1867 for W. Nicol of Liverpool. See *Lloyds Register of Shipping*, 1872.

children to the attack of an enemy against which all a man's energy of nature, and strength of frame and necessary to enable him to keep his footing? Thirteen of the Cubans assisted by August Svenson made their escape in the *Congo* on the 2nd.[61] Governor Maymo did not suspect their intention to leave, as they knew that the *San Antonio* was ordered to take them to Teneriffe.[62] They preferred to be free, however, and as, since his arrival, the guard boats have been done away with, there was no difficulty in embarking them on the *Congo*'s boats. Her Captain was William Croft. Struthers was the first to send anyone away. He got three Cubans away in his boat to Bimbia a few days after their arrival. One of them is said to be a very good, generous man, who has done a great deal of good to his native town in Cuba. His name is Balmaseda. He has made a great many proffers of friendship and assistance to Struthers and, if what is said of his doing in Cuba be true, he is the sort of man not to forget a kind act nor forget to recompense it should it hereafter be in his power to do so. The three were recommended to his kind attention by Bruce Hamilton & Co. of Teneriffe. The total number escaped is thirty-three and since their departure I am informed that the whole of their property in Cuba has been confiscated, in consequence of their escape. The voyage of the *Pinta* was a very long one. She touched at Porto Rico on her way, and as she was put in quarantine and sent on to Mabo on her arrival at Cadiz, by the time the exiles are landed and free, one year will have elapsed since their departure from Fernando Po. On board the *San Antonio* there was great mortality, thirty-seven out of one hundred and eighty having died before being landed. During the three months they were in Fernando Po only eight died. But perhaps the high rate of mortality on board may have been in consequence of their stay here. Diego Rivers, one of the two who stayed with me for a short time, is one of the dead. Poor fellow, he was a kind-hearted, retiring, modest soul, although rather troublesome with his plans for escaping. Naturally so too, I should say, when his family was thousands of miles away, and he had nothing else to think about hardly but these two subjects. I have not heard of how those fared who went by the *Pinta*. In the *San Antonio* the Cubans complained of great cruelty. The Spaniards showed little sympathy for them, or their afflictions, making themselves merry at their troubles, and it is said the doctor of the ship and doctor C------ of Fernando Po would sing and play the flute on the announcement of another death. Surely any man with a spark of humanity would not thus have outraged the best feelings of his race. A just and kind-hearted man would have naturally pitied their distress, and have done all in his power to alleviate it, and to soothe their sorrows and misery. How foolish besides, for one man to laugh at and enjoy the miseries of his brother men, when he knows not, nor can tell how soon he may be placed in the same position and have his present circumstances reversed. The Cubans we had here appeared to me too slothful, inactive and effeminate ever to gain the independence of their country. If they were a fair specimen of the Cuban race I have great doubts as to the success of their present efforts

---

[61]SS *Congo* (1283 grt) was built by John Elder for the British and African Steam Navigation Company in 1869 and was sold in 1882.

[62]Hamilton and Company had been established in 1799. By the 1860s it was operating a large banking business, as well as operating as shipping, forwarding and bunkering agents and wine merchants in Tenerife and Maderia. See A. Samler Brown, *Maderia, Canary Islands and Azores* (London, 1905), 30.

on behalf of their national independence. They might have taken this Island from the Spaniards had they pluckily made the attempt after the departure of the Borja--a guard of two soldiers placed in front of the quartel, and altogether there was not more than one hundred Spaniards to one hundred and fifty or two hundred and fifty Cubans. If they had had any organization they might have taken the gunboat and quartel simultaneously any given night. But there was no organization amongst them, and so little prudence did they show that it was unsafe to let more than one or two know of any proposed plan of escape, lest it should be revealed to everybody. I have been amused to hear them relate such and such plans, knowing that if they talked about it in such a loose way they must become known to the governor before they could be carried out. They became so greatly excited at the prospect of escaping that they must have revealed it to some especial friend or have burst in the effort. This friend would relate it to another, in confidence of course, and he to another until gradually the matter became quite public. This indiscretion on their part may have been the cause of Lauriano's imprisonment by Governor Souza.

25 August

The Consul wants me to pay half the cost of the roof of the Consulate which I put on for Frank Wilson. The Government won't pay more than half, and he thinks I have been so well paid during his absence for acting for him that I can well afford to pay this. It amounts to this--the roof will last for three years. The Government pays half, therefore as I have been acting six months and Wilson nine months, I ought to pay 1/12th, Wilson 1/8th, and the Consul 7/24ths for his 21 months. To save myself any bother with him I shall let Trello apply for payment of the bamboos as I bought them from him, and I shall thus only lose the rafters and the time my men were occupied in putting on the roof. Livingstone is a difficult fellow in money matters.[63] For instance, he thinks that I ought not to have charged anything for the boys' time in putting on the roof, seeing that I had been drawing regularly on the government for the expenses of a boat's crew of four Kroomen. I am supposed to be getting half of his salary whilst acting for him, but am put off by the Government with all sorts of excuses, such as Consul's annual absence of two months not counting, &c., &c., and receive with boat's crew allowance of £47 10s. 0d., the sum total of about £170. Of the office expenses for clerk, stationery &c., neither Wilson nor I got a penny. We had to do all the writing ourselves, and find candles, ink &c., and show hospitalities to visitors out of our own pockets. The Consul has been asking Struthers to do his work for him during his absence as he and I have had a few rough words on this matter, and I told him that I should not again have the honour of representing Her Majesty in his absence. Struthers will not have anything to do with his Post Office work as he is going into the Boobie Trade, so he is obliged to get Harry Gardner to do it for him. He has told Harry that he will pay him half the salary that may become due as Post Master during his absence. This is £3 per month for say three months in the year. Harry won't take his money, but has offered to do the work. No one will be acting as his representative in his Consular capacity during his absence.

---

[63]Livingstone was a brother of the famous Dr. David Livingstone. A brief account of the Livingstone family is found in H.G. Adams, *The Life and Adventure of Dr. Livingstone* (London, n.d.).

26 August

The Steamer *Quanza* (Portuguese mail) which came in here three months ago with a broken shaft, having got a new shaft out from England, sailed to-day for Lisbon. Godoy and Barnecho are passengers on her. There are very few Spanish officials now living ashore.

30 August

I went with Jonathan in the *Maria* for a trip to Bimbia. Stone has been doing but little there, and does not appear to be much liked by the natives. He has got the factory in good comfortable order but the landing to it is not good, and its position is not one of the healthiest, although chosen by Stone himself.

7 September

The *Janette* and *Maria* sailed together to-day. The *Maria* has hitherto proved herself the fastest vessel of any she has met with here, and I am of opinion that she has no equal on the Coast.

21 September

To my surprise Mr. Irvine came out in the *Biafra* to-day.[64] Mr. Henry, on behalf of William Cooper & Co., has also come. It is high time all the merchants came out to look after their affairs on the Coast, which are at present in a bad state. One or two Houses, supposed to be jealous of the rest, are paying very high prices. The losses of all concerned in the palm oil trade have been large this year, particularly in Bonny. Johnny Thompson is busy building a small surf boat. He is making it strong enough, but it is sadly out of shape.

2 October

The *Pinta* sailed with the remainder of the Cuban "deportados." She also takes back the majority of the colonists she brought out with her. Vergarra (a Spanish officer) also goes in her, a prisoner. This Vergarra is a good deal short in his accounts it is said, and fearing the consequences he ran away in a boat to Cameroons, where he arrived in a state of insanity. He attempted suicide, or something very like it. A Spanish officer, sent for the purpose, brought him back in the last mail steamer. He kept a shop opposite me for some time, and when the Cubans were here, did a large trade, but hardly a profitable one I think, as he bought up nearly all the trash Struthers had in his store, and used to sell things that he bought from me, for less than he paid me for them. He used to sell

---

[64]James Irvine was born in Langholm, Dumfriesshire, in 1835. He first sailed to West Africa in 1858 and six years later set up partnership with Woodward. He also established James Irvine and Company, which acted as "general brokers." He died in Birkenhead at the age of ninety-one in 1926. See Wharton, unpublished mss., 173.

the goods &c. which the Governor's nephew bought over on the mainland, and did a good deal in gambling and drinking. Poor fellow, I expect he will be the one to suffer, although perhaps he was not the only rascal.

20 October

I.N. Williams, and Victoria Macaulay, with a little girl, were drowned by the filling with water of their canoe after a strong tornado. The Krooboys, canoe, and Drucilla Macaulay were saved.

31 October

The *Minerva*, with Bruce Walker, has been eight days off the harbour before she could succeed in getting in. This has been on account of the light winds, and unfavourable and changeable currents.

15 November

The *Calabar* arrived.[65] She has been ashore in the Sherbro. On trying to get her off a hawser parted and broke Captain Hamilton's leg. He came down with her, nevertheless.

8 December

The Spaniards have made a very nice amateur theatre in the market place. They manage their dresses and acting very well. A transformation scene was not bad for such a place as this. A Spaniard named Powell has done the painting &c. and is the life of the whole thing.

1870

5 January

The *Macgregor Laird* (Captain Bremner) took away to Cameroons half a dozen Spaniards who were on board trading at the time of her departure. The authorities are making a great hubbub about it, and are sending over the gunboat to bring back the "kidnapped," some of them being petty officers belonging to her. They have promulgated a list of rules in consequence of this affair, which are to be strictly enforced and I don't know how many fines a Captain is not liable to if he does not obey them. Like all their previous orders, it is looked at, and observed, for a time, but it will soon be forgotten by themselves, and become obsolete until another similar affair again stirs them up to repeat it, with the same result.

---

[65]SS *Calabar* (1122 grt) was built by Randolph, Elder in 1864 for the African Steam Ship Company and was sold in 1873.

Figure 8: John Holt and His Family, c. 1892.

Source: See Figure 1.

8 January

Captain John Thomas died in the Spanish hospital. Frank Wilson was very kind and attentive to him during his latter hours.

I have done a very profitable business in Fernando Po. Last year, in 1868, I cleared close upon £800. This year--£2,000, although I have had a loss of about £300 on a cargo of wood per *Rothiernay* and some bad debts. I have made nothing on the South Coast trade, but I am not surprised as I did not expect to.

4 February

Bishop Crowther, on the invitation of a number of the people here, headed by Struthers, came out to see about establishing a school and missionary of the Church of England, for which most of £100 has been subscribed, and more promised.[66] It appears, however, that Prince and others have written for a Primitive Methodist missionary, and that two of them, with their wives, are now on their way out to commence work. The Bishop was

[66]Ajai, a Yoruba boy, was emancipated in 1822, ordained in 1843 and consecrated "Bishop of the West African countries beyond British jurisdiction" in 1864. See C. Fyfe, *A History of Sierra Leone* (Oxford, 1962).

surprised, but rightly concluded that there was not room enough for two different missions, and although he regretted that the Primitive Methodist missionaries had been sent for by some dozen people or so, without consulting the wishes of the Protestant population of the town, he decided upon leaving an open field to the newcomers, and the subscriptions will be returned.

21 February

News reached us of a fearful fire in Gaboon, by which the whole of the homes, stores, and property belonging to Kirkwood Taylor, Laughland & Co. and Dollner, Potter & Co. (of New York) have been destroyed. There must have been a tremendous fire, as two hundred barrels of rum, eighty cases of kerosene, four to five tons of gunpowder, and four hundred tons of barwood formed a part of it. They are all uninsured. Poor Kirkwood has lost nearly all he is worth. The gunpowder must have been very bad, as a number of kegs were found strewn about after the explosion with only one or both ends blown out.

28 February

De Cardi is over here from the Opobo, a river lately opened on account of Ja Ja, the Bonny rebel Chief at present at war with the Bonny men, having established himself near its mouth.[67] De Cardi, I should imagine, is doing a splendid trade. I have sold him my gig and a canoe. Lauriano has sold him his boat for £160 and a lot of old cannon (left with Daddy Jim when the British Government gave up possession of Fernando Po) for £100.

3 March

The Primitive Methodist missionaries arrived with their wives. Their names are Burnett and Roe. I have let Townsend's house to them, at his request, for £50 the year.

11 March

Frank Wilson, who has been staying a couple of months or so with me, leaves to-day for the South Coast where he is expecting to obtain employment.

14 March

Poor Charley Brown (or Brunn) a wrecked Norwegian sailor, whom I have had in my house close upon a year, died on board the *Maria* (of Pleurisy it is supposed) at Gaboon. He was a good young fellow, and I am very, very sorry to have lost him. He was quite well when he left me to go in the *Maria*, but Jonathan says he became unwell the same night the *Maria* sailed, and kept sick until he got to Gaboon, where he died. The balance

---

[67]For a brief account of Ja Ja's career see Cotterell, "Reminiscences of one connected with the West African Trade from 1863 to 1910," in Davies, *Trading in West Africa*, 13-92, esp. 58-60, 69, and fn. 35.

due to him was paid by Jonathan to the Consul; it was very trifling. I paid him the balance of his wages just before he joined the *Maria*. He used to work for Sparhawk, and during that time contracted a very bad ulcer, probably brought on for want of nourishing food. I kept him some months until I got his ulcer reduced so that he was able to work for me, when I put him upon pay at £3 per month.

28 March

The Consul and I went to dine with Commodore Dowell, of H.M.S. *Rattlesnake*. Conversation chiefly on the Bonny war. Commodore and Consul take the part of Bonny. I suggested the possibility of sending my schooner over to the Opobo. He thought I should be very careful, as if the Bonny men took it, I could get no redress from our government, and that if force were used on board the schooner to repel the Bonny men, it would be an act of piracy. I disagreed with him, and, moreover, supposing it was an act of piracy, it would be one punishable by the Bonnymen themselves, and not by the laws of my own country.

29 March

The Commodore has this day appointed me to the charge of the Government Coal Depot at £80 per annum. Townsend and Jenny go by the *Biafra* to-day, Townsend having been very sickly of late. I did not go to see him, and he did not come ashore. I should have gone but for Croft (with whom I am not on the best of terms) being the Captain.

A man named Thompson came out in the *Biafra* from Sierra Leone and found letters addressed to him here acquainting him of the death of his mother. He was going to the Congo to explore on private account, but as he will come into possession of a considerable fortune he returned by *Biafra* to look after his affairs. He lived with me during the few days the *Biafra* was absent at Calabar.

4 April

Received news of poor Kirkwood's death. He had obtained a little credit, and with the goods on their way out at the time of the fire he was continuing his business up at the U.S. Consul's house. He used every effort to save his property from the fire, but without avail. He lost everything, even to his and his wife's clothes, and was near losing his life by staying too long in the house, as a rafter fell and closed the door when he was inside trying to recover some books. He threw down his books and burst open the door. When the factory blew up he was struck on the head by a keg of powder but was unhurt. Some suppose that his death is to be attributed to the effect of his losses by this accident. Others say that it was not attributable to this cause. He was taken sick of fever and stoppage of the urine afterwards came on, which caused his death. He did not think he was going to die, and made no will. His sickness was a short one. He was a fine good-hearted fellow. He fell out with his employers at home (Taylor, Laughland & Co.) and they lost in him a good and faithful servant and they must have regretted their quarrel with him, as he alone, who commenced their Congo trade, knew how to manage it, and would have probably saved them the very heavy losses in that business which appear inevitable through the trust system of trading with the Portuguese. I almost expect they will retire at once from the trade, in which they have at present sunk, it is said £60,000. The French took possession of the whole of Kirkwood's claims. His brother in Glasgow has consequently had to empower the Rev. Mr. Walker, Wookey and Latta to wind it up, and he intends to assist his brother's wife in a small trade. This measure has, however, occupied a good deal of time, during which the goods have been spoiling when they might have been traded to advantage.

15 April

On the 9th inst. Struthers and I started for Basili and the peak [Fernando Po Mountain]. We had not positively resolved upon going above Basili, but on our arrival there, finding that Gazulla and Powell had left that day, we resolved upon following them the next morning. The Governor Ocana and Captain Vial, with Castillo and others, were up at Basili, and bade us success when we left on the morning of the 10th. Martin and Balboa made up their minds to accompany us, but after a two hours' march on coming to a deep ravine, they funked it, and we had to give them a guide to show them the way back. On crossing the brook flowing at the bottom of the ravine we halted for breakfast, and afterwards had to wait some time for the arrival of our Krooboys with the sail for our tent, which was a great deal too heavy and bulky, and was consequently much more unwieldy and heavier than our other baggage. They had moreover missed the path and took some time to find it. We had ten or twelve Krooboys with us. Our path was through thin bush above which spread the forest trees, and in places there was no path at all. We tracked the two ahead of us by means of the marks they had purposely left on the trees, as otherwise they might themselves have got lost in the bush on their way back. It was irksome work, however, following them, as they several times appeared to have changed their minds and after going along a path, or cutting one of their own for a certain distance, they had changed their minds and returned to cut in another direction. This often puzzled us on our way up. They had a compass with them, and were trying to get up the shortest way. So long as a path went in the required direction they followed it, but directly it diverged, they cut straight for the peak, and they had hard work of it, for the bush grew thicker as we went upwards on our first day's march, and we were astonished at the quantity of work they had done and the difficulties they must have had to contend with. We did not reach the site of their first night's encampment until the morning of our second day's march, and we did not reach their second night's encampment until the morning of the third day's march, when we found them resting from their arduous work, and awaiting supplies of food, for which they had despatched most of their Krooboys. On hearing us they began to cheer, we answered, and soon were face to face. They were very glad to see us, as we had supplies, not large, but large enough to keep us well stacked until the arrival of their boys. After breakfast (or lunch) with us, we started all four and got along pretty well considering the tangled, thick undergrowth that we had to cut through. We got a glimpse of the peak this afternoon, for the first time since we left, and found that we were going straight for it. The night was rather cold, but I felt better than the two previous days, on each of which I had an attack of fever, and felt very unwell. This made the ascent all the more trying to the muscles, and I could have wished myself anywhere but where I was. On the fourth day we were off early. We several times came across the former path to the peak, and Boobie paths, on our way up, but the former was so overgrown as to be undistinguishable for more than a short distance, and the latter scarcely ever ran in the right direction, so we had to chop away, and the more we chopped and ascended the thicker the bush became, and the thinner the forest. Occasionally this morning, and yesterday, we came across large fields of vegetation consisting of large ferns, brambles, and a sweet smelling tall herb resembling mint or balm, all growing together and forming a tangled dense mass over which we passed without touching the ground. Sometimes a couple of boys chopped at it as they passed, with their matchets. At other times Samson, a great big Krooman, would take a pole of five or six feet long, and with the weight of his body keep pressing it down before him. Early on the morning of the fourth day we got out of the bush and into the open, which appears from town as bare rock. Here we got a fine view of the town, which, with the ships and Point William (a remarkable feature when seen from this height) was quite clearly seen, and looked very pretty. The apparent rock, however, is in reality long grass reaching above the knees, and after passing through it for about half a mile, we halted for breakfast. We found that we had hit the most suitable and nearest spot of open that was possible, and congratulated ourselves on our good luck in having escaped a great deal of extra bush-chopping by emerging at this point. After breakfast we all started for the peak--about five miles distant, but oh! the horrors of the road. We little guessed the difficulty of finishing our task. That grass was something fearful to get through. Over crags and into holes, stumbling at every step, onward we pressed, sometimes falling, sometimes resting, fagged, and out of wind. Our boys, too, lagged behind, and left us short of water. I had a nasty fall on my right knee, the effects of which I have felt for weeks afterwards. At last we reached the top. Struthers was the first at the top. I rested some time on the lower edge of the crater waiting the arrival of Powell and Gazulla. Poor Powell suffered more than any of us. He was badly done up--throwing himself on the grass every few yards to gain wind. On the top we found a bottle containing several pieces of paper inscribed with the names of those who have previously ascended--Governor Beecroft, Mann (the botanist) several times, Burton, Wilson, Reinlein, Laughland, Roy, Governor Ayllon, and a number of Spanish officers, who were amongst the last who ascended--1862. We gave future aspirants the edifying information that the respective members of our party had also the honour to add our names to the list of those who had preceded us. We did not remain long at the peak, as we could see nothing but the clouds beneath us. Gazulla had set fire to the grass (which was very dry) on our way up, and to evade it we had to go a short distance out of the direct line of our descent. I was afraid we should have had some difficulty in escaping it, but although it spread fast, it did not spread so quickly as I imagined. As we went along we set fire to it in several places, and with the smart breeze the fire spread far and wide all over the mountain, for miles. It must have been a fine sight from the town, where it was distinctly seen by the people, who guessed rightly by it that we had reached the peak. On our way back we descended into a hollow not far from the peak, and found an abundance of cold water wherewith to refresh ourselves. It appeared very cold to us. A small patch of bush grew close to it. Near this place a fine red deer bounded out of the grass and made for the bush. It was about the size of a Bimbia goat, a pretty creature. We tried to get a shot at it, but could not find it. Struthers felt the descent more than the ascent. He was quite knocked up, and on reaching our tent he flung himself down on the grass with a rug on him, and slept soundly until dinner time, and dark. Our men had fixed the tent too near the burning grass, so we had to move lower down. It was a very cold moonlight night, the Krooboys lit three fires at the entrance to our tent, but they must have felt very miserable with the little covering they had on. Struthers talked of going to stalk the deer during the night, but as night wore on he thought better of it. It was too cold outside, and too comfortable inside for his resolution. I dare say he would have done it had anyone joined him, but no one cared to. We all felt the benefit of rest, and the shelter of our tent, too much to be coaxed out after night had set in. At daybreak of the fifth day Struthers and Gazulla again visited the peak--Powell and I remained at the tent. They returned at about 11 a.m. and reported the road much easier, now that all the grass was burnt off. They had a very fine view of the whole of the island from the peak, upon the very top of which they planted a pole with a sheet attached to it. On our return to the town we could distinguish both with a good spy-glass on a clear morning, but they soon were blown away. Struthers took a plunge into the pool of water above-mentioned, on his return, for the good of his spleen, he said. It must have required an effort on his part to have taken so cold a bath. They were very black about their faces, caused by the burnt grass blowing into them. We saw the steamer *Athenian*. The people on board this ship had seen the fire on the mountain and were at a loss how to account for it, some of them imagining it to be a volcano. At noon the Krooboys sent by Gazulla and Powell returned with abundance of provisions, and after a good feed we struck tent and commenced our return to the town. We slept at our encampment of the second night, and on the sixth day reached the town. I got ahead of the rest, and awaited some time at Basili. As, however, the Governor did not appear very cordial in his manner I soon left that place, and hurried home, reaching it in the afternoon. Struthers and the others came down later on. He had missed the road, along with Samson, and they were near spending a night in the bush together. By good luck, however, they hit the right track again, after a good deal of trouble, and took good care not to lose it a second time. He and I were lost together the same day. I had explored a little of the bush on our ascent, whilst waiting for the boys, and had found that the track taken by our friends Gazulla and Powell, after running some distance out of the way returned to near the spot where we had halted, but higher up. I thought it would be easy to make a straight cut with a little chopping, but we soon found that we were going in a different direction from the required one, and but for the voices of our Krooboys, which can be heard a long way off in the bush, we should have had to retrace our steps, and have followed the legitimate road. The crater at the top of the mountain one of the sides of which forms the peak, seen from below is not the only one. There are several. We passed along the edge of one equally large and deep, but five or six hundred feet lower in elevation. Grass lines these craters down to the very bottom, and along the sides, wherever the protruding boulders give it a chance to cling. On the edges of the craters the grass is shorter. Lava, stone, and earth compose the peak. Originally it had been composed of stone and lava, but atmospheric action has decomposed the lava, during the course of ages, and has produced rich soil. The action of water has had the effect of carrying this soil downward, so that there is more of it in hollows, on the sides and at the bottom of the mountain, where also the greater heat and moisture may have accelerated the decomposing or disintegrating process, and the immense quantity of ever decaying vegetation has enriched and gradually made it more and more prolific. It is astonishing, however, how little soil suffices to create, with sun and rain, enormous trees which in some places grow on almost solid rock. All the larger trees, and most of the smaller ones near the top are covered with a kind of fibre which, hanging down from every branch, and blown about by the breeze, produces a strange, weird, wintry effect. I don't know what this fibre is, whether it is grown by the trees in the shape we saw it, or whether it is simply leaves divested of the softer parts. Trees grow smaller and less numerous as they rise in altitude. In the grass at the top is here and there a short, stunted, shapeless attempt at a tree on the exposed parts (in the hollows they are more developed) interspersed with clumps of heather. The grass at the top was full of wild bees, and, of course, the bush was full of ants of all shapes and sizes. Now and then a cloud would float above our heads at the top and would sometimes envelop us for a few minutes, but most of the cloud appeared to be far beneath us. A sharp east wind blew all the time we were on the top. In the wind, and shaded by a cloud it felt cold. In both wind and sun it was pleasant. In the sun alone, and out of the wind, it was hot. The sun had such an effect on my face (with a Scotch cape over my head) that I lost all the skin off my nose and forehead. There were a number of small chirping birds in the trees near the summit. The principal one, seen seldom in the bush, is the Turavvo. It is first heard a few hundred feet above Basili and appears to rove from that limit upwards. A great quantity of dung shows that there must be plenty of deer near the summit, and here and there a Boobie hut proves that the boobies know how to appreciate their presence. We experienced no want of water, although we had to seek it. There is a vast variety of ferns on the mountain, the most notable is the tree fern--a beautiful palm-like tree. We passed through a forest of them. they do not grow above or below a certain height. We found a few ripe bramble berries, and, of course, gladly ate them as we called to mind the days of our boyhood. It is a glorious sight to see the clouds come rolling up and tumbling over each other as they pass westward of a morning. It is beautiful to see the mass of vegetation beneath you, and the outline of every nook and headland traced on the shining, glass-like sea. Once rid of the bush one feels more at home. Although the path is long and the trouble heavy, one feels a satisfaction at being able to breathe pure air, and be free of the depressing influence of that everlasting, terrible, death-like forest. The bracing atmosphere of the peak was exhilarating to our spirits. With a little more comfort, and after getting accustomed to the cold, we could have enjoyed ourselves. I do not think, however, that I shall every again visit the peak if I have to go through the same amount of toil, and suffering such discomfort. It would be a splendid place to go to, in order to recruit one's health, but to obtain that end there should be an open pathway, and two or three houses on the way where a person could rest and sleep in comfort. Horses would not do without a good road. Mules might, but men and a hammock would be as good as anything, our road at one time plunging into deep ravines, at others up steep hills, now under, then over fallen trees, and along ridges with deep hollows on each side. The night of our return (although we were very much fatigued) was celebrated. After some music and health-drinking at Gazaulla's, we went up to Struthers', and continued the festival until a late hour.

27 May

We had a very heavy tornado this afternoon, which blew down Nicolas de Castillo's house, and killed a poor Krooboy who happened to be under it at the time. Don Nicolas, Powell, and Gazulla, were inside the house when it fell and although shaken and alarmed, were unhurt. The house is a good deal twisted, and will have to be taken to pieces in order to be of future service.

4 June

Jane Campbell arrived this morning in the *Bonny* bringing news of the death of poor Townsend at Madeira. He was a smart trader who did not allow anyone to get the advantage over him. That, however, was not unjust. In all my transactions with him I have found him an honest, upright man. He would not allow rogues or fools to get the upper hand with him, and so he made enemies. He was almost entirely self-educated, was smart, far-sighted, keen in trade, hospitable, at times, amusing and good-natured, and talented. He knew a great deal of the world and understood the generality of his fellows, better than they understood him.

13 June

Harry Gardner goes home in the S.S. *Bonny*.[68] This, for him, is an event, he having been on the Coast six years without going home. Don Zoila Sanchez Ocana, our Governor, also leaves per *Bonny*. He is not very well, but I presume only makes use of that fact to excuse his leaving the colony. S.S. *Ferrol* left to-day for Spain, taking the remnant of the white colonists brought here last year, amongst others, the fair Angelita, whose profile friend Wilson much admires.

21 June

Poor old Joe Mullings, another of the old African traders, and latterly a pilot for the Rivers, died the other day in Bonny, of dropsy. He was humorous, and rather eccentric. He adopted a poor German lad named Harry Hartz, who is now agent in Old Calabar for Thomas Harrison & Co. of Liverpool, and doing the largest trade in the river.[69] When I first knew them they were inseparable, but afterwards they became somewhat estranged on account of some little differences, the particulars of which I now forget.

2 July

Bertram Sparhawk came over accompanied by Mr. Collins, of Cameroons, in the *Maria* from Bimbia, Bertram having met with a very severe accident. It appears that King William of Bimbia went to visit my brother on his arrival, and that as my brother saluted him with a discharge of his small cannon, Bertram, desirous of being heard, also fired the guns he had on Nicoll Island in honour of the occasion. One of these, being overloaded, burst, and a fragment hit Bertram (who was standing on his plazza) straight in the face, causing a fearful wound. It seems strange that those who were about the gun all escaped, Bertram being the only one hurt. It is a very dangerous looking accident. His face is horribly disfigured, eyes swollen up, so that he cannot see--blood slowly dripping from his nose, and a large deep hole straight between the eyes and at the very root of his

---

[68]SS *Bonny* (1277 grt) was built by Randolph, Elder in 1869 for the British and African Steam Navigation Company and was sold in 1890.

[69]Davies, *Trading in West Africa*, 178-179.

nose. He has lost a good deal of blood, but is wonderfully strong and in much better spirits than I think I should have been under the circumstances. We took him to the Spanish hospital where every care was shown him. His wound was examined by the doctors, who observed that it was of a very serious nature and that the patient's chances of recovery were but few. It was all the more dangerous on account of the time that had elapsed between the date that the accident occurred and that on which he arrived. He quietly requested the doctors to speak out and let him know at once if there was no chance of his recovery, as he wished to make arrangements for bidding adieu to this world, and for sending a last message to his father.[70]

17 July

I have had a good deal of bother with Lauriano Diez da Cunha about his clerk Buckle. This latter has for some time been asking me for a situation, and having one to offer him at Bimbia I arranged with him to proceed thence (he, at the time, being in the service of Lauriano but without any fixed time of service or any written agreement). I intended sending him over with the schooner, but I could not get him ready, first with one tale and then another--there was always something more to stop him. The result was that I found he was owing Lauriano some balance of account and finding this the case, on a copy of the account being presented me I gave a written promise to pay it in three months. This (Buckle told me) Lauriano agreed to, but when the time for sailing came he was not ready, and on further enquiring I found that not a three months' promise to pay but cash down was what Lauriano required. The schooner was now gone, and as I believed this prevaricating conduct on the part of Lauriano was done with the purpose of annoying me I turned the tables on him and the following night sent Buckle away to Bimbia in Wilson's boat without giving Mr. Lauriano any security whatever for his money. Lauriano, full of vengeance, sued me not only for what Buckle owed him, but what he owed Harry, Gazulla, and others, from whom he obtained copies of accounts, and presented to the Judge, stating that he was responsible for their payment. He wrote the Judge a statement of his claim and I replied to it. He again wrote the Judge, and this time accused him of partiality and injustice, threatening at the same time if the Judge did not take certain steps in the matter he should appeal to a superior authority. The Judge, highly offended, without more ado gave an order for his arrest and consigned him to close confinement for a month with the payment in addition of one hundred dollars. This I consider is a stretch or rather an abuse of power on the Judge's part, but I at the same time consider Lauriano very well served for his pains. At the same time, to somewhat soothe his feelings I agreed to pay the amount Buckle owed him and other accounts which he had paid, on receiving Buckle's request to do it. I therefore wrote to Buckle who agreeing with the amount claimed, I paid the same into the hands of the Judge, leaving Mr. Lauriano with sufficient time on his hands to consider whether or not he had been playing but a sorry part in this transaction, and to reflect on the folly of unnecessarily endeavouring to annoy a man because of an old grudge against him.

[70]It appears that Bertram Sparhawk made a good recovery; see p. 119.

Figure 9: John Holt, Taken Outside His Residence in Birkenhead, c. 1905.

Source: See Figure 1.

23 July

The thermometer was as low as 66° F. this morning. At noon it stood at 76°. Last year on the 24th July it stood as low as 65° early in the morning. This is the lowest I have every seen it in Santa Isabel, and it was for a short time quite cold to one's senses.

25 July

Admiral Bourgois of the French frigate *Bellone* invited the Acting-Governor, his Secretary, the Captain of the port, and myself to dinner with him. We had a very good dinner, but with a great amount of ceremony which I particularly dislike. I have dined with our Commodores and they had nothing like so much etiquette as this ship had. However, I made a good dinner and did my share of the ceremonial part, standing when others stood, and sitting when they sat. I had a good deal of conversation with the Admiral, as, knowing that I was the Agent of the African Steamship Co. mail steamers, he had a good many questions to ask about the dates of sailing, the proposed extension of line to Loanda, carriage of French letters to Gaboon &c.

2 August

An American whaler, the first that I have ever seen on this coast, has caught a fine large whale off the port, which they are busy cutting up to make oil. The Captain expects to get a hundred barrels out of this whale. A good many people, Krooboys and others, went to see it and eat part of it as well. I never was near one before and was struck by the monstrous size and bulk of it.

22 August

The *Maria* arrived from the South Coast with a cargo of rubber &c., on the 15th, which was discharged into the *Terrier* and she at once left for Bimbia, arriving back again on the 20th with thirty-three casks of palm oil on board. On the 22nd the *Mandingo*[71] arrived and her outward cargo for the *Maria* had to be discharged and the produce shipped by her. It was a hard day's work, and Jonathan was sick the whole of the day, although he attended to his work. He had a very wet time of it on his voyage to Bimbia, and had the fever on him during his passage across. He had also fever and what I suppose to have been an attack of bile or affection of the liver of some kind. I only learnt these facts afterwards. The day after the steamer left for the Rivers he had to lay down to it at the house, but was able to get up and go down to the *Maria* in the morning. He complained of fever and shooting pains in the bowels. I thought nothing of it (he had always been so hardy) and suggested the usual remedy of quinine for what I took to be a simple case of African fever. He took it, however, to no purpose. I had seen him sick before, to all appearances quite as bad as ever he appeared during the time that elapsed before I called the doctor. As he grew worse, gradually becoming weaker and at length unable to leave his bedroom, I became alarmed, and on the 28th when the *Mandingo* returned from the Rivers I asked her doctor to be good enough to come and see him. I was not present when he made his visit, but Jonathan told me that he said it was only a slight bilious attack and that he would get over it in a day or two. He left some medicine which was carefully administered, but not noticing an improvement, on the contrary, seeing worse and worse symptoms appearing, I called in the Spanish doctor Palan. He

[71]SS *Mandingo* (1216 grt) was built by Randolph, Elder in 1866 for the African Steam Ship Company and was sold in 1872.

pronounced the sickness to be typhoid fever. This I knew to be a serious disease, and felt all the more distressed since the doctor could say nothing to mitigate the fact. He could only "hope for the best." He could not assure me of there being a probability of his recovery. It was possible, but he regretted that he had not been called sooner. However, he set to work with his medicine and with quinine in particular, of which I gave twenty-four grain doses for several days, afterwards twenty grains and so on, gradually reducing the number day by day or every few days. I soon began to know as much of this disease almost as the doctors. I read all the medical works on it that I could lay hold of over and over again. The more I read the less hope there seemed, but I found that unremitting attendance on the sick person was a very important matter. This I was glad to give. I forsook my business entirely and gave my whole time and attention to his care. I attended him day and night, getting sleep by snatches, and with a mind so sadly troubled that I felt very unwell myself. He appeared to improve for a time. The quinine gradually looked like bringing him round. The dull heavy eye and death-like face began to brighten and although he still complained of that engine-like pumping noise in his head, he could talk and even smile. It was then that I thought about sending the *Maria* away and he gave the mate instructions what to do. He could not have done this before, so indifferent did he appear to everything round him. This was at the end of the second week of his sickness. On the third week these good appearances disappeared and worse symptoms set in. The doctor stopped the quinine as he was afraid of its effect on the nervous system, there being an increase of the noises in the head. On the 13th, Palan asked me if I wished to call in the head doctor for a consultation. This showed that he too, was alarmed. I at once said yes. The head doctor was called and although I took him into Jonathan's room and introduced him as if nothing was the matter he evidently had the clue to our thoughts, for during the night following he became worse and spoke as if he expected death. The result of the consultation was that blisters were to be applied to the arms and legs, a soothing medicine was to be administered, and a cup of light broth three times a day. No quinine was to be administered by the mouth, but was to be rubbed into the skin as an ointment. I had had so little sleep, and felt so worn out that I asked Struthers to sit up with Jonathan last night, which he kindly did, and I shall ever feel grateful to him for it. He also sat up with him to-night, and early in the morning of the 15th we found Jonathan in a fearful state. Struthers told me that it had commenced at midnight. All of a sudden he jumped up and gave Struthers a slap on the back and asked him, "How are you, old fellow?" During the whole of this day he continued in the same state--for a while he would be quiet, then all of a sudden a spasm would come on and he would get up and ask where he was, what was he doing here. Then the perspiration would break forth through his skin in streams, as if he had been making some terrible bodily effort, and then I gradually got him to lie down again when he would tell me "It's of no use"--"I'm bound to go"--"It can't be helped"--"I can't last much longer"--"There must be a change soon"--"I hope to go to heaven where I also hope to meet you and father and mother and all our family." Such as these he would continue to ejaculate, until another spasm commenced, when he would call me to him and repeat in like manner. "John," said he, "you are a decent fellow. You have been a good brother to me, but I must go." "You know as well as I do that it must be so." "Take care of Tom." I soothed him all I could, although I was little able to hide my own distress and attempted to divert his mind by asking him about the *Maria*. With an evident show of pleasure he said that he remembered her, remarking that one could do anything with her, she was such a handy vessel. This morning, when the doctor came I brought out my own medical book, and told him that it said that a patient passing two consecutive nights such as my brother had passed scarcely ever got over his sickness, and that the only remedy was a powerful narcotic. The doctor knew this better than I could tell him and therefore required no spur to apply the only remedy. Mr. Sparhawk and his son Bertram were with me most of the day. Struthers had sat up with Jonathan the last two nights, and last night I never slept a wink. Although I tried all in my power to do it, I could not. To-day I felt as I never felt in my life. I had often thought during this awful sickness that Jonathan was going to die. I was determined to leave Africa and go home for good, if he did, but to-day I felt as if there was no hope left. I became quite unmanned. I wept like a child. I prayed most devoutly that God would help me in my distress and I thought of how our parents would be grieved. I knew not how I should tell them of it. I blamed myself for the result I anticipated, as I said he would never have come here but for me. My mind was full of horrors. I half expected to get the disease myself, or to see it spread to the other members of our household here. During the afternoon I went in to see him, when, in one of his spasms, he turned to me and said "John, I have worked hard for you, and have never robbed you of a shilling." I was very much affected when he said this, and could not restrain my grief. Too hard, poor soul, had he worked for me. Alas! Alas! And as for his ever taking a shilling of mine, he knew I never suspected him. How gladly would I have sacrificed every shilling I then possessed to have seen him hale and strong again. Mr. Roe came to see him in the evening, and prayed with him. He said it was too late, it was the eleventh hours. The night of the 14th he passed more quietly. Struthers again assisted me. The opium which had been given to him in pills during the day and up to midnight (15 grains) produced their effect and brought back blessed sleep to his eyes once more. It is strange that during this sickness he has never complained of pain since the commencement, when he felt the shooting pains in his bowels. The four blisters produced no pain. He said they tickled him and in his delirium he tore them off, but not before they had taken effect. When the hospital man dressed them (on the 15th) he looked calmly on, but felt no pain. Yesterday (14th), when he came to put them on, Jonathan asked me what was the use of torturing him, that it would do him no good. He appeared to take a dislike to this man, saying that he did not care what he did but he did what he was told to do. He was rational to-day, with a heavy appearance, and very sleepy. The effect of the opium, I suppose. (16th). He was in appearance the same as yesterday. There were still certain twitchings of the tendons of the hands and of the muscles of the face, which intimate that there still remains an amount of nervous irritability. On the 18th the effect of the opium appeared to have gone off. He was very weak but, the length of his sickness considered, wonderfully strong. On the 18th Captain Smart kindly sent a piece of ice ashore. Had it come sooner it might have been more useful, but I am nevertheless grateful for the kind attention. My hopes began to rise now, although he evinced little or no inclination for food. Water vesicles appeared on his skin--principally over the bowels. At the same time the delirium and other bad symptoms commenced. On the 20th the practicante, by a careless dressing of the blister sores--threw him into a frightfully nervous state. The tendons of the hands and legs again began their spasmodic starts, and his teeth chattered. I felt much pained at this, but it was an evident sign of his recovery. He had the sense of pain again. The symptoms gradually subsided. Step by step he began to improve, but it was very slow. My books, however, taught me to expect this and besides, I had to guard against a relapse. This fearful disease ulcerates the bowels, and causes during its continuation constant diarrhoea. I therefore stuck to the doctor's orders. I even infringed them on the right side by not giving Jonathan the food that he said I might give him. The great emaciation became more apparent in him when the change for the better took place. How altered had be become! From a strong healthy man he had become reduced to a small helpless emaciated boy. He strongly resembled Tom, when his features became so attenuated. He was stronger during the time of his sickness than when he began to recover, but throughout was wonderfully strong. By degrees I gave him more and more food, but for three weeks from the commencement of his recovery I kept him on vegetable food. How anxiously he listened to the preparations for his meals! He became voracious, and the thought of food was uppermost in his mind. There was no danger of our forgetting the hour to serve him. He was too watchful. How talkative he became, too! And how bright his eyes and countenance. A most striking contrast to what he resembled when the fever was on him. He was laid up three months altogether. Although, had the *Maria* been here a fortnight sooner, he could have gone away in her. He did not look healthy when he left. His face had a bloated and unnatural look about it. A trip in the *Maria* to the Kroo Coast appeared to set him alright, but doubtless this terrible sickness has left its mark on his constitution. It seems hardly possible that he could suffer so much and so long without being for ever afterwards more or less affected by it. He has a wonderful constitution, and has ever led an abstemious temperate life. For my part, I shall never forget the lesson I have learnt, or the trial I have undergone. Until this occurred I never knew the value of my brother--or understood how dear he is to me.

9 November

Henry Gardner and Margaret Christian were this day married together at Longfield House, by the Reverend H. Roe, Primitive Methodist missionary. Struthers, Jonathan and I were present at the ceremony. We dined at Longfield House with the happy pair in the evening, and had a dance afterwards. At dinner there was a good deal of speech-making. The black men of the town had a great opportunity, which they did not allow to pass and we were favoured with speeches from most of them. In the evening a good many Spaniards came in. Struthers got so drunk that by eight o'clock he was "wound up," and disappeared. We afterwards found him fast asleep on the "marriage" bed. I strongly disapprove of this wedding, but it is useless opposing it. Harry has just returned from a visit to Scotland, and if that is not enough to cause him to keep from marrying a black girl, anything I say to him is not likely to alter his decision.

16 November

The barque *Hannah Salkeld*, Captain Massingham, owned by Stuart & Douglas and condemned some four months ago as unseaworthy, was sold by public auction for £121 to Miller Bros. & Co. of Glasgow.[72] She is to be towed to the Opobo river to be used

---

[72]*Hannah Salkeld* (535 grt) was built at Liverpool in 1845, acquired by Stuart and Douglas in 1862 and used in the West Africa trade until condemned at Fernando Po in 1870. See Wharton, unpublished mss., 153.

as a hulk there. Four hogsheads of damaged tobacco on board her were sold to Gazulla for £23. The pinnace and gig sold for £518.[73] Her cargo of palm oil has been sent home by ship and engines and sails have been taken out of her by the owners' agents.

27 November

Padre Campillo, one of the Spanish Jesuit priests of this place, sailed for Spain per S.S. *Mandingo*. He has been ten years on the Island, without once leaving it, I believe, during the period. The Civil Engineer also goes home by her. He has not been long here, but has made good use of his time. Some people think they do no great harm in robbing a government. I suppose he thought so, and a good many of his countrymen think and act likewise. He has sold a quantity of government property. The Governor offered to sell me an iron house but I knew the wooden flooring was not with it, as the Civil Engineer had sold it to Maggie Christian for building her house with.

5 December

The *Eboe* arrived to-day and reported "all well" to the visiting doctor. Shortly afterwards he was called to see the first officer, and found him dead. He then inspected the ship and found several others down with fever. Having reported this to the Governor, a fine of £100 was imposed for infringement of the sanitary laws, and regulations, and the *Eboe* was put in quarantine. Ultimately the fine was remitted but she was ordered to leave the port at once. The first officer (Smith) had to be buried at sea. The ship was in a wretched state, Captain and crew being more or less sick and unfit for duty. The Captain (Burt) ought to have gone home some time ago as he has been too unwell to attend to his duties, and the ship has been worked at a great loss to her owners, the African Steamship Co.[74]

20 December

Captain Chamberlain died in the Spanish hospital this morning early, and we buried him in the usual place in the afternoon. He came here in the *Bonny* on the 11th, ill with dysentery. He remained in Struthers' house (Struthers was away) until he got so bad that I had him removed to the Spanish hospital, where I and Mr. Roe assisted him. He died suddenly, and with a fearful fixed stare in his eyes, awful to see. The doctor did not anticipate his death, nor, of course, did I, or I should have asked him if he had anything to say to his wife and family. He is another of the steamships' pilots; Townsend, Kelly, Thomas, and now Chamberlain, have all gone.

---

[73] This is a printing error. The original diary shows that the pinnace and gig were sold for £18.

[74] SS *Eboe* (653 grt) was built by Royden in 1870 for the African Steam Ship Company and was sold in 1875.

25 December

To-day we had a baptism, a death, and a betrothal. Trello has formally engaged before the priests to marry Mrs. Macaulay. Mrs. Bennett baptized her mulatto child (by Norberto Balboa), and poor Hubert died. He was close to Chamberlain in the hospital, and has only survived him a few days. He has been, I suppose, six or seven years here, having formerly worked for Obon, Sparhawk and Gazulla. Latterly he kept a little farm of his own. Large boils in his legs appear to have gradually wasted his strength and brought him to the grave. But his blood must have been in a very unhealthy condition to have done this, I should think. He was a hard worker, and, it is said, a hard eater too.

27 December

Consul Livingstone sailed per *Calabar* for Madeira. He has been very unwell of late. He is suffering from bronchitis or asthma, or some other affection of the chest. I am afraid we shall never see him again. He has left Hopkins of New Calabar as Acting-Consul, and Harry Gardner as Postmaster.

1871

26 February

Mr. George Watts has served me a scurvy trick. I asked Struthers to buy the *Edmund* (Townsend's cutter) for me, as he was putting her up (at Old Calabar) for sale by public auction. Struthers got Watts to bid for him, and after I had arranged to have her towed over and had sent over my carpenter, Johnny, to look after her, I learnt that it was Mr. Watts' intention to keep her himself as he said he had an old grudge against me. His grudge being that I owe him £50 on a joint speculation we made in tobacco some years ago, of which he never gave me the slightest intimation. Had he done so, the circumstances of our arrangement, which was verbal, could have been easily recalled and if there was any misunderstanding about it, the matter might have been submitted to arbitration. I cannot understand how a man can let a complaint rankle in his mind four years and be on quite friendly terms with a person he intends to do an injury to on the first opportunity that occurs to him. He has since offered to hand the cutter to me, provided I paid him her cost £37, and the £50 he says I owe him. I reply by saying that I do not owe him, that by keeping her so long he has done me more than that amount of injury, besides causing me to buy a more costly though a larger and more suitable vessel (the *Mahgeda*, Kirkwood's schooner, costing £400) and that I therefore do not want her. He has made a little hulk of her in the Old Calabar river, and is trading on his own account. He has arranged with me to supply him with cargo that I can spare from my Fernando Po trade.[75]

[75]Despite these difficulties Holt joined with George Watts in 1885 to create the Liverpool African Company, which traded near Oil Rivers. See *Merchant Adventure*, 31.

2 March

The *Athenian* brought news of the capitulation of Paris.[76] Thus the horrible war between France and Germany, short but terrible in its force and effects, its at a close. France is humbled and has received a dreadful chastisement. The Germans have met with unparalleled success, but at immense sacrifice of life. Who shall reckon the sum of misery and desolation, the wreck of lives, homes, and families? And whatever may be the future influence of this war on mankind, good or bad, to the bereaved families of the victors as well as of the vanquished it can hardly prove anything but an unmixed evil.

16 March

I sold to Vivour a pretty little schooner boat called the *Sarah* which he is going to use in the yam and palm oil trade.

20 March

William L------ died very suddenly at about 7.30 p.m. He had been ill a few days, but I suspected nothing but a slight attack of fever. I was with him a couple of days back and there appeared to be nothing serious the matter with him. Although I suspected that he had delirium tremens at the time, I was very sorry and surprised when I learned that he was dead, and I am afraid that drink has been the cause of it. Harry tells me that he had been drinking a large amount of brandy since he has been here, and that before he arrived he was drinking trade gin on board the schooner, and this without eating almost. Harry tells me he tried to keep him from brandy while with him, but he made his boy go out for it, and hid it under his bed. I believe his business has been going wrong of late. He told me that several of his factories were considerably short in their accounts. These have no doubt tended to cause him to take stimulants as some people do when they are in trouble, for the purpose of procuring for a while at least a freedom from all mental troubles. When they arrive at such a state as this they ought to be put under restraint and treated as sick men. He was a decent, good-hearted soul, ever ready to oblige, but like everybody else he had his faults. I feel very sorry that he has gone in this way.

8 May

My carpenter, George Thompson, died suddenly of rheumatic fever. He had been more or less ill of it some three weeks, with no expectation of a fatal result. I had the doctor to him about a week after he commenced to be ill, and the doctor prescribed medicine, which was given him, but did not effect a cure. As he told me, however, that it would likely be a long time before it could be cured, I was not at all anxious about the result. Poor old Johnny, as we called him, tried to work with the rheumatism on him as long as he could, but was obliged to give in, on account of his legs not having strength enough in them to bear his trunk. When laid up, however, he was able to get up mostly to take his meals out of his bedroom, and latterly he was able to walk about the house

---

[76] A. Horne, *The Fall of Paris. The Siege and the Commune 1870-1* (London, 1965).

and even come down the steps one day to help me to put up a post under the piazza. Unfortunately, the rheumatism, from being in his hands and feet, attacked his chest and neck, and changed the aspect of the case entirely. I did not see him until the afternoon of the day he died, when I was told by Mr. Jones that he appeared worse. I found him breathing hard and complaining of phlegm in his throat, which he could not get rid of. I at once went for the doctor, but although I asked him he did not apprehend the result that followed. The doctor's instructions were attended to and I left Johnny intending him to get sleep. Mr. Snailham slept in the same room with him, and shortly after we had gone to bed, Thompson got up by Snailham's assistance, and sat in a chair, saying that the stuff in his throat was choking him, and that he could not lay down longer. He had not been in the chair many comments before he expired in an effort to expectorate. I was at once called, and going to his room found him sitting in his chair, his eyes wide open, and a fullness about his face as if he had been choked. He was then quite dead. The doctor was on board the hulk, so it was of no use sending for him. All we could do was to close his eyes and lay him on his bed. Jones and Snailham dressed him and laid him out, and I got the carpenters to work during the night at his coffin, which we lined with white cotton and covered with black alpaca, and furniture. In the morning we buried him and Mr. Roe read the service. I shall send for a grave stone to mark the spot where we have laid him. I feel sorry to lose him, not only because I shall miss his services very much now that I am building a new house, not only because he was a faithful, hard-working, useful man, but because he comes from the same part of England that I come from, because he leaves wife and family behind, because I have known him since I was a child, and because he was friend as well as servant. If I feel sorry, how much more so his poor wife and family who have lost their best earthly friend, their support, their bread-winner. Farewell, faithful "Johnny" until that future which, far or near, inevitably grows nearer. You were not perfection but you "strove to do good," and to do your duty. Truly God will reward you and surely he will be a protector of your widow and fatherless children.

18 May

The new Commodore arrived in the *Rattlesnake*, bringing the *Vindictive* in tow. I dined with him and our little Governor Canya. He is a very pleasant, open-hearted sort of man, and I like him better than Dowell or Wilmot. He has more amiability, more condescension, and is more gentlemanly and kind, and less eccentric than they. He has left the *Vindictive* in my hands for sale, and a launch, pinnace, and cutter, for the Coal Depot.

28 May

By the *Maria* I received news of the death of a young Scotchman whom I sent in the *Maria* last month, to take charge of my Bata factory. He tried to drown himself, they say, and so far succeeded that he died either from that, or from taking a dose of arsenic which I am told he bought from a ship to poison rats with. I don't think he died from either arsenic poison or from the effects of having too much water in either lungs or stomach. The real cause has been too much rum and gin which were in the factory for trade. He was a good swimmer, and would not easily have been drowned, had he not been weakened by too much rum-drinking and no eating, or very little of it, for several weeks. I knew he drank, and when I engaged him, warned him in a kind manner of its effects. He gave me good promises, but only to be broken. This propensity to take intoxicating drink, when it once gets hold of a man, becomes in fact a disease. I will not do it again with any other man whom I know to be a drunkard. I hear that my affairs in the factory are in a wretched state. I can imagine how they must be. I have done a foolish thing, and well deserve the loss of property which my folly has brought.

2 June

My brother Tom goes home a passenger on the *Benin*.[77]

3 June

The S.S. *Liberia* arrived, Bailey coming out in her to take Latta's place.[78]

21 June

Mr. Mayloot and his wife, Primitive Methodist missionaries intended for a North West Bay Mission establishment, arrived on the *Lagos*.[79]

16 July

I dined on board the *Sirius* with Captain Miller.[80] Captain Chapman, of H.M.S. *Dido*, who relieves Captain Miller on this station, was there too. Captain Miller is a nice old Scotch gentleman, with very agreeable manners. He is a "canny" bachelor.

24 July

I have been with Captain Chapman on a trip to North West Bay. We have only been three days absent, but the trip has done me good. On returning to Santa Isabel we found the *Torch*, with Captain Geneste, her Commander, placed under arrest by his officers, who have brought him to the senior officer, Captain Chapman.[81] It appears that Geneste, in a fit of passion, struck one of the officers. A council was held by them and

---

[77]Thomas Holt had entered his brother's employ in October 1867. SS *Benin* (1530 grt) was built by John Elder in 1869 for the British and African Steam Navigation Company; it was lost in 1881.

[78]SS *Liberia* (1470 grt) was built by John Elder in 1870 for the British and African Steam Navigation Company and was lost in 1874.

[79]SS *Lagos* (1199 grt) was built by Randolph, Elder in 1865 for the African Steam Ship Company and was sold in 1872.

[80]HMS *Sirius* (1755 grt) was a single-screw, wooden sloop built at the Portsmouth Dockyard in 1868. See Cox, *Cox and the Ju Ju Coast*, 68 and 81; *All the World's Fighting Ships, 1860-1905*, 48.

[81]HMS *Torch* was a three-masted sailing vessel fitted with an auxiliary steam engine. See Pedler, *The Lion and the Unicorn*, 140, fn. 2; *All the World's Fighting Ships, 1860-1905*, 109.

they were determined to place him under arrest, and put the charge of the vessel into the hands of the First Lieutenant, which they accordingly did. The result will likely be the dismissal of Geneste from the service, but I question if the Admiralty will approve the action of the *Torch*'s officers. I expect they will be reprimanded, if not forced to retire or even dismissed. The precedent is such a bad one to set before the Navy.

13 September

A.J. Jones died early this morning. He was one of the largest traders in Boobie. As he is owing £600 or £800 in the town (Couper & Co. holding £600 of it), Harry and I asked the Judge to take possession of his effects which he did at once, sealing everything.

1 October

The Spanish gunboat *Prosperidad*, having been succeeded by the *Ligera*, sailed to-day. Her Commander Don Felipe Canya de Arguelles has been Acting-Governor nearly the whole of the twelve months he has been here, two Governors having been invalided in that time. He has done a good deal of work in the time, the principal being the garden in the square, the jetty, the church tower and clock. He was bent upon beautifying, and has certainly improved the appearance of the square. I attribute this to the influence of the Jesuit missionaries, of whom he appears to be a thorough supporter. At first he and I quarrelled on the occasion of his fining me $5 for one of my bullocks having strayed into the square, then in process of transformation into a garden. From the top of the church tower he cried "A fine of $5 on the owner of that bullock, and the next time $20." I thought this arbitrary with a vengeance. It looked as if he were commanding his own ship. I plainly told him I would not pay it, had a very stormy meeting with him, and at length settled the matter by paying the $5 to shew my deference to the superior power, and then receiving it back as an acknowledgement of my right of appeal against his measures. After this palaver we grew more and more friendly, and latterly he has scarcely allowed a day to pass without visiting me at my office or at the new house I am constructing in the square, in which he takes great interest, and would have me spend a good deal more on it than I intend to do, in order to forward his pet idea of improving the appearance of the square. His officers, too, Caniargo, Vera, Cosi, Doctor Pardo, and Paymaster Canova, were all decent fellows, and I felt regret that they have to leave us. These officers however, made a great mess of their visit to Elobey a month or so ago. Caniargo was in charge, and went there for the purpose of inquiring into the complaints of the traders. The officers and three or four men landed, and a palaver was held at Walker's factory. The natives became noisy and threatening. The officers were unarmed, the men having nothing but guns and bayonets, without ammunition. The officers took fright, ordered the men to the boats "at the double," the officers following at full speed and rushing into the water to get to the boats, the natives in the meantime yelling and hooting around Walker's factory and not attempting to hurt the Spaniards. This is Gazulla's statement. He was ashore with them, and according to him, Dr. Pardo and himself were the only two who did not run. The natives swear death on Walker about the palaver and he durst not leave his factory. The Spaniards would not land to assist him. On attempting to leave the beach at midnight in company with his cooper, he was fired upon and his cooper was killed by his side. Caniargo wanted to bombard the Island, an absurdity against which all the traders protested, as they would be the only sufferers. The palaver, however, was settled between them, and the natives and Walker. I expect the latter would have to pay sweetly for it, Caniargo having told them that if they did not settle it within a given time he should bombard the Island. Before he left, they intimated to him that in future they should endeavour to settle their differences with the natives as best they could without appealing to the Spanish authorities for assistance. The natives after this will become bolder and more arrogant in their conduct than ever. They have seen white men run away from them in a fright, almost without anything to fear, and white men whose profession is war. They must have the greatest contempt for such men, unless their eyes be opened by force. Ignorance of black men, their appearance, mode of speech, action, and manner, has been the cause of this act of cowardice. They have exaggerated the meaning and intention of all these. Surely had they known the negro better they would never have "cut and run" before two or three score of them.

8 October

The *Volta* and the *Soudan* had a race from Old Calabar, the former beating the latter by twenty minutes, contrary to the expectation of most people.[82] The *Soudan* however, was three feet by the stern, and consequently somewhat out of trim. They had a collision in the river. The Soudan caught the Volta's stern and tore away about fifteen or twenty feet of her bulwarks aft as she was crossing the bows of the former. The *Soudan* lost her jib-boom by it. The *Volta* did the distance in seven hours.

Figure 10: SS *Roquelle* of the British and African Steam Navigation Company, c. 1870.

Source: Courtesy of Dr. Sam Davidson.

[82]SS *Volta* (1477 grt) was built by John Elder in 1870 for the British and African Steam Navigation Company and was sold in 1891; SS *Soudan* (1603 grt) was built by Royden in 1870 for the African Steam Ship Company and was lost in 1875.

10 October

Measles are very prevalent in the town. Abel Moses, one of the carpenters employed in my house-building, died of them to-day.

11 October

William Bell died. He has long been sick.

4 November

Struthers returned from Scotland on the *Roquelle* in very good health.

5 November

H.M.S. *Dido* arrived, bringing over Hopkins (acting Consul).[83] He and Captain Chapman have been making a settlement at the Bonny, Okrika, New Calabar and Brass palavers, I believe to the satisfaction of all concerned, at least the letter of thanks from the traders at Bonny and New Calabar is gratifying to them. The Opobo nut (yet to settle) will be hardest to crack. The Government at the instance of the African Association have given the senior officer and Consul powers to use force in the settlement of these palavers.[84] Thus their hands are strengthened. Hopkins does the Consul "heavy." He has his boat crew dressed man-of-war style with H.B.M. Consulate in gilt on their caps, and has himself got the rapier, cocked hat and other fixings of a Consul's uniform.

10 November

The two Sparhawks go home by the *Roquelle*, they having sold the *D.N. Richards* for £275 to Jim Hemingway.[85] This schooner came over here on the 4th August after an attempt to reach Bonny. In anchoring off the mouth of that river she drove her anchors and went ashore on the Balour Bank, over which she bumped. A survey was held in her by two Spanish carpenters, Sparhawk being loud in his condemnation of her as unseaworthy. Willis, his brother-in-law, who was on board her, figured in her papers as owner of vessel and cargo. Sparhawk was with him (the vessel having been over at Bimbia) as his adviser in trading, I suppose, or as supercargo receiving a commission on the sales. The Spanish carpenters condemned the ship, not because she was unseaworthy,

---

[83]HMS *Dido* (1755 grt), a wooden corvette fitted with a screw propeller, was completed in 1871; *All the World's Fighting Ships, 1860-1905*, 48.

[84]The African Association was originally founded in 1843 with membership open to any partner in a firm of West Africa merchants. It was reorganised as a limited concern in 1889 and John Holt took a major interest in its affairs. See Davies, *The Trade Makers*, 94-95 and 425.

[85]SS *Roquelle* (1283 grt) was built by Randolph, Elder in 1869 for the British and African Steam Navigation Company and was sold in 1882. See the illustration on p. 127 of this volume.

as they only found that her false keel had been partially knocked off and her copper aft a little wrinkled--but because she could not be navigated without a new false keel, which they said could not with safety be put on her here. She was then put up to auction, the ship in one lot and the cargo in another, both lots being bought by Sparhawk in his son's (Bertram) name. Sparhawk was the auctioneer and bought her for his son for $1,060, and her cargo for $2,600. Some of the cargo has been landed at Sparhawk's factory at Bimbia, and a little sold here before she left this for Bonny, but directly she and her cargo was sold to Sparhawk, he had to go hunting about the town for buyers of his tobacco, and he opened a shop in Lynslager's old house to obtain a little cash, and by both means managed to obtain sufficient ready money to give Willis to enable him to pay off the captain and crew of the schooner, not without a good deal of trouble and after being summoned before the judge by them. The captain noted a strong protest against the whole of the proceedings, the matter having been taken out of his hands by Willis, who verbally undertook all the risk attendant thereon. After disposing of the crew, Willis acted for Sparhawk in reloading the schooner, and after considerable delay and expense she was towed over to Old Calabar by one of the African Steamship Co.'s steamers, for the sum of £50. They met with some opposition there, and had to dispose of the cargo by public auction. The supercargoes combined to prevent anyone but their own party being present and agreed amongst themselves not to bid against each other. The cargo, Willis assured me, cost him $14,000 in Boston. The part taken to Old Calabar fetched, I am told, £650. The ship sold for £275. The tobacco was sold to Jones at a sacrifice, and a hogshead sold to Vivour with other small things sold by retail may have brought in £250, total realized by Sparhawk £1,175. He bid £762 for them, and his expenses might have reached £50, so I reckon he has cleared about £360 by the transaction.

11 November

Captain Chapman, of the *Dido* a day or two ago when here, wrote me a letter on service stating that he had given orders to have the two Government lighters hauled up for repairs. This morning, on going to the Coal Beach with the intention of seeing about the shed to be built over them, I found them lying broadside on to the beach at high water mark. Fortunately, the sea has been very quiet the last few days, or I should have gone down there only to find them in pieces. I have since had them taken round to Bligh Beach and hauled up with my own people. I am sorry to observe so little zeal for the interests of the nation by those who are so well provided for at its expense. They, as a rule, slur over their work anyhow and care to do as little as possible. They are a most unmanageable set. The *Vindictive* was beached where she now rests, by the Commodore's own officers, and orders given me to put coal in her upper and lower decks. She, of course, being in a very leaky state when beached, goes as far into the water as the beach will allow her, heels over, and consequently about a hundred tons of coal on the lower decks is lost to the Government, as well as the vessel herself, which could have been sold at Lagos for £300, but the Commodore, thinking that too small took the trouble to tow her here, and then beached her in such a manner as to lose both her and the hundred tons of coal placed on board her. Then some of the captains presume to blame me, and the Government ask why coal was put on board when the ship was actually sinking, why she was put ashore to sink, and said it was a miscalculation on the part of those who beached her, and ordered coal to be placed into her. Had she been hauled as far up on the beach as she could have been put, instead of allowing her to have two feet of water under her bow at low water, the loss of coal would not have occurred, nor would it have been difficult to have pumped out the vessel.

Figure 11: John Holt, Wife and Eldest Daughter, December 1913.

Source: See Figure 1.

15 November

The *Maria* has returned from the Kroo Coast. I had almost given her up as lost, she having been twenty-two days from Bereby, an almost unparalleled passage I should think. Calms and head currents have been the cause of the delay. She brought me five canoes, four casks of Kroo rice, and forty-eight Krooboys.

24 November

I have been ordered both by Commodore Commerell, and Captain Chapman, to sell the *Vindictive* for the highest price obtainable, after notifying the latter that I did not expect to get more than £50 for her, if put up to auction, and being still requested to sell, after giving due notice of the sale to the Rivers, she was this day put up and knocked down to my own bid of £20. There were only Gazulla, Struthers, two Spanish officers, and myself present. There were only three bids, $10, $70, and mine of £20, or $100. I expected she would have gone higher than this, and almost feel ashamed to take her for the money. I was prepared to offer £50 at least. I shall see the Commodore or senior officer about it when he comes, but in the meantime intend to go on breaking her up.

28 November

My new store was finished to-day at 2 p.m. and we at once commenced moving the goods from Couper's store into it, finishing the removal on the 29th at sundown. The house is not yet ready, but I hope to be into the new premises altogether by the end of the year. I have been forced to build these premises on account of Couper having given me notice to quit, as in consequence of his having sold Longfield House to the Primitive Methodist mission, he required his own place to carry on his business. In the meantime, he occupies Harry Gardner's house at a rental of £50 per annum. I offered Couper £400 for his premises to prevent the trouble and expense of removing and building, but he considered that the offer, if accepted, amounted to buying him out of the trade and consequently declined it. I then purchased the premises where I am now building, from Gazulla, on behalf of Obon & Co., to whom it belonged, for £100. This was dear, but I could not help myself. It was the most suitable place to be had. The house on it had to be knocked down and the timber of it will be of little value, unless I can pick out a few planks for building kitchen &c. It was not worth £5. Therefore, I may be said to have paid my money for the land alone. I have raised the shop floor on low brick pillars. I expect the whole affair will cost about £600.

2 December

Little Frances Lynslager passed in the *Benin* to-day on her way to the United States under the care of Dr. Nassau, and his sister. She has grown greatly since as a baby almost when she could only just prattle, I used to nurse, play, and sing to her. She did not remember the appearance of the town. Did not come ashore, and it was only by accident that I knew she was on board. Poor little Frances, I feel sorry to see her leave us, perhaps for ever. It seems unnatural too, that she should be going amongst people who are strangers in blood to her. Mr. and Mrs. Walker are very fond of her, and she is going to them, but really they have no right to do what they are doing with her. It was I who recommended her grandmother Mrs. Lynslager, now Mrs. da Cunha, to send her to the American Missionaries in Gaboon to receive an education. It was I who sent her. She has been with them six or seven years I suppose, and things and people have changed since then. Mrs. Lynslager then thought of no one but her grandchildren, then she was well off and was her own master. Now she is under her husband's thumb, and her property is under his control. He is a young man, she an elderly woman. She has been much to blame, but now she is much to be pitied, and I know she will keenly grieve when she learns that Frances has passed within sight of her house, without even seeing her. Mr. Walker may be doing a good and Christian act in desiring to adopt Frances as his child, and in rearing and bringing her up in a good and virtuous way. If left here she would be too much in the way of corruption and vice to long resist their contaminating influences. But for all, I think they should have had the grandmother's permission to have taken this step, and at all events that permission should have been asked.

25 December

I had Bruce Walker staying with me for a few days before and after this day. Just after dinner we saw a steamer come into the harbour, and shortly afterwards received a letter from Captain Wharton, stating that his ship the *Macgregor Laird* had ben lost on a rock near Cape St. John. We at once went off to see him, when he told us that on the morning of the 13th, on his way to Small Elobey, he struck on a rock off Crown Point, Cape St. John, his vessel being under the charge of Captain Chanzy, who, he says, was acting as pilot. She filled with water soon after she struck, her stern being in four or five fathoms, and her bow nearly out of water altogether. After some time the natives boarded her and assisted his men to land passengers &c., at a town near the point. They afterwards boarded her in numbers, and pillaged her from stem to stern, the Captain being either unable afraid, or unwilling to keep them off by force. His reason, he says, for not doing so, was because he had only twenty rounds of ammunition. He and his men were gradually driven from the officers' quarters forward under the forecastle, and at last he called together two of the white traders at Elobey, Bremman and Downey, to put a value on the ship. They valued her at £500 and on that valuation, he sold her to them for that amount. The plate, boats &c., were taken to Elobey, and sold by public auction at good prices. When Bremman and Downey bought the ship they sat on the fore hatch all day, and were able to keep the natives off, they having plenty of plunder to dive for aft. During the night they got off some thirty dry bales of cloth, out of the fore-hold, which they reckon will more than repay them what they paid for her. As the natives were taking everything they could get, the purchasers gave permission to my man there, and to others, to help themselves to anything they could get. Hill, and John Scott, saved a good deal, but that saved by Hill was principally stores, which were soon eaten up and indiscriminately given and squandered away. Property easily obtained is lightly valued. He bought one of the lifeboats, and with the *Macgregor Laird*'s crew saved a lot of stores which they afterwards helped to consume. I don't think Wharton did all he could have done to save the cargo. With eighty men on board he could, with sticks, have kept off the whole of the natives of that part of the Coast. But he appears to have been afraid of them, and the white men at Elobey were doubtless afraid or undesirous of advising him, if they had an opportunity of doing it. A boat was despatched to Gaboon for assistance, but when the French man-of-war arrived, the natives had taken all that was worth taking, and she did nothing more than bring the crew here. During their stay on Small Elobey some palaver between the Kroomen of the ship and the natives arose, and the former ran to the Master and officers for protection. the natives fired into them indiscriminately, killed one Krooman, wounded several others, and wounded the doctor and assistant purser. I had some six or seven of them staying in my house, two were with Harry Gardner, the Krooboys ashore, and the white crew on board the pontoon *Alcedo* until the arrival of the *Calabar* from the Rivers, when they all went on to the Consul at Bonny. Wharton reported to the Governor in writing what had happened, and I sent a copy of his letter to the Consul and Commodore.

1872

2 January

I ought to have commenced a new book with the new year, but I have not got one. Captain Hopkins, H.B.M. Acting Consul, arrived on the *Volta*. H.M.S. *Bittern* also arrived shortly afterwards.[86] Hopkins has come down to catch the *Bittern* for the purpose of proceeding to Elobey in order to obtain satisfaction for the outrages committed by the natives of that place, and of Corsico, on the crew of the *Macgregor Laird*.[87] I accompanied him and Captain A. St. Clair when they called on the Governor, and interpreted for them. They demanded satisfaction of him as Governor of possessions owned by his country, the inhabitants of which had wantonly plundered an English vessel in distress and afterwards fired on her crew. The outrage on Walker, the killing of his cooper, the continued insults, violence, and outrages committed on English subjects visiting and resident on Small Elobey were also brought before him, and the punishment of the offenders demanded. He said that the gunboat had gone to make enquiries, and he could say or do nothing until her return. We told him that enquiries were not sufficient, we wanted redress. After a good deal of shuffling we got an order to the Commander of the gunboat stating our object, requesting him to obtain redress, and whilst opposing active or hostile measures being taken, required him to bring the offenders to him for punishment. Having been invited to accompany the Acting Consul, I went on board the *Bittern* on the 3rd, and we left on the evening of that day for Elobey. I took the liberty of letting her have thirty-eight tons of patent fuel belonging to the African Steamship Co. as the Government Depot is without coal. I suppose the Directors won't object to this, seeing that it is about their vessel and people that we are going. On the 5th we arrived off Cape St. John, and boarded the wreck. She is on a rock about a mile N.W. of Crown Point. The chart is not far (if anything) out. Captain Wharton was decidedly too near the land to be safe. I'm afraid he will lose his certificate. The water washes over her poop at high water, and all her starboard deck as far as a little abaft the main hatch is under water. Her port deck, and the engines, are at all times clear. Her bow, of course, is far out of water. From the stern to the after hatch we found about four fathoms at low water, the soundings gradually lessening to six feet under the bows. The rock on the port bow dries well at low water. Everything of any value that can readily be got has been taken out of her, but her masts and spars are all standing and her anchor and chains are untouched. I saw a few shooks and empty casks floating about, and a great deal of spoiled powder, of which she smelt strongly, and by which she was covered with a coat of black from stem to stern. The decks had been burnt and cut open in many places, and

[86]HMS *Bittern* (755 grt) was a wooden gun vessel constructed at the Pembroke Dockyard in 1871; *All the World's Fighting Ships, 1860-1905*, 109.

[87]See fn. 59.

all the cabin and officers' partitions demolished. Even the forecastle was knocked down. We then went to Small Elobey where we anchored. We found the gunboat *Ligera* there, her Commander apparently waiting the day fixed for his departure. During his stay he had done nothing, had scarcely spoken a word to or seen anyone. We delivered the Governor's letter and told him what we had come for. We arranged to leave together for Corisco, stating that we should be glad to co-operate with him in obtaining satisfaction. We then went to have a look at the factories. I stopped at my own and was regaled by Mr. Hill with several different wines, taken out of the *Macgregor Laird*. He tells me that trade has been stopped since the wreck took place, several of the natives have been drowned in her, a good deal of fighting had ensued and one man was found with his throat cut, lying on the beach. They are thinking of nothing but the plunder, and making themselves drunk. Trade is likely to be injured for some time to come. I have told Hill to buy the plunder if he can do so, cheap. They must have a lot of valuable property in their hands of no use whatever to them, and of the value of which they will be altogether ignorant. Hill gave me a meerschaum pipe, one out of a number found in a case of fancy goods. He had a lot of stores but has eaten, "dashed," and squandered them away. Seven barrels of ale alone, he has gone through. On returning to *Bittern* we found that the First Lieutenant had given chase to a canoe and captured her with three men and three women, the women being the wives of Corisco men. We kept them. the men we let go, as they were bushmen. We then, by permission of the Spaniards, dropped a few shells into Big Elobey, just to let them see that we could reach them, and perhaps to drive some of them out of it, but we were mistaken, for although we sent out boats round to the back of the island, they saw no boats attempting to escape. The natives fired on our boats and got their fire returned. We steamed round the banks, Parkinson piloting, and were followed by the Spaniards. Night coming on, and the boats not being in sight, we steamed towards the south side of Elobey, and anchored there for the night. We saw the firing quite distinctly. Boats came off at 8 p.m. and at midnight were sent away again to try and catch some more hostages. The First Lieutenant brought off one canoe and six men. He had fired at them, to make them stop, but the more he fired, the more they paddled. One shot struck the steersman behind the left ribs, and going along one of them, lodged in the left breast. Our doctor extracted the ball, bandaged him up, and sent him away in the canoe with one of his comrades to paddle him ashore. I expect the fellow was never so surprised in his life. Within a couple of hours he had been chased, caught, fired at and hit, the ball cut out of his body and shown to him, a prisoner on board a man-of-war, and then free and among his people again. Certainly so many important incidents never crowded into two short hours of that man's life before. I hope he will recover. I think so. As soon as these men were went away we up anchor and steamed to Corisco. Boats were sent by both ships to keep guard between the Island and mainland in order to prevent anyone escaping during the night. It having been reported that a large boat was on the beach apparently ready for us, orders were given to one of our boats to bring her off. On nearing the beach the boat was fired into, by the natives, and the fire was returned by her and a Spanish boat in company with her. The next morning the boat was sent off in charge of three or four sailors. Kemble, the First Lieutenant, having learnt that one of our boats had been fired on during the night, himself landed the following morning, and ordered the other boats to do the same. The Spaniards following, they marched up to the town, which belonged to Koomba, and burnt it down; leaving it burning they proceeded from town to town, burning each in succession, until they reached the ones opposite the ships. Eight or nine villages were thus destroyed besides all the boats and canoes met with on the beach. the boats brought off a few fowls, ducks, and sheep, and some plunder out of the *Macgregor Laird*, but the natives had taken the precaution to move most of their property out of harm's way, as they moved themselves when they saw it dangerous to remain. The Spaniards were rather hard up for chop, and so paid more attention to foraging than our men. They took some half dozen dead goats to keep on board. The Consul had sent John Scott ashore to the principal town the previous day, with a letter and message to the Headmen, stating our object in visiting them, requesting delivery of those concerned in the murder of the *Macgregor Laird*'s Krooman, and of Walker's cooper, particularly of the Chief Koomba, who was said to be the root and origin of these, and most of the other outrages committed. They replied that Koomba was reported to have left the Island but that they would try to find him the following day and let us hear from them. Next day John Scott was again sent ashore, a letter having previously been sent to the Consul by the native missionary Ibia, in the name of the Chiefs, asking for more time. Consul replied that he required ten hostages for Koomba's appearance, and should move the ship up to a position opposite their town with a view to enforcing his demands, if not complied with by 12 o'clock the following day. On the morning of that day, the missionary accompanied by one Chief and two of his people who had summoned up resolution to come off to the ship, arrived on board to see the Consul. They stated that they were unable for want of power, to get hostages for Koomba, but that the Chief had brought two of his men for that purpose, that Koomba had been at the beach and promised to come off, but at the last moment had refused to come. Consul told the chief that on account of his having brought two hostages, he would spare his town, but that he must have Koomba. They offered to go back and endeavour to get him to come off, if he would wait. He gave them until one o'clock. the boats were got ready before the hour, expecting to have to destroy most of the other towns, but a white flag on the beach announced that we had obtained the man we wanted, who shortly afterwards arrived alongside and was put in irons. One of the hostages was detained, as he had been recognized by Scott as the person who took the books out of the German factory, the other one, and the three women were set at liberty. It was arranged that the Chiefs were to meet us at Elobey the next day. The sailors were ill-pleased that they could not continue their burning amusement and regretted having left it so soon on the previous occasion. We informed the Spaniards of what we had arranged and accomplished, and left for Elobey, where we arrived the same night. Next morning two boats were sent to Big Elobey to pay them for having fired on our boats, and they did not return until they had burnt every house on the Island. They met with no natives, but found traces which proved they were about. In some places holes were half dug, in which they had intended to bury their property for safety. One or two explosions occurred in the towns, but no one was hurt. A good deal of property was destroyed here in houses, boats, canoes, and the wrecked plunder. Several casks of rum were found, and smashed to pieces. the boats brought a lot of plunder off with them, but nothing of any value. The same day Walker's Kroomen pulled down all the native houses on Small Elobey. On the following day a meeting of the white men was called on board, and a few words of reproval, counsel, and advice given to them by Hopkins. After hearing the charges against Koomba and the other prisoner, who were present, it was decided to take them down to Fernando Po and deliver them to the Governor. Koomba offered $500 for his release, which was not accepted. The Chiefs of Corisco having come on board, the

Consul gave them a sound rating for their past behaviour, told them what he had decided to do with the two prisoners, requested them to obtain the four people who actually fired on the Krooman and cooper, informing them that the four hostages would be handed to the Spaniards' gunboat and kept until they were produced, imposed a fine of $1,000 to be paid the Spaniards, and $40 to my factory for having taken my books, and ordering them not to build again on Small Elobey. The Spanish Captain was also informed of this, in which he acquiesced. The Consul then wrote a formal letter embodying all he had said to them, threatening to come again if more outrages were committed, and remove the whole of the factories away. This letter was signed by the Spanish officer, Commander A. St. Clair, and the Acting Consul. On the following day (13th) we left Elobey and steaming down to the wreck, took about eight tons of coal out of her. At the same time two boats were sent ashore to destroy the town on Crown Point, opposite the wreck. This was done, the Mission House excepted here, as on Corisco, from the general conflagration. We left that night, and touching at Benito arrived at Fernando Po on the 15th January, 1872. The Coriscos have had a lesson, which I think will do them good. Walker was afraid to leave his cargo on the beach and had it taken off to his hulk along with all his people. But I think he need not fear. I have left mine.

End of *The Diary of John Holt*

Memorandum of Sundry Occurrences During a Passage from Liverpool to Fernando Po in the Schooner *Maria* of Liverpool, and Whilst Trading on the West African Coast

1869

10 February

Having the past two days been ready for sea, and anxiously wishing the weather to moderate, resolved to go out to-day, blow high or low, and for this purpose hauled away in the morning to the Pier Head. About three the pilot came down and said it was blowing a fresh gale at Holyhead. The telegraph gave news of a hurricane at Brest and the mouth of the Channel, and the gents of the Meteorological Society prognosticated it would reach all the ports in a few hours, and as a warning the drum was hoisted. The Dock Master, Mr. Palmer, advised me to wait a day, remarking that he would not like to hear of us receiving damage after the particular care he had taken of us whilst under his authority. I must say he took a great interest in the welfare of our craft, not allowing any other craft to come near us or even make fast to us. In fact all the people belonging to the Queens Dock I found particularly obliging, I suppose from his orders.

At 3 p.m. hauled out of the dock and under canvas went into the river, just high water and nearly calm. A great many people were down to see us out and a great many different opinions were expressed as to our seaworthiness; some would like to go whilst others said she would never get out. The general opinion was we ought to remain a few days longer till the weather was settled. Even the underwriters mentioned that we ought not to go with a westerly wind; yet it is more satisfactory to go when ready, even should you have, through stress of weather, to return. I thought we should manage to fetch Holyhead where I could at any time get in, if necessary.

Proceeded down the river in charge of Mr. Evans, the pilot. Fresh breeze right up. This was the first time I had an opportunity of testing her sailing qualities against those of one of the pilot schooners--No. 4--beating him under the same canvas about four miles between the dock and the bell buoy.

7.30 p.m. The pilot left after wishing us a pleasant passage. Wind W.N.W. fresh breeze, hauled two reefs down in the mainsail and set the watch.

12.30 p.m. Very dirty appearance with drizzling rain, tack'd several times during the night.

11 February

Surprised at daylight to find Holyhead bearing W.S.W. on the lee bow, wind N.W. by W., stiff breeze, shook out reefs. I found afterwards I had done this too early there being a very nasty head sea. She dived completely under and washed us throughout. During the day the wind became light and weather hazy.

12 February

Wind on the quarter very light. Tuskar light bearing S.W. by W. about 12 miles. The binnacle light would not burn. Having sent a hand to trim it several times I resolved to see what was wrong and for this purpose I took it into the cabin. Upon getting into the steerage I pulled off the knob of the cabin door, consequently could not get in. During the time I was looking for a something to open it the passenger--R. P. Fowler--came out. I asked him if he opened the door. He replied yes (rather slowly). I had just placed the lamp upon the table when I heard a splash with an exclamation from the man at the wheel (a black man) "My Lord hab marcy pon me."[88] Before this was finished I was on deck just in time to see a ripple, I caught the end of the main sheet and threw it over the side, yet he was unable to catch it. He evidently could not swim as he never made a second appearance, neither did he make the slightest noise. The carpenter, hearing the cry "man overboard" was pretty smart at throwing over plenty of wood. Altho' the main sheet was off she came round like a whip top--lowered the peak and she came round over the same place in a few minutes, yet we could not see or hear any noise. I remained hove to till 4 a.m. although I knew it was useless, it being very smooth and moonlight. Had he been above water we should never have lost sight of him. At this time, the wind freshening, I made sail to the westward, putting all the proceedings in the official log. Lost sight of the Tuskar about 8 a.m. bearing N.N.E., wind westerly, rather shy, throughout the day.

21 February

Light winds rather shy. Several vessels in sight all of which we passed. Towards the evening freshened a little, coming a little free, sea rising.

22 February

Fresh breeze W.N.W. nasty head sea which made us pitch a great deal. One of the seamen "Solomon" laid up, "belly hurt him," a Krooboy complaint, what I termed the "channel fever," it being rather cold and he having little or no clothes to cover himself.

23 February

Strong breeze N.W. hauled two reefs in the mainsail--the sick man turned to, asking me for an old coat, should I have one to spare he would purchase; taking pity upon him being a negro in high latitudes I gave him one.

---

[88]For John Holt's reaction to Fowler's death, see *Diary*, 97.

24 February

Strong wind from N.W. nasty sea which at times tumbled on board rather heavy and made me feel fidgety about my two boats. The sea being abeam it rolled over more amidships: to avoid this I kept her away a point, bringing it more astern, after which she went tolerably easy. Yet at times I had to tell the man at the helm to look out for a stray one I expected to poop us. It is a common saying that yachts will not run in a breeze. Certainly they will be drier and more comfortable hove to, yet I have found this vessel thus far to run, I think as long as any other craft of her dimensions. My idea is that with carrying a press of canvas the sea loses all power and should one or two come over the stern, it appears to be spent. Lat. 44.13 Long 15.29 W.

25 February

Wind pretty fresh with a heavy sea. A sea came over the poop, causing the vessel to lurch and take over "Sambo" who was looking over to leeward. Not wishing to part so sudden I put the helm down when, as usual, she came round with all sheets off. In a few minutes we had him on board again, hoping he will not continue these practices or at sometime I may be compelled to leave him. Lat. 41.41 N. Long. 14.50 W.

26 February

Wind northerly, strong breeze. Hove the log during the dog watch for the first time when she took it all off, the reel being marked not further than nine knots. Should she continue at this we shall have to get it lengthened altho' I anticipated we should not want it so long.

27 February

Fresh breeze northerly. Nasty sea. Nothing occurred worthy of note. Several vessels in sight all of which we seem to pass. Lat. 39.3 N. Long. 15.29 W.

28 February

Fresh breeze N.W. nasty sea. Weather very gloomy. Barometer very high. Nothing interesting.

1 March

Wind veered to the eastward still blowing fresh. A ship named *Peter Penney* of London in good trim, with passengers, passed us this morning. Still in sight so that as soon as the carpenter finishes the boom I anticipate returning the compliment by setting the squaresail. Yet should the wind freshen he will no doubt overpower us.
6 p.m. Set the squaresail. Wind less.

2 March

The *Peter Penney* this morning is again on our quarter, thanks to the *Grey Mare* which, tho' light, draws with a breeze. This is the first fellow that has annoyed me and hope the last. I do not fear him troubling us again this passage--when passing us he hauled up close to, yet when it was my turn he sheered away to windward.

3 March

About 4 a.m. the wind died away completely after having a strong breeze; lowered down the mainsail. We had a very heavy sea which struck her very hard under the counter, shaking her throughout. A continuation of this kind of weather would certainly knock off her stern. I tried the pumps and imagine she made a little more water, tho' not much. This lasted about two hours, when a light breeze sprang up and gave her headway. During the calm some of the seas came right over the taffrail, filling the cockpit and partly the cabin. During the day the wind freshened. At some times I put her rate at 11 knots.

4 March

Fresh breeze from N.E. I expect the commencement of the Trades--at least I hope so. If this be them we are likely to make a pretty good passage to Cape Palmas. Spoke a schooner, who promised to report us upon arrival in England. Both of us being smart vessels we had not much time to "parlez vous," yet to make sure of his understanding the chief object, I chalked our name on a board, wishing him a stiff breeze in his jib.

5 March

Wind very light with heavy sea. Lowered down the mainsail to prevent chafe, being desirous that this sail shall not receive any more wear and tear than I can possibly help, as it is not likely I shall ever have another half so good, or as well cut. 'Tis certainly large, tho' small enough for this kind of weather. I sent up the square topsail this morning which, with light winds, is a first rate sail. The gaff topsails too, are fine light weather sails, yet very unhandy with such yards, the yard of the main one being 26 feet long--no trifle to take in a breeze with sea in proportion, it nearly takes charge.

Lat. 22° Long. 19° 58' W. Opened the after hatch and took out several things now wanted, such as chalk, rope. I found the vinegar cask had leaked upon the hoop iron, and rusted it considerably. I noticed too, several leaks in the deck, altho' I was very particular in having them caulked in some places twice. Put the lost passenger's luggage down, his chest not being opened, I have not seen the contents to take any inventory, but put it away thus.

6 March

Light winds from N.N.E. If these be the Trades they are very light--rather too much so. I sincerely hope they will not continue long at this. I do not want too much, neither do I care for it calm, yet this is too good--makes every one feel too lazy. The other seaman is laid up to-day with the old complaint "belly run"--"No can work, sar." This leaves in my watch, to steer, me and myself--rather too much of a joke to steer four hours at once. I'll soon have him cured.

Fitted to-day new topping-lifts, the old ones being completely done up, and not safe to hang the boom which, should it come down, would spoil the appearance of our skylight, as well as other fixings. The old ones are to go for square topsail halyards the first opportunity.

Saw a large turtle, yet not having a boat handy we could not make any attempt to catch him, and perhaps spared some extra trouble for nothing.

Harpooned a porpoise, yet did not succeed in getting him on board, the harpoon drawing. In sending down the old lifts the sheave and pin was lost overboard. I've promised the fellow it shall be put down to his book, which may have the effect of making him more careful.

Wind freshening towards evening. Lat. at noon 20° 44' N. Long. 19° 54' W.

7 March

This being the third Sunday at sea. Wind a little fresher than yesterday tho' very light north east Trades, much lighter than I anticipated. I have been through them several times but have never known them as light as now. To windward about 8 miles is a barque steering south. I suppose a coast of Guinea trader. He is like the other unfortunates we have met with. Dropping astern I would edge up and speak him if I could, yet the moment he sees I wish to be near him he will luff, so that I may not be able to make him out. Consequently, I will let him go in peace.

The sun has been exceedingly hot to-day--I imagine hotter than I've felt it before. I put this down to the fine run we have had; fourteen days ago, the wind northerly, it was the reverse. Lat. 18° 30' N. Long. 19° 55' W.

8 March

The Trades to-day are very light. Have had the mainsail down most of the day. Towards the evening it begins to freshen. Have seen during the day a quantity of seaweed in patches, similar to the gulfweed. I tried to catch some yet did not succeed. The mate is bothered with a bad thumb. I hope it will soon be all right as he is the only sailor that is on board, and the one that will be most missed. The A.B. Solomon was unable to get up to the main topmasthead to reeve gafftopsail halyards, had to send up the other, promised to give him a Paddy's rise. Lat. 16° 30' N. Long. 19° 55' W.

9 March

Wind fresher and further to the westward, ship at eight bells. Nothing interesting. Lat. 14° 37' N. Long. 19° 53' W.

10 March

Wind freshening from N.N.E. Fell in with a quantity of flying fish. The A.B. complained of having the scurvy 20 days out, and had fresh provisions most of the time.

What would become of him should we have a four months' passage? I don't wonder at him being sick, he is so confoundedly lazy. I don't think he has been washed since leaving Liverpool; afraid, I suppose, of the water running short. Busy making ridge-ropes for the poop. Lat. 12° 17' N. Long. 19° 47' W.

11 March

Fresh breeze this morning--something what I expected of the Trades, putting us along about 8 knots, falling light towards the evening, to revive shortly I hope. I anticipate Cape Palmas on Tuesday and if we meet this anticipation it will be what may be termed a tolerable good passage. Employed about the head gear. Carpenter puttying decks &c. Gave the usual allowance of medicines. I don't know what I should do if I were in a large ship with regard to the medicine. There are only three coloured fellows on board and they take me one half of my time weighing out medicine. One complains of rheumatism, another--scurvy, the other--"belly run." They undoubtedly must have mistook the *Maria* for the *Dreadnought*, or some other floating hospital. They have certainly made a mistake in coming here to be sick at leisure. Off work, I put them on low diet which soon has the effect of bringing them to their bearings. Lat. 10° 3' N. Long. 18° 42' W. Distance run: 160 miles.

12 March

Wind very light. Nasty sea, causing the sails to chafe and knock about. Carpenter busy with the putty. Self employed with man-ropes, covers for sundries. Wind freshening towards evening. Black clouds rising to the eastward, bringing to mind I am again advancing towards those tornadoes, some of which we shall no doubt feel before we reach Fernando Po. Attended to the sick as usual. Lat. 7° 47' N. Long. 17° 52' W.

13 March

Wind fresher. Smart breeze carries a white feather for'ard. Falls light towards evening. Set the balloon jib to see what it is like. Expected to find it larger. Busy with the skylight. Carpenter at the putty. Found some of the bread mouldy and put it in casks. Lat. 6° 7' N. Long. 16° 29' W. S.S.E.

14 March

This the fourth Sunday out. I did not anticipate being this far to-day, three weeks back. I hope we may be able to keep it up without much detention on the Kroo Coast &c. To-day I would like to be as near Fernando Po as we now are Cape Palmas, yet I'm afraid we shall be short of this. I am wondering where Kirkwood's vessel is, and if she be ahead. I rather think I am not much astern as we have had light winds and I think in this kind of weather we shall be more than a match for him, being I think, able to spread much more canvas than he; fortunately we sent our flying kites up before we crossed the Bay, from that time they have not been down. The squaresail has been aloft seventeen days without touching, such a spell as I did not imagine. The wind is fresher with a nasty sea, which does not agree with the mainsail being continually upon the move, and for which I cannot get much sleep. Lat. 5° 11' N. Long. 14° 57' W.

15 March

By way of commencing the week it began with a tornado, causing us to reduce our canvas considerably, and the vessel to skelter. Pretty well moderated towards 8 a.m. Light airs S.W. till noon, since which time it has been a completely dead calm, the helm moored, and all sails furled. Found out at 4 p.m. the chronometer had run down on account of my neglecting to wind up yesterday. We are certainly not far from the land or this would be a serious annoyance. Very hot and sultry. Very light wind. Nasty sea. All sails furled. I don't ever remember being at sea in this manner before, generally something set--yet everything is one the move to chafe.

17 March

Saw at daylight a sail on the port bow, hull down, wind very light from S.W. Just enough to steer. Came up with him about noon. Found him to be a Frenchman--three masted schooner *Sylvius*, Marseilles, bound to the Congo, 38 days from Havre. He admired our vessel and spoke of her sailing qualities being pretty good and having gained upon him eight miles in six hours, and our vessel would never go more than two knots. He gave me his time also--Longitude 13° 48' W. from Paris. At 6 p.m. we could only just discern him on the weather quarter.

18 March

This makes the 28th day since our departure. I anticipated a wider distance this day. If this kind of weather holds there's no likelihood of our getting much further, yet this infernal weather is worse than the Channel. A squall or tornado every 12 hours, afterwards a dead calm. The sails are up and down like signals. As for the weather, I don't think I ever felt it hotter than to-day. I would like for it either to dry up altogether, or blow, not in this manner. Lat. 11° 39' N. Heavy swell from S.S.W.

19 March

Light breeze from N.N.W. Should it keep this I have slight hopes of now getting in with the land, tho' squalls are continually threatening and if they step in the breeze goes at once. Heavy swell from S.W.

20 March

Hove to 4 a.m. having on the port bow a light which I took for Cape Palmas not any other being on the chart. At daylight hauled in to the eastward and found it to be sixty miles to windward of, yet true to, our reckoning. Bore up for the eastward about mid-day. Wind very light. This makes from the Tuskar to the Kroo Coast twenty-seven days. I hope we shall keep it up to our port.

KROO COAST[89]

21 March

We were visited this morning by about one hundred canoes of Grand Botou--who appeared to be very anxious that I should drop anchor at "we place." I was sure to get everything I wanted. At first the spokesman denied having a canoe large enough to hold my cask. Afterwards, when he found this was what I could not do without, he suddenly said "I been forgot one boat he live dere, savvy take two punch." Having heard of these infernal liars and rogues I put not the slightest confidence in what they said. I agreed to lay anchor at Sass Town if he would send canoe for beach to bring Kroo boy, which was done. I found I could not get water at either of these places unless I had a boat to carry it off, which I have not. Consequently will have to trust to places to leeward. I engaged (or at least attempted to do so) 18 boys from Botou, yet upon my wanting to put them below after giving them advance, they objected to it, saying it was too hot. They had nearly got off with one boy's pay. Had it not been on the look out for something of this sort and wanted them to remain on deck, they would no doubt have cleared out. Upon my refusal to let them remain on deck they jumped overboard and left with a blessing, although none of them got a drop of grog. After this I took six boys from Sass Town. I also saw Tom Peter, one of the lot of Kroo boys I had at Fernando Po. He told me that Moses and all the other boys had gone to sea yesterday. He also told me Kirkwood's schooner had been at Botou and had left the day previous with sixteen boys. I wanted him to come, yet he pleaded sickness. Left for Rock Town 4 p.m.

Upon the boys coming on board this morning, "Sambo" took fits for about two hours, after which he died. Whether it was from the effects of something they may have given him, or from the heat, I can't say.

22 March

Hove to off Cape Palmas. Wind very light. At daylight calm. Found we were drifting to leeward. Being now off Cavally and still calm I anticipated a strong current and hove to early, yet not being able to see the light on Cape Palmas I did not expect we were so far down. I anchored off Cavally about 4 p.m. the sea breeze having just set in about 5 p.m. canoes came off I sent ashore for "big canoe" which, upon arrival, we found too small for our casks. I got them to fill four of my beakers, promising to come early in the morning with big canoe, when I will try to empty the cooper's stores to enable us to get it sooner. I am afraid we shall be at a loss for water and think it would have been better to have gone to Cape Palmas, at which place I could have procured a boat at once, and although this would have incurred extra expense otherwise, it will amount to the same in the end. To-day makes three days on the Coast with only six boys. Had I plenty of water I no doubt would have had thirty from Sass Town and Botou. A French barque dropped anchor about two hours after us. I suppose he wants boys too and will, I dare say, give more advance than myself, which will at once put me in the shade. Although

---

[89]For John Holt's views on the Kroomen, see *Diary*, 24-25 and 75-76.

I tell them "I go river" they appear to be doubtful as to the truth of this. Particularly want to know the name of the firm which I tell them is a new one. They no savvy.

23 March

Canoe came off at 8 a.m. with water, yet would not return without knowing how much I go pay; to get them off I gave them rum and tobacco. They can see I am hard up for water so will try to put the price up.

I got four more canoes with water, which took till three p.m., when, seeing they began to tire, I hove up anchor. They at first told me "plenty of boy live for beach" yet would not come off till I had paid for the water, and if I paid good plenty of boys come. I gave them 3 gallons rum, 1 jar, 36 hhd. tobacco, 2 bar soap, 2 bunches beads, I piece beef. This they grumbled at and refused to take, saying they would not take anything rather than this. With a good deal of palaver they departed, but said no boys fit come. I proceeced down to Tabou Point when, falling calm, brought up in 10 fathoms water.

8 p.m. A steamer passed during the afternoon--I suppose the *Roquelle* appearing similar to what the *Bonny* is. Showed the burgee, and he dipped his ensign as he passed. I anticipate from this he got my name, and should he arrive in Fernando Po will report me.

24 March

Anchored off Tabou River, at which place we were visited with several canoes. From here I took nine boys. At 10 a.m. hove up and proceeded to Grand Tabou. The big man Tom Liverpool came off and gave me six more boys. I had a great deal of palaver with this fellow about the rum, some of the boys having seen water passed into the cabin. All day I have been continually palavering. Anchored at Half Bereby at 8 p.m.

Some canoes came off early this morning, yet none large enough for buying. Palavering with the King who promised to fetch canoe, suppose I give him rum. I did this, at the same time thinking this was only a draw; in fact I don't put confidence in any word they say. However, one came at 9 a.m.; another half hour palaver for put anchor, which I refused, having weighed to meet the canoe. From 9 until 3 p.m. we were palavering for this canoe. I don't think they wanted to sell it. However, I did not like to see it pass, so I paid their price, rather than lose it. I consider it very dear, yet as I stopped for canoes I don't like to go from them for fear I may not be able to pick up any further to leeward. Anchored at Tabou at 5 p.m. close to the beach. Had several canoes off at once, and before dark bought another canoe, smaller than last. I certainly don't know where to put her now I have got her, but I will try on deck to-morrow. Have faithful promises for to-morrow for canoe.

ADVANCE PAID KROOMEN ex *Maria*.

Sass. Town	Bars of Soap	Gallons of Rum	Empty Jars	Romalls	Heads of Tobacco
Angry	2	1	1	-	8
Friday	2	1	1	-	8
Boy George	2	1	1	-	8
Davis	3	1	1	-	0
Black Will	2	1	1	-	8
Tarpot	1	1	1	-	-
Tabou					
Jack Liverpool	1	1	1	2	6
Black Will	1	1	1	2	6
Tabou					
Tom	1	-	-	2	6
Davis	1	1	1	2	6
Tom Brown	"	1	1	2	6
Tom Pearce	"	1	1	2	6
Jack Never-fear	1	1	1	2	6
Black Will	1	1	1	2	6
Spy-Glass (Head Man)	1	1	1	3	6
Gang-Tabou					
Yellow Will	1	1	1	1	12
Spy Glass	1	1	2	1	12
Tom Peter	1	1	2	1	12
Pea Soup	1	1	2	1	12
Rope Yarn	1	1	2	1	12
Liverpool	1	1	2	2	6
Bereby					
John & Ben	4	2	"	2	12

Paid at Half Bereby for one Canoe "Big"							
					£	s.	d.
1 c/s Guns at 6/6	...	...	...	...	6	10	0
10 Romalls (scarves)	...	...	...	...		15	10
3 Iron Pots--3 gals	...	...	...	...		2	6
3 Jars--2 gal., 1 gal., 1 gal.	...	...	...	...		2	0
1 Box Soap	...	...	...	...		9	0
10 heads Tobacco	...	...	...	...		1	6
5 Gallons Rum	...	...	...	...		10	0
					£8	10	10

Paid at Tabou for Canoe No. 2							
					£	s.	d.
5 Guns at 6/6	...	...	...	...	1	12	6
4 Romalls at 1/7	...	...	...	...		6	4
5 Matchets	...	...	...	...		2	1
2 Iron Pots--3 gallon	...	...	...	...		2	6
10 Bars Soap	...	...	...	...		4	6
100 Pipes	...	...	...	...			9
28 Heads Tobacco	...	...	...	...		3	6
4 Gallons Rum	...	...	...	...		8	0
					£3	0	2

Dashes.		Rum	Romall	Pipes	Tobacco
1st		Gln.			
Canoe	...	1	–	5	6
2nd					
Canoe	...	½	–	4	2
		1	–	20	6

Ship Victuals.	Tobacco	Rum	Pipes	Romalls	Soap
Water and Stores	14	1	70	4	
Plantains ...	10	½	24	"	
1 Goat	3	–	20	1	2

26 March

Tail end of a tornado visited us during the night which caused our vessel to roll very much--so much that no one could lay with ease. We had canoes off early telling any quantity of lies about big canoes coming off if I would only wait. I not being ready, having the canoe to take on board, consented to wait, altho' I could see that no other canoes were coming. They kept pressing me to lend them glass to look, but having heard of several of these valuable articles being missed I carefully carried mine in the case. The people who sold me the canoe last night took away, in mistake for something of more value, the carpenter's hammer and cook's axe. I have had a great palaver about it this morning and raised this excuse to ward off the sundry "dashes". Seeing nothing more for sale I hove up at 12 a.m. when a small canoe came off saying, as I had not any powder, the party who owned the "big canoe" would not sell it but, having two, had sent this small one, and the price was 2 guns and 1 gallon rum. By the way he talked I could see he did not want to sell it, and when I offered what he asked he made an excuse that it was 3 guns. However, I made him stick to his price and took the canoe from him. He palavered a great deal about the guns being unfit and the rum watered, and persisted in having back the canoe which, by this time, was inside the other one on deck. It certainly does not take any room for freight a/c, yet it is not a cheap canoe, having paid $11, and it will not carry any casks--merely a message canoe.

Whilst off Half Bereby two of the boys I engaged at Tabou got into a canoe and started for the beach. I had the carpenter and an A.B. keeping watch over the boys as I anticipated something of this sort. I seeing the canoe crop the bow, called. Receiving no answer I jumped into the cabin for the revolver, but when I got on deck they were out of range, the King being on board sent two of his "big men" who caught them and brought them back, giving fits to three fellows who were in the canoe with them. Paid for small Canoe--

					£	s.	d.
2 Fuzees 6/6d.	...	...	...	...		13	0
1 Gallon rum...	...	...	...	...		2	0
6Hhd. tobacco	...	...	...	...		1	0
						16	0

KROO COAST

27 March

Wind very light and current to the westward. Drifted off Half Bereby where a canoe came off, expecting we had some boys from sea. I made up to proceed to Fernando Po. Having spent 7 days on this coast I have not got the quantity of boys I would like, yet I don't think I shall be able to get more to leeward. They all seem to be under the impression I am for Townsend.

28 March

Light airs from S.W. Ship making little or no headway. Lahou right abeam. Current still to the westward. Gave to the boys rum and beef. Took the bread out of the locker; it having got damp and mouldy I spread it in the sun to dry. The temperature is 89.20 which with no wind makes it boiling hot.

29 March

Light winds from south. Commenced the painting and scraping. Nothing remarkable or worthy of note.

30 March

Light winds from south. Since towing the canoe our vessel appears to have lost all her smartness. Even when we have a smart breeze she does not appear to go through the water as before. The canoe I should say by the look of the water stops us 1½ knots.

31 March

Smart breeze making about 5 knots. Ship appears quite dead. Saw Cape Three Points abeam at 8 a.m. Busy painting.

1 April

Commenced All Fools' day by the capsizing of the canoe, after which the man at the helm let her come up in the wind bringing the canoe alongside, which exasperated me so much that I could not refrain from ropes-ending him.

2 April

Fresh breeze with little rain. Distance from Fernando Po 330 miles.

4 April

Fernando Po in sight distance 90 miles. Fine weather. Wind light.

6 April

Heavy tornado off Cape Bullen. No sea breeze. Got out the boats and commenced towing ahead. 6 p.m. Towed into anchorage in the Bay when a light breeze sprung up and sent us into the harbour at 7 p.m. after a 48 days passage, ten of which were spent on the Kroo Coast.

7 April

Banecho and the doctor on board. The health boat told me I ought to hoist my colour for the doctor to come on board. I mentally ejaculated that he and the doctor might jump up the rigging.

8 April

Discharging cargo in Fernando Po.

FOR BIMBIA

10 April

Weighed at 2.30 a.m. had a very heavy tornado. The jib sheets, for the want of not being properly secured, unhooked during the breeze and split the sail from clew to earing. I have lost my best jib through sheer carelessness

14 April

Arrived in Bimbia 12 a.m. brought up in a place of Captain Stone's recommending. After letting go the anchor I found we were in 2 fathoms. I at once went into the boat and sounded--afterwards shifted into 3 fathoms 1 foot.

15 April

Left Bimbia for Victoria arriving at 12 a.m. Went ashore and saw Daddy Wilson. Left at 7.30 for Rumby.

16 April

Anchored at Rumby at 10.30 a.m. Weighed at 7.30 p.m. for Fernando Po.

AT FERNANDO PO.

17 April

Arrived in Fernando Po 2.30 p.m.

20 April

Weighed at 2 p.m. for Bimbia. Wind very light. 10.30 p.m. arrived in Bimbia about the same time as the longboat which sailed the previous evening from Fernando Po.

21 April

Commenced discharging the mats and other articles for Captain Stone. I found upon going to the beach he had cleared away the bush and was upon the point of commencing to build. Finished about 3 p.m. and beat out of the harbour, a manoeuvre not very often practised in Bimbia, or I think not.

22 April

Had a heavy tornado about 4 p.m. afterwards throughout the day. Calm.

23 April

Wind light 12 p.m. Hove to in a tornado off Bata. No lights. I could not make out the anchorage.

GABOON

24 April

Brought up in Bata harbour if such a place there be. Went on shore and had a look at King Toma Condie's factory.

25 April

Being Sabbath, it was of course honoured with nothing being done save the decks and pumps attended to carefully.

26 April

Put on shore Charlie and his baggage into the House of the Kings, for which place I have agreed to give rent till the factory is completed. Sailed for Gaboon at 2 p.m. Wind very light.

27 April

At 6 a.m. Benito hove east when we had a good land breeze which took us off Corisco about 2 p.m. The sea breeze came and at 7 we were off Gaboon. Hove to for daylight. Not having been here before I did not care to run in the dark.

28 April

Anchored in the river the ebb tide coming out. Wind light. Weighed at 2 p.m. and anchored shortly after at Glass Town. Went on shore and saw Wookey and Kirkwood. Found Mrs. Kirkwood in the ship acting shop man.

Took up to Plateau the ship's papers. Saw the Commandant about a grant for a factory &c. Was told to come again to-morrow. Had a look at the ground which is near Plateau and chose a pretty good site with a good beach and at once resolved to build there near the second tree from the slaughter house.

IN GABOON

30 April

Went to the Commandant again and told him I had struck upon a spot when he sent a fellow with me to measure. Upon getting down he informs me it belongs to a Gaboon man and that I must go further on. The ground further towards Glass is much lower and a very bad beach. I sent him away, telling him I will look again.

1 May

Went on shore with the boys and commenced operations in the best place I could find, yet not a good one by far, having a bad beach is situated low and a bad road down to the beach. The only advantage it that it is as near to Plateau as I can get. For this reason I build it in this place. All the land betwixt this and Plateau town is occupied. I have made an offer to the owner of the other ground to exchange and give him or her ten dollars. Whether it will be accepted or not, I can't say. I shall know to-morrow. I do not meet with the assistance I might have expected from the white neighbours. Whether they think me an intruder or not, I can't say. Unfortunately R.B.N. Walker and Bailey are away, so that no one is here but Kirkwood, and he too busy.

2 May

Painted the life buoy by way of recreation. About 10 a.m. a boat came from the guard ship asking what I wanted down at Plateau. I informed him I was making a factory. He parlez vou'd a great deal with both his tongue and hands, and said it is not good that the Commandant did not know what was on board and that I must make out a manifest for him to see what we had on board, and I was not to be surprised to see a small steamer pluck me away to Glass. I told him to go to the Custom House for the manifest, and as for the steamer taking me to Glass--I wouldn't care if he took me to Fernando Po. He shrugged his shoulder and left saying I was to see the Commandant to-morrow, which I don't intend unless he sends for me. I don't care to see him, as I have got the ground.

3 May

Tom down with the fever--the effects of yesterday's scorching. Cut all the bush and commenced squaring out the house. Gave trust for bush rope and rafters. Sent the boat with four boys for posts. The *Oriel* came in this afternoon, and was hove to for more than 2 hours awaiting the health boat, which I think never went off. Mr. Walker tired of waiting brought up and went on shore. This treatment is certainly worse than that of the Spaniards in Fernando Po.

4 May

Finished the squaring and dug holes for posts. Cut down all the roots of trees and received from the boat 20 short posts. Gave out $20 trust for bamboo and mats at the rate of $2 per 100, counting two two. Bush rope is 5 bundles for $1 understand it takes 30 bundles; if this be the case, Captain Stone will run short of this article. I do not yet see my way clear to leave this on the 10th, let along arrive in Fernando Po, after calling at Elobey, Benito, Bata, Biappa. I intend directly the dwelling apartments are roofed to put cargo into it and clear out. The mate tells me one of the boys tried to hang himself and he prevented him. I tell him to let him do it next time for if he will rid the world of such rubbish as himself, he is at liberty to do so. I am told that the boy who ran away the day we arrived is working for the government on the roads. If this be the case, and they know it they certainly are a mean set of devils. He imagines because I have not made any enquiries for him he is free, yet I think will be mistaken should I get a glance of him.

5 May

Went to the bush at 3 p.m. having had four boys cutting the past two days. On account of the strong ebb tide we did not reach back before 9 p.m. after having been on the stones once or twice with the surf boat. 'Tis a bad beach to run along in the dark, there are so many stones about.

6 May

Went again to the bush for four corner posts, but owing to the stupidity or laziness of the boys I had to come away with only two, or I should not have been able to get back before 6 p.m. I only wish they had a few months pay due, 'twould be a little sharper for their eyes; upon getting down to the boat I found another of the boys missing. This makes two that have skedaddled, and for what? I can't say.

7 May

Shipped a cook from Louis Town who says he can cook proper, engaged for one year, if he stays. Got all the posts up for the dwelling part.

8 May

Much rain all night, making the ground too soft to work upon. Found at daylight the steward and cook had flown with the surf boat during the rain. Saw her on the beach; upon getting her found they had taken two axes, two cutlasses. I expected that everything would have been stolen, which would have included most carpenter's tools. Sent the boat for bamboo. Painted ship throughout. This is the first day I have remained on board since we commenced work.

9 May

Went and dined with Mr. Walker. Upon landing on the beach I surprised one of the runaway boys and pursued him, yet managed to lose him after Wookey's cutter arrived.

10 May

To-day expected in Fernando Po, and the house frame not yet up. No bamboo down, neither likely. Hired a canoe for $2 to fetch the stocks. Afterwards found she could not bring them, being too leaky. Expected the boat with mats &c., but did not arrive.

11 May

Sent the boys for sticks. Canoe leaks too badly, could not bring. Went to the Commandant respecting some clothes which the steward took on shore. Informed him also of my two runaway boys. Found the boy had stolen hat, shirt, and trousers of mine, and sundry other things from the mate. Boat came back with 260 mats, 200 bamboos.

12 May

Commenced with the house sides. Finished the front, when the men and I had a palaver, they saying they understood $4 each to build the house along, store not included. I knocked them off and had another understanding. With a blessing and a lot of palaver the day finished with scarcely anything done. Sent away the boat.

13 May

Morning done, all hands off up to the Commandant to try to make me pay 1 franc per day. He coolly told them to go to Harry, and I wanted them there too, and some others in their stead.

14 May

Engaged ten men at $5 with a proper understanding to work daily and not stay away. Tom's 21st birthday.

15 May

Went to the bush for more posts. House progressing slowly.

16 May

Had sailors' prayers down in the cabin. Afternoon went to see Bailey. Upon getting to the beach I found everyone expressing a wish to kill R. B. N. Walker about some palaver. During the afternoon five of the crew of the *Erronanga* came on shore without leave and brought the boat, which the Captain sent back. After getting half seas over and money spent they returned at dark for the boat, but not finding one came up to Bailey's whilst we were at dinner. Mr. Bailey told them to depart, which they did, but only to arm themselves with sticks and stones, using some very expressive language respecting their Captain, and what they would do. Two of them came up, I suppose to storm the castle. Mr. Kirkwood at once seized one and so did I (generally being first where I have no business), not observing the other fellow who, upon seeing me collar his chum, came down with his stake on my arm, making me see stars for some time after, and giving it a nasty cut. This was certainly an introduction and I did not forget to improve the acquaintance. With the help of my remaining arm, the others succeeded in securing the whole of the them, and tied them together, after which they were taken to the stone jug--thus ended a good day of palavers.

17 May

Got my clearance and was informed that I should give for the future, 48 hours notice previous to my departure. House progressing slowly. Mr. Walker on board.

18 May

Put on shore Tom and his effects with the carpenter. Sailed 5 p.m. Flood Tide. Wind shy. Carried out 6 fathoms. Heading N.W. Westerly. Surf boat astern.

19 May

6 a.m. Cape St. John S.E. 8 mi. Wind light, nasty sea causing boat to toss very heavy.

FROM GABOON TO FERNANDO PO

20 May

Arrived in Bata, found little or nothing done in the shape of building. Went into the bush and cut 200 sticks with my boy.

21 May

Weighed at 3 p.m. for Fernando Po. Fresh breeze. Nothing strange.

23 May

Arm very swollen and painful. Had a dose of fever for the first time since out. Arrived in Fernando Po 2 p.m.

FOR BIMBIA

26 May

Weighed for Bimbia at 3 p.m. Wind from eastward--light, with a strong set to the westward, did not make much of it.

27 May

A.M. off Cape Horatio. Wind light and easterly 9 p.m. anchored off the point with King William's house just open. Very heavy sea rolling in, carried away the boom guy and turned over the binnacle.

28 May

Sent on shore a load of shooks. 10 a.m. light sea breeze. Got under way. Dead low water. Getting opposite the house we took the ground and remained grounded half an hour. Sea quite smooth, though the reverse outside. Anchored off the end of the island at 2 p.m. in 3½ fathoms.

IN BIMBIA

30 May

On account of so little work being done yesterday I made them continue all to-day which did not fit my sailor man whom I had sharpened up with a substantial persuader before he could see the force of working on Sunday.

1 June

Left for Bata at 8 a.m. light air off. Came to outside for the sea breeze. Weighed again at 4 p.m. Wind light.

3 June

Hove to off Bata at midnight.

IN BATA

4 June

Came to 7 a.m. in 3½ fathoms. Went on shore and found the carpenter laying the floor of the house. It will by the present appearance be some days yet before ready for cargo.

5 June

Sent the boys and mate to fetch bamboos and poles to take to Gaboon, so that in remaining here I shall not be wasting time, or stopping their progress in Gaboon. I expect they will be short of these.

7 June

Landed all the cargo into the sleeping apartment where it will remain until the factory is finished.

TO GABOON

8 June

Finished landing cargo and sailed for Gaboon, having on board Mr. De Heer, passenger to Corisco, so that for the next two or three days we shall have to be better than generally.

12 June

Arrived at Gaboon. Found the house further than I anticipated. I also find the carpenter suffering from the first attack of fever so that his work is much behind.

13 June

Went and saw Bruce Walker, also No. 2 Walker, whom I found at the Stone house, both looking pretty well. After went and saw Mr. Bailey and Kirkwood.

14 June

Discharged most of the cargo into Tom's sleeping room, intending to sail as soon as possible.

IN GABOON

15 June

Completed discharging and sailed for Fernando Po about 4 p.m. Passed the *Mahgeda* off Cape Esturias about sundown.

23 June

Arrived in Fernando Po.

24 June

The *Biafra* arrived in Fernando Po with the mails. Left at night.

25 June

Sailed for Bimbia. Arrived at 10 p.m. Anchored in 2½ fathoms off the Point of Meolls Island.

26 June

Took in four puncheons of oil and talked palaver about the trade being stopped. Swore I would take away the factory &c., left at 8 p.m.

IN FERNANDO PO

27 June

Arrived in Fernando Po about 1 p.m. Anchored inside. Had to remain on board until sundown on account of the doctor being on the spree, after which I was relieved by the health boat.

28 June

Rainy weather with a nasty sea. On the beach fitting the gaff for cargo.

29 June

The *Biafra* arrived on her homeward voyage. No one allowed to board her without a permit from the Governor. Left in the evening.

30 June

Took in cargo for purchasing yams &c., and sailed for N.W. Bay about 3 p.m. having been denied a permit from the old Governor, but who afterwards came to and allowed me to sail.

1 July

Daylight, off Goat Island. A fresh breeze S.S.W. heavy sea. Lost lifebuoy overboard, but picked it up with the boat. Anchored in North West Bay about 3 p.m.

2 July

Put on shore Krooboys at different places to purchase yams, myself going to Bocoko. Found a very nasty surf on the beach which filled the boat, and wet most of the cargo.

IN GEORGES BAY

3 July

Returned from Bocoko after the third attempt to get off the beach with the small boat. Arrived on board 4 p.m.

4 July

About 2,000 yams came down this morning--more than I have seen before. I hope they will keep it up.

5 July

Yams came down very slow. War palaver is the excuse and laziness ought to be the other. They certainly are too lazy to dress, or even put on a cloth to-day. At Bocoko out of 22 women and girls only two had on cloth--the rest as naked as they were born. I suppose the weavers are on strike up in their town.

6 July

Bought to-day 1,200. Much rain with a very heavy sea. Moored the vessel with a kedge to prevent her from tailing on the beach.

7 July

Bought to-day but a few, they don't come at all fast--weather is very rainy and sultry.

8 July

Rain all day but a very few Boobies came down, and those that did came for the glass of rum to keep the wet from penetrating.

10 July

Rainy as usual. Went to Bocoko, returning the same evening. Found the boys alright with but a very few yams.

IN WEST BAY

12 July

Fine weather. Bought no yams. Commenced painting outside.

14 July

Fetched "Doc" from Bocoko, being short of pigeon shot, and he, not doing any trade, bought his yams.

15 July

Completed painting &c. Did not buy a single yam. They appear to be getting tired.

16 July

Went to Bocoko, off Charles' Folly. Fell in with the *San Antonio* coming into the Bay. Gave him course to Fernando Po.

17 July

Returned from Bocoko, bringing the boys, having only bought during 4 days seventeen hundred yams, instead of as many thousands. Rain all the afternoon. It is such an infernal place for rain as I never came across, every day almost hourly, a continual stream.

TO BRASS RIVER

29 July

Took in all the yams during the night, (total bought 17,644) the weather generally being finer than in the day; yet this time, unfortunately for the yams, it was not so, most of which were a complete mass of mud. Finished about 4 a.m. These yams are much smaller than those at the other wharves. The surf boat will not carry more than 3,000 of the others, whilst here she takes five quite easily. Weighed kedge and anchor about 3 p.m.--calm with a nasty roll inwards. Gave "Jim Doe" cargo with orders to remain until Saturday, then proceed to town with what yams he may have bought. Calm most of the night. I believe the person who calls himself King of North West Bay anticipated something handsome by way of a "dash". On account of not getting this he tried to stop the boys from taking water, but they were too old to be fooled by Boobies. I intended giving him a couple of heads of tobacco had he not made a palaver saying I did not pay good and refused to bring more yams. Rain all day.

21 July

Coming to purchase yams here, it is better to place factories when bound to Gaboon, leaving them until you return, then remaining a few days in North West Bay with the vessel until the boat is fetching them. During the first week you would buy 10,000 with the vessel. They bring them down faster when you are there than when left to Krooboys. The things I would bring would be rum, powder and pigeon shot, tobacco, sufficient to buy the whole quantity; should you fall short of any of this it stops trade. Romalls, satin stripes, pipes, shirts, guns, knives, only a few as they only get spoiled with exposure, the wet &c. Got clear of the Bay about 2 a.m. Very heavy head sea. 9 a.m. went about, on the main, in 9 fathoms. Saw a fore and aft schooner.

TO BONNY

22 July

Spoke the *Ariel* for Liverpool. Asked for the buoy right ahead--which turned out to be the lee fairway buoy instead of the weather one. Took the lee channel and went pretty well in, but seeing breakers ahead, and not being too well acquainted tacked in 3 fathoms and went round to the weather one.

23 July

Anchored in Bonny about 2 p.m. off the *Charles Horsfall.*[90] Took 1,000 yams.

24 July

Found this morning the boat boys and all appurtenances thereto flown. Taken in their flight a beaker of water and beef, yams &c., intending I suppose to have a picnic in the bush. Thus I am a prisoner until I get relief from some of the ships. No one appears to care for yams.

IN BONNY

28 July

Went to Bonny Town and found it not what I expected just a mud hill with numerous stakes stuck up. I suppose it was better before the fire.

TO FERNANDO PO

2 August

Received from the *Arabian* a boat to take round for sale--price £35. 10% commission in case of sale. Weighed at 8 a.m. and stood over the flood tide. Wind light 4 p.m. fairway buoy abeam.

3 August

Fernando Po visible at daylight tho' hazy, hauled up and found ourselves off Badgely having gone too far to windward. Anchored at 5 p.m. Saw the *Minerva* outside.

---

[90] *Charles Horsfall* (860 grt) was built at Aberdeen in 1855 for Horsfall Brothers and was later hulked and used for trading at Bonny. See Wharton, unpublished mss., 59 and 144.

5 August

Sailed for Bimbia. The S.S. *Benin* arrived, having been on Bonny Bar.

IN BIMBIA

6 August

Arrived and anchored at 8 a.m. Much rain. Discharge part cargo. Too much wet to work.

8 August

Weighed about 3 p.m. Wind light, strong flood tide. Made little or no headway for some time. Sailed close to the point of the island. 2½ fathoms.

9 August

Arrived in Fernando Po. Went alongside of the *Terrier* and discharged.

12 August

Left Fernando Po 3 p.m. for Victoria, for a bullock.

13 August

Calm, did not get in before midday.

14 August

Went on shore and found we could not catch a bullock, being too wild and took to the bush. Sailed in the evening.

TO BATA

15 August

Drifted near to Cape Horatio, where we remained all day, being no wind.

18 August

Arrived in Bata. Took on shore the cargo.

19 August

Weighed for Gaboon 7 a.m. Light breeze. 6 p.m. off Benito.

21 August

Anchored off Santa Maria Villa at 4 p.m. Took on shore the papers and gave notice to depart.

23 August

Intended to sail, but could not get the papers, the clerk being sick. Took in ten casks for Brookey.

24 August

Sailed for Fernando Po via Bata 7 p.m. Cape St. Johns abeam

TO FERNANDO PO

25 August

Anchored in Bata Cove off Hope Factory in 4½ fathoms. Went on shore and headed up the casks with rubber. Took away the carpenter who I found had been stealing to the amount of $90, 60 of which had been recovered, leaving to his account $30. This he acknowledges.

26 August

Weighed at 10 a.m. Fresh breeze. Course N. by W. Saw the *Lizette* steering S.E. Distant from Bata 20 miles.

27 August

About 3 a.m. the tow rope of the surf boat broke and with difficulty we managed to find her, yet not before drifting to leeward. At daylight found the bottom in 13 fathoms. Have drifted out of our course 40 miles to the eastward. Daylight, saw a steamer which proved to be old *Diggs* who kindly gave us a tow into Fernando Po, where we anchored at 4 p.m.

TO BIMBIA

30 August

Sailed for Bimbia via Victoria at 2.12 p.m. 7.12 anchored in the Bay.

31 August

Went on shore and found the bullock still at large and likely to be. Could not catch him so came away to Georges Town where we took in some oil and weighed and anchored in Bimbia 5.30 p.m.

1 September

Went and brought off a boat load of stones for ballast, afterwards took on board shooks and hoop iron, also four casks of oil.

2 September

Took in remainder of cargo and weighed for Victoria at 3.15 p.m. Anchored in Victoria at 8 p.m.

3 September

Found the bullock still free. Took two goats and a few beakers of oil from George. Weighed at 3.12 p.m.

4 September

Anchored in Fernando Po at 8.30 a.m. Discharged the cargo. Rainy.

6 September

Took in empty casks and sundries for Kirkwood and Wookey, intending to sail in the evening, but owing to calm did not.

IN FERNANDO PO

7 September

Pulled out of the Cove. Hove to for the boat. At the same time the *Janette* passed. Owing to the yard rope getting fouled we were some time in getting canvas set after the boat returned, so that she was a couple of miles ahead when down at Trello's Farm. Passed her off Horatio at 5.30. Were becalmed all night.

8 September

P.M 2.30. A smart breeze from west. Lost the *Janette* astern. Laid up S.S.W. until 12 p.m. then S. till daylight.

10 September

Anchored in 3½ fathoms off the factory. Took on shore most of the cargo before dark. Gave the natives a dance in the factory yard which they kept up until morning.

TO GABOON

11 September

Weighed at 11 a.m. for Gaboon. 7 p.m. saw a schooner off Benito, which I took to be the *Sunbeam*. Make her out better in the morning.

13 September

Off the Gaboon, wind light. Anchored off the factory. At 3.30 went up and saw Mr. Kirkwood, who is to send the *Mahgeda* down to Fernando Po this month.

14 September

Discharged cargo and cleared out. Weighed at 4.30 p.m. for Elobey.

15 September

Arrived at 5 a.m. saluted the *Minerva* and anchored under her stern. Went on board. 10 a.m. the *Minerva* and *Ann* sailed. 3 p.m. weighed and stood into the beach anchoring in 7 fathoms close to.

IN ELOBEY

17 September

Had on board a quantity of my old traders who owe me slightly. They appear to want to pay, yet want other trust first, saying I stay away too long, they have kept the rubber for a long time but finding I did not come were obliged to sell it to other man. As for keeping, I don't imagine they tried, or cared to do so, selling to the others I dare say is right.

18 September

Wrote to Fernando Po by Wolber's boat going through the creek. This boat was stopped yesterday on account of a palaver they have got up amongst themselves respecting the weighing of rubber. They want the rubber to be sold by the number--100 pieces to the $1 or, if by weight 8 lbs. to $1. If not agreed to, trade is to be stopped.

20 September

Bought or received 18 pounds of rubber being the first old trust. The barque *Carrol* sailed for Hamburg. Much rain throughout the night.

RIVER MUNI

27 September

Received a note from the Lords of Elobey commanding me to come down to Elobey within two days, if not they would come and fetch me. Sent message I should wait until they came. If they did not come I would come to take them.

28 September

Bailey returned from Elobey very much cut up having had a palaver with John Scott, he wanting to come up with his cutter. At the same time he was urging the Coriscos to fetch me down. Bailey considered he had not any business above me. Took him and his cutter back to Elobey and told them I can go up if I wish, but they shall not, and if any of the Coriscos come to disturb me, I have his assistance.

29 September

Jacob returned with 700 lbs. rubber.

RIVER DANGER

31 October

Weighed and went down to Elobey, at which place I find them in the midst of palavers, yet keep at a respectable distance from me, and I think they are likely to.

11 November

The *Minerva* came in from Fernando Po. 8 days' passage.

12 November

Put up in Bailey's, a punkah, being the first I have seen upon the African coast.

16 November

Went off alongside to the *Minerva* and brought up in a line with the *Ann* and *Sunbeam*, all intending to ascertain which is the fastest vessel to-morrow.

TO GABOON

17 November

At 4.30 a.m. the *Sunbeam* tripped. I imagine he intended to give us the slip, not hearing him heave up. Upon seeing him make a move I immediately hove short and made sail. At 5.25 tripped anchor, the *Sunbeam* then out of sight. Observed him at daylight about three miles off. At 7 we were alongside and about five miles from Corisco, from then until we arrived we kept the lead. Anchored off Onward factory at 5.10 p.m. The *Sunbeam* anchored off the guardship some time during the night, it being too far to make her out.

18 November

Entered and cleared. Took in and discharged cargo and made all ready for a start in the morning.

19 November

Weighed about 7 a.m. Wind light. Drifted out of the river. Had a squall off Corisco and split the gaff topsail. Broke the peak halyards &c.

IN GABOON

6 December

Discharged the cargo. Mr. Wookey went on shore a little better

8 December

Sailed at 7.30 a.m. Mr. Kenyon passenger. Anchored off Corisco at 4.30 p.m.

9 December

Took in bamboos and mats and sailed for Elobey at 4.30. Arrived at 7 p.m.

14 December

The S.S. *Pioneer* came in at 2 p.m. reporting the *Minerva* ashore in Cape Lopez.[91] At this time we were stripped. At 5.30 we weighed intending to render assistance to her if required.

15 December

Sighted the *Minerva* at 11.30 a.m. off Mbanya. Spoke her and she reported making little water. Promised to report him to R. B. N. Walker. 5 p.m. spoke the Elobey who returned 5.15. Spoke the *Pioneer* with *Ann* in tow. He immediately slipped and returned. Having a smart 6 knot breeze, perhaps a little more, we completely doubled the whole, leaving the steamer a good one-third of the distance in. We anchored inside at sundown.

---

[91]HMS *Pioneer*, was a small wooden paddle steamer based at the Lagos Bar as a tender to the flagship. See Cox, *Cox and the Ju Ju Coast*, 68 and 75.

17 December

The small boat this morning sank and broke her headpost. Had the canoe after her all the day, yet without success.

IN ELOBEY

19 December

Captain Brown came with the *Janet* on his route to Benito. Mr. McLachlan's eyes, much inflamed, were doctored with native medicine (blood from a man's leg put on with a red feather from a parrot's tail).

31 December

Finished the dwelling apartment of the house.

1870

1 January

Commenced discharging cargo into the new house. Finished and made ready for sea.

2 January

Sailed for Gaboon about 8 a.m. Wind light. Arrived 10 p.m.

3 January

Commenced to take stock at the factory.

TO FERNANDO PO

5 January

Cleared out. Waiting for Tom who is not very well. Took in 12 barrels flour, 4 casks beef, 2 pork, 10 c/s. kerosene. Kerosene $52.50., beef at $25., pork $28., flour $10. Some few things for Bata.

6 January

Sailed for Bata 6 a.m. 12 a.m. off Laval.

7 January

Arrived in Bata 8 a.m. discharged one boat and took in one cask rubber. Took stock and sailed 4 p.m.

9 January

Arrived in Bimbia at 8 a.m. Took in cargo and shooks from Sparhawk. In receiving the shooks I find them rotten and useless.

10 January

Light winds and very thick. Hove to at 8 p.m., supposed off the town.

IN FERNANDO PO

12 January

Hauled alongside the *Terrier* and discharged cargo. Took in from Mr. Struthers as per his a/c 6,500 yams as per a/c on board--6,176.

14 January

Finished loading and sailed for Bonny at 6 p.m. the gig giving us a pull out about a mile.

16 January

6 a.m. Spoke *Lady Alice* riding off Andony, also a schooner off Apogo. 2 p.m. sighted the weather channel fairway buoy. Anchored for the sea breeze which never came.

TO BONNY

17 January

Weighed at daylight with a light land breeze which freshened towards mid-day. Strong ebb tide. Beat as far as the third buoy, bringing up in 6 fathoms. Weighed at flood, light wind off shore, beat in and anchored during afternoon. Very thick. At present there are three buoys, the outer one a red can, flat top, in 6 fathoms; the second--red can, flat top, in 4½ fathoms; the third--striped, in 5 fathoms; the fourth and last black spiral on the outer point of the spit. It is very narrow against the third buoy. Keeping to the westward is not less than 4 fathoms, and more nearer the breakers which are pretty steep.

18 January

Went alongside the *Onward* and discharged the stone ballast, finishing about 6 p.m.[92] Afterwards hauled into the stream in thirteen fathoms of water.

---

[92]*Onward* (911 grt) was built at St. John, New Brunswick, in 1850; in 1868 the vessel was acquired by Irvine and Woodward and fitted out as a trading hulk at Bonny by Harry Cottrell. See Wharton, unpublished mss., 59 and 130: and Cotterell, "Reminiscences of One Connected with the West African Trade from 1863 to 1910," 38.

IN BONNY

19 January

The S.S. *Norway* sailed for Brass.[93] Received and took in thirteen puncheons of palm oil from Mr. Curphy, paying him for the same at the rate of $85 per cask. Short of cash. Remains owing $17.50.

20 January

The *Lagos* sailed for Fernando Po. Took in from Watts 80¼ barrels and 2 hhds. rum, 1 case matchets, some yams and 10 barrels powder.

21 January

Weighed and sailed to Fernando Po. Calm. Towed out of the lee channel with the small boat. Water 8 fathoms.

22 January

Arrived in Fernando Po and anchored 8 a.m. in Clarence Cove. Discharged the 13 casks of oil and sailed into the other bay ready for loading on Monday.

24 January

The S.S. *Lagos* arrived and sailed. Shipped the 7 casks of palm oil. Went to the theatre in the evening.

25 January

Finished loading and sailed about 3 p.m.

27 January

Made sail at daylight, fairway buoy bearing S.S.W. Went alongside the *Onward* at 10 a.m. without dropping anchor. Half discharged at 5 p.m. when, with a strong sea breeze and ebb tide the head post broke and we sheered off until morning. During the night we had a tornado, not very heavy, yet much rain.

TO FERNANDO PO

28 January

Hauled alongside the hulk and discharged the remainder of stone, finishing about 12 a.m. Took in 40 shooks from Mr. McDonald, and refused to sign for the sizes, which he

---

[93] SS *Norway* was chartered by the African Steam Ship Company from mid-1869 to mid-1870. See Davies, *The Trade Makers*, 61.

seemed to think was, or ought to be, natural to me. At the same time he objects to sign for any quantity of my cargo. Sailed about 5 p.m. Got down to Rough Corner at 6.30. Too dark to see the buoy. Made two more tacks to the W. and then kept away S.E. which carried us out through the lee channel in three fathoms. A very strong breeze, with much lightning and thunder.

30 January

In coming into the harbour there was a strong set to the eastward which set us with our keel on the reef. Fortunately, the sea was very smooth. Got off at once and anchored.

IN FERNANDO PO

3 February

Took in cargo and sailed in the evening for Bimbia; most of the white Fernandonians coming to see us off. Mr. McLachlan passenger.

TO GABOON AND SOUTH

9 February

Anchored in Elobey. Charlie rather sick. Put on his chest a mustard plaster.

10 February

Sailed after landing sundry cargo. Mr. Parkinson sick with fever, hard tornados throughout the night, never leaving the deck. Hove to midnight off Esturias.

11 February

Came to off the factory at 2 p.m. Charlie apparently better and eating heartily. Went on shore to enter. Upon getting on board at 10 p.m. I found him quite dead.

12 February

Buried Charlie at Baraki. Landed cargo and repaired the staysail. Being alone some Krooboys took inventory of Charlie's effects.

13 February

Went to Church at Baraki, being the first time in a place of worship since April 1866. Wrote to John for guns.

14 February

Weighed and stood off. Flood tide running up and sea breeze. Tacked and dipped to the *Janette*. Sent McLachlan away to her in the boat. 8 p.m. outside.

TO SOUTH COAST

17 February

Off the Cape, having made during the night little or no headway. Stood to the westward all the afternoon intending to try a long tack into the beach as it is evident there is a strong current running inshore. The new sailor is down to-day, having a swelling in the groin, and which will take him some time to get rid of. I am again left to keep all the watches.

TO LOANGO BAY

25 February

Smart breeze during the three hours in the afternoon, afterwards falling light. Made out the Loango land before dusk. Hove to at 11 p.m. in 12 fathoms. Head to the westward.

26 February

Made sail at 4 a.m. Stood in with the land breeze but falling calm when off the Bay, drifted out to the southward. A small white Portuguese schooner sighted inward bound to Loango, he sailed in over what is called the Indian Bar, a bank of stones running in a northerly direction from the point. I followed until we suddenly went from 11 fathoms into 2, which to me appeared too little water to be pleasant, with the nasty roll then on. Hauled up N.W. till we had 7. Afterwards keeping away gradually, and coming to in 4 fathoms. Went on shore and saw the place which consisted of three factories, one of which was a very snug place, the outer walls being built of stone, making a safe enclosure against any intended raid by the natives. In fact it appeared to have been built for a slave barracoon, and that a pretty secure one. It is a Dutch house, and appears to do most of the trade. He is a very intelligent and hospitable person in charge. He does not trade directly with the natives, but gives trust to Portuguese about the Coast, they trading with the natives, or being what I call the retailers, ivory, rubber, and oil. The oil is nearly white, something of a cream colour. Stock appears to be very dear, goats at about £1 cost price. He being so pressing for us to remain until the morrow. I left McLachlan intending to come ashore in the morning and sail by the sea breeze. Got on board at 7 with wood and water. Paid out 30 fathoms of chain. Sea smooth.

IN LOANGO BAY

27 February

Went on shore early intending to get away as soon as the sea breeze put in. Had some difficulty in getting up the lagoon, it being low tide. Upon getting ashore we went along to look at the village some little distance in the bush, our mode of travelling being in hammocks going at the jog trot rate of East Indian palanquins, only not quite so comfortable, having no awning to keep off the sun. We found the houses (of which there were about one dozen) to be just the roof of a house rested upon the ground without sides. One or two were a little better, yet very small, being a house within a house, each having its own door and windows. The town was called La Martinique. We afterwards came down to breakfast. Afterwards went off to the ship where we arrived at 2 p.m. Got under weigh immediately for Guiloo River.

AT GUILOO RIVER

28 February

Went on shore at 6 a.m. without getting wet. Found on the beach a salt house belonging to the natives. A little further up we came to a Portuguese establishment, the late Doctor Hilliard's, where we found an American very sick with bilious fever. We then crossed the river to another house of the Company of Portuguese Merchants in charge of Senor Galatz. He took from us a few things causing me to remain on shore all night, Mr. McLachlan kindly going off and sending ashore what was required.

1 March

The boat came on shore this morning with the things. I went on board by the launch of Senor Galatz with the produce exchanged, getting under weigh at once.

TO MAYUMBA

2 March

Calm, with little sea. Did not get the sun at noon. Scraped the small boat. Found her bottom completely wormed through. I only hope I may be able to get hold of Mr. Hyder's boats. I will have the value of this out of her if possible.

3 March

Wind still light, making but very little progress. I am afraid my calculations will for this time run short unless I am favoured with more wind, it being impossible to get over the ground without. I anticipated Gaboon on Saturday, and that with ease, had we been at all lucky. Ran along the land in 7 fathoms; at noon south of the Makandakio. It has a large factory upon its south side. There are several rivers and factories between this and point Banda, also one about a mile beyond this, off which we were at 7 p.m. becalmed, off our course.

IN MAYUMBA BAY

4 March

At daylight off Matooti Point with a little land wind through which we managed to get soundings in the Bay and brought up in 12 fathoms at 8 a.m. Went on shore to the nearest house, which appears to have been a factory of the Companía's, yet through some palaver the trader is away. There is a river running parallel to the sea at about fifty yards behind the house. Breaking on to the sea some three miles nearer to Cape Yumba on the other side are two Portuguese factories, and two other, we are told, further up the river. Not having much spare time we did not go to the other houses. Filled our water and came off about noon. Got under weigh with the sea breeze. We saw another factory south of Cape Yumba, and one or two miles north of it, also another house which may be a salt house about one mile further north. Rubber, oil and coconuts are bought here, the former supposed to be the best from the Coast.

TO GABOON

Wind during the afternoon very light, ran along the land in making the Cape from the north. A white patch of sand is seen near to the water which in the sun resembles a sheet of white paper. The land is also high with trees without bush, and when seen from the south it is quite steep to the water. Made another factory about midway betwixt this and Point Pedros.

5 March

At daylight 10 miles south of the Point observed two Portuguese factories in the bight a few miles from Point. Two canoes came off, yet did not come alongside. Passed the town in the bight north of which B. N. W. had a factory. Made Lattas southern factory about noon. Had a squall during the afternoon. The boy at the helm jibed her, unshipping the boom and injuring one boy by its falling upon him, split the mainsail, pulled the clew out of the foresail, tore the squaresail, and laid up the sailor with the old disease, afterwards fine.

6 March

This morning a little south of Fernan Vas, which we passed at 10 a.m. Wind very light. Repairing clew of the foresail. Light breeze throughout the day, not making much. Mesias at dark.

7 March

Daylight off Cape Lopez; going slowly; wind light. Noon lat. 0.15 south. Distance to Gaboon 45 miles at which place we, with patience, may arrive, but when?

8 March

Hove to at 3.30 off the River.

9 March

Took in from town 16 casks produce--Kirkwood 7, Wookey 7. Finished and sailed at 7 p.m. Light land wind.

TO FERNANDO PO

10 March

Wind light. Still off Point Clara. No signs of further progress 7 a.m. Wind freshening towards noon. Came to inside at 11 p.m. Found a barque, the *Rattler*, loading wood from Kayan George, the captain of which was over at Corisco very sick. Squally throughout the night.

11 March

Discharged two casks of salt and took in four casks containing 3,768 lbs. rubber, 266 of which belongs to Mr. Hill. I found the long boat with the starb'd side knocked completely out, timbers, plank, and copper; a bright beginning, only having her down new about a month, and now useless. I am sure had either Krooboy or native taken the slightest interest in getting her off she could not have made much hurt, yet when two white people with three boys and natives at their call acknowledges they saw her on the beach, and were not able to get her off, they were afraid of the surf, and did not exert themselves, or care. Sailed at 2.30 p.m. Wind light from N.W. Brought up in the tail of the bank at 6 p.m. Calm. Weighed at 10.

12 March

Fresh breeze from S.W. at noon lat. 2.2 N. Made Fernando Po at 6 p.m. Calm, with a tremendous heavy sea from south causing our sails to suffer from chafe. Split the clew of the staysail.

14 March

As usual wind very light. Off Boteller Rocks daylight. 8 a.m. spoke the *Janette*, hove to and went on board. Heard of the death of McGowan, and young Stewart in Bonny, also Kelly. Arrived in Fernando Po 7 p.m. Mr. McLachlan went on shore.

IN FERNANDO PO

15 March

The steamer *Calabar* (Preston) came in. It was 9 a.m. before I was boarded, and the steamer having too much cargo for me I am unable to do anything until noon, thanks to these infernal Spaniards, whom I should like to punch. Discharged into the *Terrier* 37 casks rubber loaded from the steamer and discharging the *Terrier* into the steamer, completing at 1 a.m.

16 March

Reported to the Consul the death of the sailor in Gaboon. Was ordered to sell his effects and remit the cash. Took in stores for Bimbia.

17 March

Finished in Fernando Po and departed to Gaboon. Bimbia at 2 p.m. Wind easterly and light. Drifted near Cape Bullen, at which place we remained all night.

20 March

Sailed about 7 p.m. Able to get out with the light breeze in the afternoon.

21 March

Arrived in Fernando Po about noon. Discharged the oil and took in the remainder of the South Coast cargo. Owing to mismanagement in the steering we were a long distance to the northward, or we ought to have been in before daylight, yet a fellow cannot always be awake even though he intends to.

TO GABOON

24 March

The S.S. *Biafra*--Captain Croft--came in at daylight. I went on board and found a few packages for south, yet not the guns I wanted, which will, of course, come when I don't want them. Discharged from the steamer and got all on board, taking Mr. Skertchly, a passenger, to Gaboon.

Captain Hopkins came round with an intention of chartering the schooner to trade in the New River, Opobo. Sailed in the afternoon. Wind very light, having to tow out with the boat ahead.

26 March

Had a squall during which the staysail sheets were adrift and sent through the jib. This is the third time the same carelessness by the same boys. I stop from their pay the amount of damage in hopes of making them more careful.

29 March

Made Cape St. John' at daylight, having had a very heavy squall from N.E. in which we were put rail under, yet thanks to our masts and gear everything held. All anticipated getting in, yet when off the Point it fell calm and we drifted about all night.

30 March

Brought up in seven fathoms near the tail of the bank. Becalmed. A light breeze sprang up about noon, which enabled us to get in at 4 p.m. after a passage of six days from Fernando Po. The same ought to have been done in two or three at the most, in any reasonable weather.

Upon arrival I find R. B. N. Walker away to the northern factories. The Captain of the *Rattler* is dead. Jamieson, too, the master of Wookey's cutter had rolled overboard and drowned whilst up Gaboon River.

31 March

Discharged 2 casks rum, 1 case of pipes, 4 soap, 4 gin, 5 matchets, 3 hats, stores, 40 pieces prints. Hauled upon the beach the surf boat and put upon her bottom tar and arsenic. Hauled up on the hill the broken long boat. Found 17 of her timbers broken. The whole of the copper will have to come off in order to get her done properly, also recaulked. Was extremely sorry to hear by Wolbers boat of the death of Mr. Kirkwood from the effects of bilious fever. I scarcely believed the report at first, yet sorry afterwards to find it too true. He is certainly the last I should have taken to have dropped off in that manner. Poor fellow. I suppose it is the result of the fire.

1 April

Finished caulking the decks to-day and sail immediately, having waited for this, or we should have sailed last evening. Grounded on the flats, being dead low water, and drawing 11 feet soft mud. Remained half an hour.

2 April

Wind light--off Cape Esteiras most of the day. Towards evening we had the sea breeze. Anchored in seven fathoms. Wind done, ebb tide.

3 April

Arrived and entered. Went to the beach. Nothing new. Found the French had taken possession of Kirkwood's estate and turned off the wife, they considering the marriage to be illegal, and she not being able to produce the certificate,it being burnt with the house.

4 April

Discharged the cargo, as much as was not wanted to trade with up the river. Had to carry it up to the house, the boys being absent.

5 April

Making a shop of the after hold, and opening the goods to be in readiness. We shall be much pressed for time when up, no other vessel being up now, and cargo being scarce we ought to do a little.

IN GABOON

6 April

No sea breeze--did not make a very early start, our intended pilot not being too well to-day, from the effects of lifting his hand to much to his mouth. Anchored about 8 p.m. off Bangia Creek.

7 April

Made a start at daylight--land breeze--anchored off Island Lika till the sea breeze put in, after which we again anchored Chimby at 7 p.m. Bought 4 parrots.

18 April

Discharged and took off a little cargo for Bata. Cleared out expecting tow down during the night. Did not sail till morning.

19 April

Wind light--drifted out of the river. Passed the *Sunbeam* off Esteiras. Anchored in Elobey during the night.

20 April

Took in 4 casks rubber. Found Mr. Hill had been too sick to attend to the trade much. Sailed at 4 p.m.

23 April

Sailed for Bonny at 4 p.m. Fresh breeze outside, yet had difficulty in the calms.

BONNY

24 April

Made the fairway buoy at 8 a.m. Kept away and came to off the *Onward* at noon. Not a bad passage.

25 April

Took on board from Curphy seven casks rum; from Johnston of the *Onward*--10 cases fuzees, 3 cases pipes, 2 kegs flints, 200 pieces assorted madras, prices of which I am to get from H. Cotterel in Fernando Po. Sailed at 3 p.m. Wind S.W. In standing over to the westward on the second tack we took the ground, having stood over too far, and she going too fast to get the bottom before touching it, being very steep. Remained thus until midnight, all our efforts to get her off on the falling tide being useless.

26 April

Came out with a light land breeze. Had to come off Rough Corner spit in five fathoms. In getting under weigh with a very nasty sea we carried away the starboard hawse pipe, yet got the anchor up, and without cutting her head.

TO GABOON

27 April

Arrived in conjunction with any amount of rain and anchored about 8 a.m. Found to my annoyance the steamer had sailed yesterday and that we had passed her during the night. Took in 150¼ barrels powder, and 500 yams. Sailed at midnight to Bimbia.

BIMBIA

30 April

Did not get on board before 3 p.m. to breakfast. King William came to the factory to settle price for the King guns, and also to talk sundry palavers relative to the man now in charge not being too civil with them. After leaving our factory he was intending to pay Sparhawk a visit, and for the honour Sparhawk was giving him a salute with three guns, one of which burst, and a piece out of the breech struck him on the forehead and smashed his skull very very much, closing up both eyes, and nose, and knocking out his upper teeth, leaving a fearful gash above his eyes. I went up as soon as I got the news, but was not sufficiently versed in the art of surgery to do much.[94] Mr. Coakeley, with myself, remained with him during the night, doing what we considered most advisable, and sending for Mr. Thormaleu to come down with a doctor at once, expecting him the following morning.

1 July

Bertram Sparhawk to-day pretty sensible, and not quite so self-willed as yesterday. Asked him to go over to Fernando Po with the *Myrtle*, yet he appeared to have more faith in Thormaleu than in the doctors of the Spanish. Went over to our factory where a quantity of oil was waiting for the guns. Returned to the Island shortly afterwards. Mr. Thormaleu, with Mr. Collings, came about 2 p.m. when a consultation was held as to what was the best to be done with Bertram, they remarking that it was a great pity he had not gone over to Fernando Po with the *Myrtle* (she having sailed at noon). Had Hemingway have asked, or offered a passage, I would have persuaded Bertram to go, yet he did not care for passengers. He even ran away and left Coakeley who was ready to go with him at his previously appointed time. It was agreed that it would be the best

[94] An account of Sparhawk's arrival in Fernando Po is given on pp. 114-115. He apparently made a good recovery; see p. 129.

for him to go, and that I should take him over to Horatio in the *Maria*, from thence Mr. Collings would take him in his boat. Came on board at seven and sailed immediately.

IN BIMBIA

3 July

Heavy sea. Wind about south. Tacked off Campo at 4 p.m. Hove to off Bata during the night.

4 July

Anchored off the factory and discharged what cargo I could spare. Talked palaver about Charlie's shooting a couple of the bushmen who were owing him, and running away; concluded by their wanting a jar of rum. Left at 4 p.m.

TO GABOON

7 July

Anchored at Gaboon off the factory at midnight.

8 July

Found Tom just down the river with 12,000 lbs. of rubber, having got rid of all the guns and powder. Discharged cargo.

10 July

Went to church, where we arrived just in time to be too late. Our clock and Mr. Walker's were keeping different time. Went and chopped with Wookey. Returned to Plateau at 7 p.m. where I found two of my boys had deserted.

TO RAMBOE

11 July

Sailed at 2 p.m. with a light breeze--flood tide. Anchored at the mouth of the Ramboe at 8 p.m.

12 July

Gave Tom in the two boats a considerable quantity of cargo, then weighing and proceeding up to Chin Chua, anchored at 5 p.m. Bought a little rubber.

13 July

Removed a little further up the river into 4½ fathoms, being only 10' at low water when our stern was tailed towards the beach, with a stony bottom. Bought a little rubber, yet very dear. Put on shore Rufus Anderson.

14 July

Weighed from Chin Chua at 4 a.m. proceeded in tow of boat till high water, anchoring near the first Mpangwe town. Came to till flood tide, then weighed and came to off Sixth town, the previous townspeople begging of me to stop as they had plenty of rubber, yet I was unable to take it, being overfull.

UP THE RAMBOE

16 July

Bought to-day a few more hundreds of pounds of rubber. Owing to a Gaboon trader I had on board I was rather sold, he cheating them too much, causing some of them to go away with some rubber, yet seeing this I was particularly careful not to let any more pass and found it not very difficult to please them cheap, with the exception of guns. These they want for less than I can let them have them, and remark I don't go to the bush and cut guns in the manner they do rubber, and that if I did I would appear to consider its value. This I do, as well as the gun.

17 July

Weighed at 5 a.m. and proceeded up to Agunjo. Bought a few more hundred pounds of rubber.

18 July

Weighed at 6 a.m. Went up to Gumongoys town at which place I considered we were high enough, having very little room to swing, occasionally touching the mud. Bought a few more hundred pounds of rubber. I dare say I have 4,000 on board, which is not so bad for four days' trading, some time of which we were under weigh.

19 July

Remained at anchor all to-day, intending to go down to-morrow should the rubber trade cease. Arrived on board to-night.

20 July

Bought this morning a few more hundreds. Weighed at 2 p.m. and went down to Agunjo. Anchored at 5 p.m. Amount of rubber about 6,000 lbs.

RIVER RAMBOE

21 July

Weighed about 2 p.m. Proceeded with the ebb tide down to Bote's town. Anchored at sundown.

22 July

Brought on board Lassein's rubber, he having given out some trust. I am obliged either to wait a day or leave him, which I don't care to do, as I do not know when I shall be back.

23 July

Brought on board Lassein with the remnant of his cargo. Weighed and went down with the ebb. Anchored at flood tide; did not trade any. Weighed with the ebb, yet owing to the strong sea breeze we could not get far down. Anchored at sunset.

24 July

Weighed and proceeded down to the entrance, bringing up at flood tide, about 1 mile above Chin Chua. Got under weigh at high water, yet owing to the strong sea breeze brought up again when in sight of Chin Chua.

25 July

Came down to Chin Chua, anchored and took from Rufus 1,853 lbs. rubber. Returned him more money. Gave also Anguilla 400 lbs. trust.

26 July

Weighed from Chin Chua and proceeded down. Brought up about 9 a.m. Proceeded up the Como at flood tide. Anchored at Ningam Windam at 7 p.m. having been without sea breeze.

27 July

Weighed and proceeded with the flood tide up the river. Anchored opposite the *Commander Gordon* at 6 p.m. Found Tom with 10,000 lbs. of rubber.

28 July

Taking rubber from the boats. Had a proper dose of the fever, and ague.

RIVER COMO

5 August

Came down. Went up to Chin Chua with the boat. Brought down 2,000 lbs. rubber. Gave out more cargo, sailed at 7 p.m. On Saturday eve anchored in Gaboon at 12 p.m.

9 August

Sailed, and arrived in Elobey at 3 p.m. having come from the anchor in 8 hours to anchor here, and beat up inside against a flood tide. Took in rubber and got ready for off.

TO FERNANDO PO

10 August

Sailed from Elobey at 8.30 a.m. I found most of the people here half screwed. It looked as if they had been celebrating someone's birthday. I had on board a box of coats, some brandy, which fell in at a seasonable time, being demolished in less time than it took making. There are too many people here without work and chop.

11 August

Finished and sailed from Bata. Wind fresh. Took 5 casks rubber.

12 August

Anchored Fernando Po.

13 August

Discharging produce into the *Terrier*. To November 20th too unwell to attend to duties and remained during this time in Fernando Po, from 20th August to 20th November.[95]

TO BIMBIA

22 November

Weighed at 1.30 a.m. Slight breeze off. Not having sufficient sickness during the past three months had a little fever and took quinine. Anchored in Bimbia at 4.30 having had the wind for the most part of the day from the eastward. Found Thormaleu's factory building upon King William's Beach. Not much trade doing.

---

[95]See above, 117-120.

24 November

Sailed at 6 a.m. light land breeze, ebb tide drifted out. Sea breeze. Set in about noon.

25 November

Arrived in Fernando Po. Discharged upon the beach, and took in a quantity of cargo.

IN FERNANDO PO

27 November

About 12 a.m. the *McGregor Laird* came in. Took from her 1,399 kegs powder. According to the ship's tally we were 11 short.

28 November

Waiting for the arrival of the *Valla*, having, or expecting, 60 cases of fuzees by her.

29 November

Working at the boom guys and topping lifts. No *Valla*.

30 November

Took on board the Krooboys bags and boxes. Sailed about midnight. The seaman Hodgson went on shore last evening and did not return until just before sailing.

1 December

When off Victoria we had a light squall which took away our jib boom by the cap. Anchored at 3 p.m. Landed all the cargo--10 rum, one case cloth.

TO KROO COAST

2 December

Measured a 40" cask by the keg measure. The cask by gauge was 208 gallons, whilst by the keg it was 162 gallons, making a difference of 46 gallons per cask. Allowing these 46 gallons to have been dirt, I find Mr. Buckle, exclusive of this, to be by the last two shipments, 940 gallons of oil short. According to his books he says Brass Bell is owing 8½ kroos, though Mr. Sparhawk says he knows for a fact Bell is owing sixteen kroos, as well as some trust given to buy goats. He denies having given any cargo out of the factory for keeping, until he is able to fetch it; also denies having sent any goats to Victoria. I searched his box for money, yet found none. I found some madras, satin stripe, single caps, singlets, and several other things which he acknowledged having taken out of the factory, and not passed to his a/c. One singlet he said Moni had given him, yet Moni, who was present, said that he received for it one gallon of rum. His chest too, has been bought lately, I suppose from Victoria, being country wood. Knowing he had not anything of his own to pay for it, I imagine this has been paid for out of the factory.

Sailed about noon. Wind easterly. Tacked at 6 p.m. heading up S.S.E. to S. ½ E. Wind light. Sea smooth.

6 December

Anchored to Bata 11 a.m. Discharged cargo. Sent the canoe to fetch a spar for jib boom. Did not succeed.

7 December

Took the boat and fetched a spar from the river. Weighed for Elobey 11 a.m.

8 December

Arrived in Elobey about 4 p.m. Found Mr. Hill on board the barque *Gartsherry* in company with the other factorians, most of whom appeared to have been drinking something stronger than water. Paid off the boys.

9 December

Landed all the cargo and sailed about 4 p.m. out of the weather channel--not less than 3½ fathoms.

10 December

Threatening tornado off Corisco early in the morning. Made Cape Esteiras at sundown. Anchored in Gaboon at midnight.

11 December

Found trade very dull, the *Commander* being up the river blowing down some towns for the late robberies upon trading boats. Cash very scare.

12 December

Landed cargo with the exception of powder. Cooper hard at work with the casks.

13 December

Finished with the powder. Cooper not finished with the casks.

14 December

Found the casks purchased at Bimbia would not hold water, being wormed. This will cause our water to be short of what I intended.

15 December

Sailed at 12 a.m. Light wind.

16 December

Hove to at sundown off Cape Lopez.

17 December

Came to inside the harbour about 10 a.m. in 3½ fathoms. Went and reported to the Governor, Received on board a Customer officer.

18 December

Went on shore. Found Bethancourt had 11 boys, and Mello 6, for home. They appear to be sorry to lose their boys, and would have been glad if I had not come. The boys here appear to be very comfortable, and feel it at leaving. Have been here for a long time. They have got wives and most have children.

19 December

Weighed at 2 p.m. Found at clearing that the Customs dues and charges were not so much as reported to be, for the officer and anchorage $4.00 and 6 francs charges for pass on articles. $3 I paid for two pigs, which makes the sum total of my expenses here $8.20. Received for boys' passage from Bethancourt $110--Mello $60.

TO CAPE PALMAS

30 December

Squally with nasty sea. We were struck with a squall in the starboard quarter about 9 a.m. I had been watching it rising, yet having had them nearly every day I imagined it was as before, plenty of rain with little wind. It however, turned out with too much of both. It hove her on her beam ends, and being so far aft it was some time ere she came up to allow the sails to come down; the jib sheet went, and the squaresail tack. We, however, lost nothing worthy of mention. Made the land at about 2 p.m. Cape Palmas E.S.E. and Grand Cess N.N.W.

31 December

Had much difficulty in getting canoes to come off, they having a palaver with piccaninny seas. They were afraid to leave the beach. Anchored at Sasstown at 4 p.m. Landed the boys and had loud promises of having a ship full of boys to-morrow.

ON KROO COAST

1871

1 January

Remained at anchor until 9 a.m. Finding that not a single boy had come off I asked the reason. They replied that the King wished me to go to the beach having brought their boys back to their town. "I do good too much that he King want to make book for me belong to him town proper and that I must take him a drop of rum and some smoke tobacco." After a long palaver and seeing no boys were coming off, I hove up. Some Bassa boys wanted to go beach here and asked for their traps, which I gave to them. These Sasstown people appeared to be anxious to take their trunks which they passed into canoes. I cautioned them about losing them, yet they said "we no fear, we country men live beach." After a while I saw that all the canoes had cleared out with the whole of their boxes, and left them (fools that they were) on board whilst they went to the beach, and stopped further communication. Bore up for Rocktown. Made Cape Palmas at 11 p.m. Came to near Rocktown at 1 a.m.

2 January

Wrote to Fernando Po and sent on board a schooner for some twine. Mail expected to-day. Did not come. Got from here 26 boys. Weighed at 5 p.m. towards rising and very heavy sea.

3 January

Drifted east of the Cape Tabou. Landed the boys and shipped 4 more proper bush boys. In fact, I have nothing more save 3 boys from Sasstown. Have loud promises of to-morrow to have ship full of boys and rice. Agreed to anchor, which I intended to do, going in the night. It was nearly the next night, before we got to anchor. Very heavy sea, ship rolls very much.

4 January

Charlie, with his big father, came about 8 a.m. yet did not bring any boys. They, like the others, wished me to go on shore, as they said to get me some because my not going was the reason I could not get them. Weighed at 10 a.m. Came to about 5 p.m. at Wappoo.

5 January

Shipped 22 boys. Bought a few more kroos of rice. Got a better sample of boys here than I have hitherto done. Weighed at 9 p.m. Hove to off Half Bereby for a canoe jammed. At last, after a two hours palaver in which was as much talk and noise as ought to have been in buying the whole country, and goodness knows where it would have ended had the vessel not been drifting down too fast and me occasionally helping her with a bear-up to make them clear out, came to at the Devils Rock villages. Paid for canoe 20 barrels of powder, 9 gallons rum. 1 c/s gin, 44 heads tobacco, 2 iron pots, 10 matchets, 5 romals, 2 neptunes, Total about £9 10s. 0d. This is more than I paid previously, yet this is a much better canoe; is appears to be rather dear, yet I don't fear getting back this amount. It is too large to take in, consequently will have to be towed, which I did not intend to do any more. They are too much trouble, yet I don't care to let a chance escape. Should I lose her it will make me more careful again.

6 January

Another larger canoe came off from this place which I could not resist the temptation of buying, paying about the same price as before--£9 8s. od. She is about the best canoe I have seen. What I am to do with her, or how to get her to Fernando Po I can't say. Weighed and came to off the Tabou villages and Grand Bereby. King Tom with his force came on board and bored the life out of me for liquor.

7 January

Bought this morning another canoe for which I paid about £3 10s. od. It is a pretty good one, yet rather small and not too cheap. It is so very difficult to tell when these large canoes are around what kind of a canoe will do for Fernando Po. They all appear so very small during the day. Bought another, smaller, for which I paid about £1 8s. 0d.--another, smaller, for about 17/-, and when about done I found that our lead had been stolen, so I chopped another smaller. Should the lead be returned I will give back the canoe. Bought about 18 kroos of rice, about 60 small fowls, 12 ducks, and plantains. Engaged 7 more boys, took on board all the canoes save one which I am compelled to tow, being far too heavy for my gear. Total bought, 5 canoes, 3 casks rice, and engaged altogether 61 boys. For ducks I paid 2 bottles rum; fowls--1 small beer bottle rum; rice, for 4 of my wash basins (about 7 gallons wine) I paid 4 bottles rum, or 8 heads tobacco, or 4 brass rods, or 3 fathoms rope.

8 January

Weighed from Tabou villages at 6 a.m. John coming off, when passing his town, he tells me he has talked all night about the lead palaver. He has got from them one that I did not know had been stolen until he showed it to me. I still stick to the canoe until the lead is brought back. Came to off Half Tabou at 12 a.m. Bought 20 kroos of rice and have faithful promises for to-morrow. I intended to have sailed this evening, yet have been unable for the want of wind, not having any sea breeze.

9 January

Bought a considerable quantity of rice and weighed at noon. Light breeze.

11 January

Threatening tornado or squall--came on about 2 p.m. without much wind at first. Saw a water spout during the breeze. When it freshened I started the peak halyards and the sail ripped from clew to head, up the second cloth. We were repairing all the night and had not sufficient twine to finish.

12 January

No wind. Used up all the twine and set the mainsail. Made more twine during p.m. out of canvas. Wind towards evening freshening, sea rising, and any quantity of fish around.

TO FERNANDO PO

13 January

Calm, nasty sea. Plenty of dolphin around yet could not catch any. Making more twine for repairing old jib (distance to Fernando Po 600 miles).

14 January

Wind very light with nasty roll from S.E. Have not made much during the past 24 hours. Although we are slowly drifting with the current it is almost a standstill. I expect Fernando Po by the next Xmas should the weather continue.

17 January

Fresh breeze blowing, at times pretty strong. Carried the squaresail tack away. Broke the tow rope of the canoe--a 4 inch hawser, first time used. I don't think much of it.

18 January

During the day we had a couple of tornadoes in our teeth. I never arrived yet in Fernando Po without something of this kind flying around. Nasty sea during the night, and no wind.

21 January

10 a.m. made the Island about N.W. Bay. Wind light Anchored at 10 p.m. in the Cove.

Report of Proceedings on Kru Coast On Board *Peep o'Day* Chartered to Remain Thereon 10 days for the Purpose of Enabling the Undersigned to Procure Krumen, Canoes &c.

1867

23 November

Peep o'Day arrived at Cape Palmas.[97]

25 November

Landed nine shooks[98] and 11 bundles of hoop iron which I arranged to have made up (with Mr. Cooper) and filled in readiness for my return from Settra Krou--to which place I have decided upon going as having found Townsend's headman at this place (on my arrival by steamer) sent hither to procure 30 Kroomen for his master in readiness for the *Peep o'Day*--I despatched him by one of McGill's cutters to get as many boys ready as possible previous to my arrival at his town. Sailed for Settra Krou at noon.

26 November

Anchored off Settra Krou at 10 a.m. Found that the headman I sent from Cape Palmas had only reached this yesterday on account of some stoppages for the purpose of trading, made by the boat on her way hither. This was communicated by a Kruman named Purser who with a lot more canoes came off to the schooner. Got three boys.

27 November

Engaged 57 Kruboys. Total engaged at Settra Krou 60 boys--In the afternoon finding no more boys coming off we raised the anchor and left. The headman meeting us off Fishtown with three boys (included in above number) he told me that he had been obliged to go down to that town before he could get a canoe to bring him off his own townspeople having refused the loan of their canoes in consequence of my not having sent the old or chief people a dash of rum &c.

---

[97] *Peep o'Day* was a 481-ton iron barque built at Newcastle by Marshall in 1863. See *Lloyd's Register of Shipping* (1872), 112.

[98] A *shook* is a barrel or cask that has been broken down to its constituent parts and packed into the smallest possible bundle.

29 November

Arrived at Cape Palmas at 8 a.m. Procured eight casks (40") of water which I found already filled the ninth not having been made up for want of sufficient hoop iron, as the ship was short of water her two 36 inch casks were also filled and brought off besides wood and sand for filling the tub, and upon which is made the fire required to cook the men's rice. Two of our Krumen ran away here I suppose on account of what they heard from the Cape Palmas men of Fernando Po--this was the more easy as I had employed ten of them in the boats belonging to Mr. Cooper--used for bringing off the wood and water. I engaged fifteen more boys belonging to this place and seven small boys were brought me by Townsend's headman, to whom I gave no advance--Total engaged here 22. Total on board 80.

30 November

We should have left last night, but it was pouring without any breeze. At 10 a.m. hove up anchor, but as it was almost as dead calm all day we made no headway and in the evening had to bring up off Cavally where we were visited by a canoe with some boys in her whom I know, they told me that my old headman Tattoo was ashore and would be glad to go down with me. As we were leaving Cape Palmas I engaged three boys belonging to Rock Town, making my present number 83.

1 December

Early in the morning we were visited by three or four Canoes which bought off two boys whom I engaged, some (a few) plantains bananas, eggs, fowls, ducks &c. Old Grandan the chief came off and excused Tattoo's absence by saying that as he was most desirous of going down with me, and as he had on his last voyage heard me recommend him to take down his wife he had gone to *seek her* and make preparations for leaving at once--at the same time begging me to wait. This of course was only an excuse for getting me to stay and to get a dash--but I did not see the force of their arguments and at about 10 a.m. hove up anchor and with a very light wind proceeded down the Coast. Our number of boys at this place reached 85. During the day we passed Rock Bocca where other canoes came off, chiefly for the purpose of begging a dash, but they bought me one Kruman, which makes my total on board 86 exclusive of Townsend's headman.

2 December

Anchored off Grand Bereby at noon, hoping to be able to buy some Canoes. Last evening being moonlight and this morning we have been visited by canoes as we passed each town, with the usual object (a glass of grog). They told us that they had everything we wanted, canoes, Kruboys, Rice &c., and begged us "do cappen put anchor for we place" "you sabe catch all ting for we place s'pose you fit put anchor". This is not the first time that either Captain Morgan or myself have been on this coast, therefore we knew how little reliance was to be placed on what they said. I bought a little rice today at Grand Bereby and have received great promises for to-morrow.

3 December

Bought a very large soft wood canoe of King Tom which will be towed as it is too large to be hoisted. I got a little more rice but as I saw no further chance of getting more of either rice or canoes we left at 10 a.m. During the day we bought a few hundredweights of rice at about 4/- invoice but no canoes. We were frequently begged to "lay anchor for we place" but upon our proposing to lay to until they brought off the canoes they would not promise to bring them off. It appeared to be indispensable that the anchor be let go.

4 December

Canoes visited us with a little rice--full of what might be done if only we anchored. As it was calm we promised to anchor until morning to put their promises to the test.

5 December

Last night we anchored off Drewin and Grand Drewin, and this morning some canoes came off--but I verily believe none came for sale--the only one that I would have bought was rather small and the owner of it refused to sell it on account of my not having any cloth. He had found out what I had *not* got and so pleaded this as an excuse for not wishing to sell, this was at Drewin, from Grand Drewin I got some firewood but the canoes they promised never came off. All the time Accra and Freeman (two headmen) were on board they said the large canoes were coming off soon--at one time they offered to send men to hurry on the others if I would give them tobacco, I gave them five heads intending to seize some of the men if the canoes did not come off, but just before doing this I had bought a necklace of god, coral and shells from one of the boys who after making the bargain--rued and wanted back his necklace, but I refused to give it him, and seeing that no boys had been sent off for the canoes, I took back my tobacco, and sailed on, leaving them to go ashore without a dash. This master Accra like most of his country men is a plausible rogue. On leaving Grand Drewin I gave up all hopes of getting more canoes, and told Captain Morgan that my business on this coast was finished, but upon passing Sassandra we were again visited by canoes and the men who came in them stated that they had several for sale. I told them I did not believe them but agreed to lay to until the canoes came off if they would send for them, this they agreed to and sent away a small canoe with orders to bring off the others. The small canoe however came back at sunset stating that the headmen wished the ship to anchor until morning as it was too late to send off the canoes--I agreed to wait provided they would leave me six boys on board as guarantee of their sincerity. They concurred--pointed out the boys to me--got my order for a dash of a gallon of rum and would have soon been off with it had I not stopped it on being unable to find the hostages whom I wished to secure previous to the departure of the others (for I had my suspicions that they would be swimming off after them if I did not) but when I came to look for them I found they were all in their canoes and refused to come out of them stating they were afraid to stay on board lest I should take them away during the night. They were loud in their protestations of truth but after a parting blessing on their whole race and themselves in particular I left them taking with me the jar which held the rum I had got already drawn for them--and I dare say they thought they escaped on easy terms--much better than they really deserved.

6 December

Wind S.S.W. lat. 4.45 N. Long. 5.2.W.

7 December

Noon. Lat. 4.46' N. Long 3.30. N. Distance 91 miles.

8 December

Noon. Lat. 4. 12' N. Long 1.27' N. Distance 129 miles. Gave a gallon of rum 6 hds. tobacco and 12 pipes to the kruboys.

9 December

Noon Lat. 16' N. Long O.36' E. Distance 123 miles.

10 December

Noon Lat. 3.57' N. Long. 2.21' E. Distance 103 miles.

11 December

Noon Lat. 3.40' N. Long. 3.59' E. Distance 100 miles.

12 December

Noon Lat. 4.3' N. Long. 5.13' E. Distance 75 miles.

13 December

Noon Lat. 4.10' N. Long. 6.51' E. Distance 99 miles.

14 December

4 p.m. 3.46' N. Long. 8.47' E. Distance 116 miles.

Winds on the Coast light and variable but after leaving Sassandra we had for the most part light fair winds and generally a current of from one to two knots in our favour (we had couple of rainy days). On the 13th when off the Bonney we had a good strong breeze which kept up the most of the night and on the 14th we had rain and little squalls from the N.E. We anchored in Clarence Bay at four p.m. The rain finished at noon. Thus we have made the passage from Sassandra in 8 days 21 hours.

(Sgd.) John Holt

REMARKS

If I were again to have a vessel call on the Krou coast for boys I would have shooks and hoop iron sent out to somebody in Sierra Leone with instructions to have them made up and filled with water in readiness for the ship so that on her arrival she would not be detained. Sierra Leone would be better than Cape Palmas as the vessel would, after watering, at the latter port, have to go to windward for men. If goods are to be got at or rather if arrangements have been made when loading the vessel to have the proper goods at hand in the event of any trade being met with--a person might during the oil season, buy some oil as he passes down the coast while at the same time if his vessel is sufficiently large he can buy fowls, ducks, goats &c. and at Fresco pigs &c. in addition to canoes and engaging Krumen. Settra Krou is claimed by the Liberians but their claim is contested by the natives who would protect any ship trading with them, and if the ship had no necessity for going into any of the Liberian ports of Entry of which I believe there are six, she might be employed in trading with any part of the Liberian coast without having to pay the duties or at present have reason to fear any force sufficiently strong to stop her if she is provided with means of defence as the Liberian government has no ship of war to prevent an infraction of its so-called laws nor has it the means of enforcing payment of duties if the person engaged in evading them has no interests ashore such as trust to Liberians, and is perfectly independent of them. Equally impotent would it be to punish any outrage which might be committed on a vessel by the natives living under its rule.

The Liberians of Cape Palmas make that port a sort of depot from which they issue their goods and in return receive their produce either for payment to the white captains from whom they generally receive credit or for sale to trading ships in exchange for fresh supplies of goods or for shipment per steamer to England. They have factories along the coast between which and Cape Palmas their boats and other small craft are employed. The captains of most of these act as traders as well at such places of call where no factory belonging to the owner exists. In Cape Palmas a Kru of oil is four wine gallons, but that used by the Liberians in trading with the natives will measure six wine gallons. It is sold by the Liberians to trading ships at 40 cent per wine gallon. I am informed by William (Townsend's headman) that during the oil season (Decr. to April or June) a vessel of from one to 200 tons could load between Monrovia and Cape Palmas within one month. The system appear to be one of trust to trade men at each port or place of trade or by factories in charge of a clerk or agent. This is the system practised by the Liberians, and used to be so conducted by the whitemen until their trading with the natives was stopped by the Liberian government, and trade between them and Liberia limited to the ports of entry, a policy well calculated to enable the Liberians to monopolise all trade with the natives, and to make their services indispensable to trade both to the whitemen and the native producer. The natives kick against Liberian rule, but as they are divided against themselves they are powerless to prevent it and as our government thinks fit to acknowledge the jurisdiction of some 9,000 Liberians over 150,000 natives or more and an extent of coast about 300 miles long the English trader is compelled to submit or become liable to prosecution for infringement of the republican laws by the Liberian agents in England (?) I was told by Mr. Cooper that as a rule he finds the native traders as worthy of trust as the Liberians he employs in his factories. At Settra Krou the price paid by the natives (kru equal to 6 wine gallons) for:

	On Board Ship		If to Native Trader on Trust
One Long Dane Gun	3 Krus Oil		3 Krus
One Fuzee	2½		3
20th Gunpowder	1		1
10 Gunpowder	2		2
¼ Gunpowder	3		4
One Gallon Rum	1		1
7 lbs. shot	1		1
18 yds. Satin Stripe	2½		3
18 yds. Blue Baft	2½		3
8 hkfs. Fine Madras	2		2½
8 hkfs. Comn. Madras	1		1½
1 Pce. Silk Hkfs. (7)	7		7
20 yds. W. Baft	3		4
18 yds. Print	3		4
½ Gln. Iron Pots 4 for	1		1
1 Silk Umbrella	3		3
6 Iron Bars	1		1
3 bars of 5 hds. each tobacco	1		1
5 bars soap	1	4 for	1
6 axes or matchets	1	4	1

If trust is given to a trade man, a loss of at least ten percent may be expected as he will pay that quantity short which he deducts as a commission, a large red case of fifteen bottles gin sells for 8 Krus.

Care is requisite to prevent the boys engaged from running away. Those belonging to the westward of Cape Palmas will not run away to the Eastward. Oil might be got in small quantities supposing a day's (or two) detention at each place after Settra Krou, Nannakrou, Gran Sestro, Garraway, Cavally, Taboo, Gran Bassam Half Bereby, Tafou, Drewin, Sassandra. Most Kruboys will be procured at the first seven places. Canoes at the last four and Grand Bereby. Rice may also be bought from Cavally eastward as far as Brewin from November to March. A Kru of rice at Cape Palmas weighs 30 to 33 lbs., a native kru or 5 wine gallons will weigh 40 lbs. and will cost about 1/3 invoice. I paid 5 hds. tobacco or 2 botts. rum, or one 2 or 3 gallon iron pots for each Kru. I might have bought a good deal had I paid these prices at first, but I caused some of the Grand Bereby people to go away by trying to get it cheaper. Cloth, matchets, soap and gunpowder all of which I was out of were very much asked for. The canoe which I bought here although large was of soft wood, and I consider it dear at the price £6.12.8. invoice. I might have bought a smaller one at Drewin of hardwood, if I had had a supply of cloth, matchets, soap and gunpowder. I paid fuzees, jars, brass rods, iron pots, gin, rum, tobacco hats pipes for it. For two small canoes I paid one fuzee, 23 gall. jars, 3 bottles rum 3 heads tobacco invoice value 10/5. All along the coast I bought paddles, paying for good large ones a bottle of rum or one head of tobacco each, if small I paid half these quantities. The Kruboys I engaged for two years and paid them various rates of advance from $4 (trade price) to $2 according to size. 1 bar soap $½, 2 cutlasses $½. 6 heads tobacco $1. 1 gallon jar $½ 1½ gln. rum $1½ going for $4 (invoice price 7/-) and the smaller advances in proportion. It is better to have a supply of rice on board sufficient for the use of kruboys before going to the coast, so that in case of being unable from any unforseen cause to purchase Kru Rice, no predicament would arise. I got 86 boys, and that number was as many as could be well stowed away in and under the long boat. Had there been room for more in the hold and if had not been pressed for time I should have called at Gran Sestros, Garraway, Taboo, Gran Bassa, and have made greater efforts at Half Cavally. I should also have gone further eastward of Sassandra in search of canoes. A person visiting the Kru coast for the first time would think from the number of people who crowd on board with the noise and tumult they make that he was going to be taken by storm or that for the time he was in the midst of Bedlam. They are a tremendously noisy importunate set of beggars, full of lies, indeed I think it is hardly possible to find a kruman capable of speaking the truth when his interest lies in telling a falsehood. They all ask for something to drink which when got will lead to a desire for tobacco and after this to pipes which if granted may lead to goodness knows what, they are never satisfied. Still I think it is good to give the first man a little something as it tends to encourage them to go off miles to a ship, and many a captain on making the Kru coast is glad to learn from the canoe men the name of the point they come from. There is a class of men who come off in the canoes and who have acted as assistant in procuring stock, men, water, rice or oil to some of the captains and others who call along their coast, most of them have "books" given by those captains in proof of the assistants' fidelity and power to do what he professes. I have been told that these are sometimes forged by the blacks or others capable of writing (for a consideration). They are also said to be lent one to another so as to be used by anyone or everyone. I think a person who goes to the Kru Coast should be on his watch against any imposition of this kind, and bear in mind that they will swindle him if they can. I should not like to trust even those who really owned the good books, for I can readily understand why they may have on several occasions behaved sufficiently well towards those who are in the habit of trading on their coast as to secure a favourable certificate. I never employed any of them either on this voyage or my last, and I do not think I have lost anything by it.

Fernando Po, 14th December 1867

(Sgd.) John Holt

Brass foot rings, copper rods, brass kettles, beads fluted and round (large) of various colours, Madras, blue baft, Chelloes, satin stripe, white baft &c are wanted along the coast in addition to those goods with which I on this occasion paid advances to kroomen and bought rice, canoes &c.

Expenditure of cargo on board *Peep o'Day* in advances to Kroomen, Purchase of canoes &c. December 1867

	Guns Fusees	Jars	Brass Rods	Iron Pots	Gin	Rum	Tobacco	Straw Hats	Pipes	Beaver	Soap	Cut-Lasses	Scent
Large canoe	5	5^{38}	50	8^{38}	1	8	30	5	1c	1			
Cash				1^{12}		12	9						
Kroomen		46^{11} 4	12	1^{10} 1^{14} 1^{3}		76	356			1	75	120	1 box
on a/c ship						5½	5						
Dashes						5 g	26		34				1 box
Small canoes	1	2^{3}				3 b	3						
Stock		1^{3}				6B	24						
Rice 32 krus of 5 imp glns. or 40 lbs.	1^{1} 1^{1}		9	15^{3} 3^{1} 4^{2} 4½		2	33	11					
Paddles 33						20B	13	3					
	6	9 4 47	71	24^{3} 1^{12} 1^{10} 1^{14} 3^{1} 4^{12}		113	499) 10)	5	1 case & 48	2	bars 75	120	boxes 2

Note: The significance of the numbers and letters attached to the quantities in the table above is not known but they may refer to ledger accounts.

Total		
4 cwt Rice for Krooboys food	13/6	£2.14.0.
6 Fuzees	6/5	1.18.6.
82 gallons empty jars	5d	1.14.2.
71 Brass Rods	4½	1.6.7.
113 gallons Iron Pots	6d	2.16.6.
1 case (Green) Gin	5/10	5.10.
113 gallons rum	1/10	4.16.0.
499) 10) Heads or 128 lbs. tobacco	9d	10.7.2.
5 Straw Hats	1/9	8.9.
1 case and 4 doz. pipes	14/6 & 8d	15.2.
2 beaver hats	14/6 & 10/-	1.4.6.
75 bars soap - 1 box of 2 cst.	17/6	1.15.0.
120 Cutlasses or 1 box of 10 doz.	7/6	3.15.0.
2 boxes ea. 3 bott scent	3/-	4.0.
		34.1.2.
Dash to Captain - one case Brandy		1.3.0.
		£35.4.2.

Canoe			Kroomen		
5 Guns @	6/5	1.12.	1. 46 1 gln. jars	5d	1.2.6.
5 3 g. jars	1/1½	5.	7. 12 brass rods	4½	4.6.
50 brass rods	4½	18.9.	39 gln. iron pots	6d	19.6.
8 iron pots 3g.- 24g	6	12.0.	356 head tobac.89 lbs.	9d	3.6.9.
1 green case gin	5/10	5.10.	1 beaver		10.0.
8 glns. rum 15 u.p.	1/10	14.8.	75 bars soap		1.15.0.
30 heads tobac.8 lbs.	9d.	6.0.	120 cutlasses		3.15.0.
5 straw hats	1/9	8.9.	1 box scent		2.0.
1 beaver hat		14.6.	76 glns. rum		6.19.4.
1 case pipes	14/6	14.6.			
		£6.12.8.			£18.14.7.

2 small canoes			
1 fuzee	6.5.	Peep O'Day	
6 glns. jars 5d	2.6.	5½ glns rum 1/10	10.1.
½ gln. rum	11.	5 hds. tobacco	11.
3 heads tobacco	7.		
	£0.10.5.		£0.11.0.
Cash sales		Dashes	
12 glns rum 1/10	1.2.0.	5 glns. rum 1/10	9.2.
9 hds. tobacco	1.9.	36 hds. tobacco 9d	6.9.
		34 pipes	6.
	£1.3.9.		£0.16.5.
Stock for food & c		1 box scent	2.0.
			18.5.
3 glns. jars 5d	1.3.		
6 bott. rum	1.10.	Rice 32 krus of 5 imp. glns or 40 ea.	
24 hds. tobacco	4.6.	4 glns jars 5d	1.8.
	7.7.	9 bars rods 4½d	3.4.
33 paddles		50 glns iron pots 6d	1.5.0.
20 botts. rum	6.4.	2 glns rum 1/10	3.8.
13 hds. tobacco	2.5.	33 hds. tobacco 8 lbs.	7.8.
3 pipes	1.	11 pipes	2.
	8.10	Total 1280 lbs. or 11½ cwt.	£2.1.6.

FAMILY TREE OF JOHN HOLT

William Holt, Baptised 19 July 1815 at Luddington. Buried there 23 February 1816.	William Leonard Holt, Baptised 7 February 1824 at Burton-upon-Stather. Buried 24 March 1828 at Luddington, aged 3 years.	Married secondly his cousin, Elizabeth, daughter of William Holt, of Clee, Farmer, Born *circa* 1824. Married. Buried 18 July 1900 at Burton-upon-Stather. County Lincoln, aged 76 years.	Thomas Godfred Holt, of Luddington and Broughton, County Lincoln, Shipowner and Mariner. Baptised 29 June 1817 at Luddington. Buried 10 February 1909 at Broughton, aged 92 years.	Elizabeth, daughter of Jonathan Cockin, Born *circa* 1822. Married 26 July 1841. Died 31 January 1879, aged 58 years, at Broughton aforesaid, and there buried 31 January following.	John Holt, of Goole, Shipowner and Master Mariner. Baptised 20 July 1822 at Burton-upon-Stather. Buried 2 June 1887, aged 64 years at Luddington.	Sarah, daughter of James Naylor of Garthorpe, Farmer. Born *circa* 1824. Married 16 October 1845 at Luddington. Buried 9 April 1887 at Luddington.	Elizabeth, Baptised 17 September 1820 at Burton-upon-Stather. Died 22 April 1836, aged 15 years. Buried 25 April following at Luddington. Mary Ann, of Epworth aforesaid, Baptised 27 December 1827 at Luddington. Died 1903.

William Holt, Baptised 27 February 1843 at Luddington. Buried there 9 February 1855.	Jonathan Cockin Holt, Master Mariner. Born 27 July 1844 at Garthorpe. Baptised 27 July following at Luddington. Died 14 September 1896, aged 52 years, at Broughton. Buried there 18 September following.	Florence Mary, (cousin of husband) daughter of John Holt of Goole and Sarah Naylor. Born 26 January 1862 at Garthorpe. Married 3 October 1881 at Snaith, County Lincoln. Died 1950.	**John Holt, sometime of the Grange, Broughton and Halstead House, Oxton, County Chester, African Merchant. Born 30 October 1841 at Luddington. Baptised there 30 November following.** **Died 22 June 1915, aged 73 years, at the Grange Broughton.**	Eliza Ball, daughter of Robert Longstaff, of Stixwould, County Lincoln, Farmer. Born 7 April 1848. Married 25 February 1875 at Misterton, Nottinghamshire. Died 22 April 1934 at Broughton, aged 86 years.	Thomas Holt. Born 16 May 1848 at Luddington. Baptised there 11 June following. Died 1921.	Emily, daughter of George Lamming. Lived at Bridge Farm Broughton. Died leaving his wife (maybe another relative).	Louis Holt of Garthorpe, Baptised 3 January 1858 at Luddington. Died 1930. Married Florence Holt, widow of Jonathan Cockin Holt. Jane Elizabeth, Born 15 January 1850, at Luddington. Baptised there 6 March following. Married to John Lamming. Died 1920.
Jonathan Cockin Holt. Born 1 December 1875. Died 14 August 1959.	Constance, Born 6 November 1876. Died 1929.	Robert Longstaff Holt,[1] Born 9 February 1878. Died 11 March 1948.	Godfrey Ball Holt, Born 26 September 1880. Died 14 September 1923.	Ancell Ball Holt, Born 9 February 1882. Died 2 June 1946.	John Stanley Holt, Born 2 August 1883.	William Gordon Holt, Born 23 April 1885. Died 5 January 1887. Rosa Dorothy, Born 10 December 1887. Died, 1934.	Elisa Winifred, Born 3 August 1889. Died 1959.

Cecil Raymond Holt[2] of the White House, Damhead Lane, Willaston, Wirral, County Chester. African merchant. Born 2 March 1911 at 4, Blundell Drive, Birkdale, Lancashire. Died 24 May 1969.	Audrey Louise, daughter of Alfred Ernest Gardner, of Hoylake, Ship-broker. Born 1 March 1914 at 10 Drummond Road, Hoylake. Married 12 September 1936.	John Alphonse Holt.[3] Born 27 August 1906 at Birkdale, County Lancaster. African merchant of Dellside, Delavor Road, Heswall, County Chester. Died 10 October 1968.	Pamela Esther Holt. Daughter of John Holt Jr. Son of Jonathan Cockin Holt. Born 12 October 1914. Married 1937.	Dereck Jonathan Holt.[4] Born 2 April 1919 at Geneva, Birkenhead Road, Meols, County Chester. Of Halstead, Delavor Road, Heswall, County Chester.			
Robert Clive Holt. Born 27 March 1941 at Rosslyn, Huscote Park, West Kirby, County Chester.	Derek Rodney Holt, Born 2 August 1944 at Brookfield, Brookfield Gardens, West Kirby, aforesaid.	David Cecil Holt. Born 6 September 1948 at Rosslyn, Huscote Park, West Kirby aforesaid.	John Christian Holt, Born 3 June 1939. Died 1964.	Sarah Elizath, Born 14 November 1948. Died 10 December 1978.			

Notes: [1]Robert Longstaff Holt played an important role in the running of the Company and was Chairman from 1917 to 1947. [2]Cecil Raymond Holt became a director of the company and was responsible for the publication of the first edition of the *Diary of John Holt* in 1948. [3]John Alphonse Holt enjoyed a distinguished business career with the company, as Chairman from 1949 to 1968, and was also a director of Cammell Laird, of Martus Bank, and of the Sea Insurance Company. [4]Derek Jonathan Holt worked for the company for seven years before taking up a position as a teacher in West Africa. He subsequently retired to London where he now resides. He currently holds the family papers and the present work has been published with his permission and support.

Printed and bound by CPI Group (UK) Ltd, Croydon, CR0 4YY

16/09/2026

14963469-0002